VMEbus User's Handbook

VMEbus User's Handbook

STEVE HEATH

Heinemann Newnes

Heinemann Newnes
An imprint of Heinemann Professional Publishing Ltd
Halley Court, Jordan Hill, Oxford OX2 8EJ

OXFORD   LONDON   MELBOURNE   AUCKLAND   SINGAPORE
IBADAN   NAIROBI   GABORONE   KINGSTON

First published 1989

British Library Cataloguing in Publication Data

Heath, Steve
  VMEbus user's handbook.
  1. Computer systems. Buses. VMEbus
  I. Title
  004,6'4

ISBN 0 434 90722 7

Filmset by Deltatype Ltd, Ellesmere Port
Printed and Bound in Great Britain by
Billings of Worcester

Contents

Acknowledgements

The following trademarks mentioned within the text are acknowledged:

MC68000, MC68010, MC68020, MC68030, VERSAbus, RMS68K, VERSAdos, EXORbus, MC6800, MC6809 and VME130bug are all trademarks of Motorola, Inc.
PDP–11 and DEC are the trademarks of Digital Equipment Corporation.
CP/M and Concurrent Dos are the trademarks of Digital Research, Inc.
UNIX is the trademark of AT & T.
MTOS is the trademark of Industrial Programming, Inc.
VRTX is the trademark of Ready Systems, Inc.
PSOS is the trademark of Software Components.
PDOS is the trademark of Eyring Research.
OS–9/68k is the trademark of Microware.

Figure 10.9 is courtesy of Concise Technology.
All other photographs are courtesy of Motorola, Inc.
While the information contained in this book has been carefully checked for accuracy, the author assumes no responsibility or liability for its use, or any infringement of patents or other rights of third parties which would result.

As technical characteristics are subject to rapid change, the data contained are presented for guidance and education only. For exact detail, consult the manufacturers' data and specifications.

Preface

For many VMEbus users, the only guide to designing with the bus is the bus specification itself. While this document is extremely readable and provides a lot of useful practical information, it falls short of providing total system information encompassing software, integration and design. With the VMEbus so widely available, many engineers and students from an 8-bit microprocessor background are finding themselves using VMEbus systems that are more akin to a minicomputer or supermini than that of an 8-bit microcomputer. As can be imagined, there is a large potential for making mistakes or misunderstanding the concepts used.

VMEbus systems have such a close interaction between the hardware and software that it is very unwise to consider these as separate entities, and indeed many of the common problems encountered with VMEbus designs arise from such preconceptions. Unfortunately, much of the currently available information is biased towards one aspect or the other.

The VMEbus User's Handbook provides a total system perspective and brings the hardware and software aspects of designing with the VMEbus together. Chapters 1–4 cover the basic bus concepts behind the VMEbus and give a good grounding before the next section. Chapters 5–8 cover system concepts such as operating systems, single and multiple processor concepts and designs. Chapters 9–12 describe the practicalities involved: it covers system integration and fault finding techniques for VMEbus systems, a design methodology and gives several case studies as examples. Chapter 13 covers VMEbus interfaces and identifies the design requirements. Chapters 14 and 15 cover more specialized applications and high integrity designs and networks. Chapter 16 describes future developments. Finally, several appendices are provided whose subjects include common system errors, contacts and addresses and other useful information.

The Motorola MC680x0 microprocessor family is the most common-ly used processor for VMEbus boards and the microprocessor aspects of

VMEbus have been based around this processor series. However, many of the topics are relevant for other microprocessor families.

The text uses several conventions:

1 All active, low signals are indicated by an asterisk after the signal name, e.g. DTACK★, DS0★, etc.
2 All references to VMEbus MASTERS and SLAVES are given in capitals. All other references use lower case, e.g. master–slave configurations, master reset, etc.

I would like to express my thanks to Tim Coombs of Concise Technology, Lennart Svensson and Gordon Stubberfield of Motorola and to the many VMEbus users that I have worked with for their inputs and comments. Special thanks must go to Sue Carter, who not only edited the text, but provided much feedback, support and coffee.

Steve Heath

1
Why VMEbus?

Why use a bus at all?

Since the advent of the electronic digital computer, there has been tremendous interest in the electrical buses used in such systems. These bus structures, like their associated processor designs, tended to be proprietary and this meant that system expansion (adding, for example, extra memory or mass storage) was often restricted in choice, expensive or frequently both. The high costs were necessary to recoup the design investment and therefore difficult to reduce because of low volume production runs. The wealth of differing bus standards prevented third party specialist companies from expanding the choice and opening the market. As a result, only a handful of companies could provide the total system solution the market required.

With the advent of the microprocessor in the 1970s and the realization that not only could they supersede discrete logic but also provide the functionality of a computer processor core, low cost computing became available. This gave the system developer the ability to build his own low cost computer system without developing his own processor from scratch. Off-the-shelf microprocessors provided a stable software environment which allowed system developers to add their expertise to the product, instead of having to develop everything themselves—often with disastrous results.

However, each microprocessor had its own particular bus structure which required a new circuit design every time the system was upgraded or modified to any extent. Many designs produced at this time were low volume products and this only compounded the problem. Low volume production runs again prevented reduction in costs. Many of the high prices were associated with the design costs, and not with the price of the materials, e.g. semiconductors, power supplies or printed circuit boards.

This was clearly an inefficient design methodology, especially for low volume production runs. It would be far more efficient to build systems from a series of discrete 'building blocks' connected electrically, so that changes would only affect the module(s) to be modified. Memory expansion could be achieved by adding more memory modules, mass storage could be increased by adding a disc controller, and performance could be increased by replacing the processor module with a faster one.

As a result of this requirement, microprocessor buses were specified to provide such interface standards and this enabled third party companies to provide specialist functions, establishing the basis on which a wide range of system components would become available. A typical bus standard from this time is Motorola's EXORbus, supporting MC6800 and MC6809 microprocessors.

Unfortunately, these buses had two fundamental limitations:

A   they could only address 64 Kbytes of memory, and
B   they only supported single processors.

Attempts to run multiple processors on such buses often imposed strict limitations on system software design—there would be no checking or prioritizing of bus access, resulting in attempted simultaneous accesses causing, for example, data corruption, bus lock ups and system crashes. This was clearly unacceptable. The requirements for the next generation of microprocessors and electrical buses were being defined. These new designs were being based on the restrictions that the current 8-bit microprocessors placed on system design.

The introduction of the MC68000 family was the first step in realizing these requirements. It offered a microprocessor architecture that was more akin to a minicomputer than a micro, and was far more suitable for system designs. Its development gave the VMEbus many of its concepts.

The introduction of the MC68000 microprocessor

The MC68000 was introduced in 1979 with the message:

'Break away from the Past'

It did not extend the existing 8-bit microprocessor architecture. It exploited ideas previously used only in a minicomputer design and new VLSI techniques to increase both functionality and performance. Figure 1.1 is a photograph of the die showing its functional blocks. Its architecture was more like a Digital Equipment Corporation (DEC) PDP11 minicomputer than its predecessor, the MC6809 8-bit microprocessor.

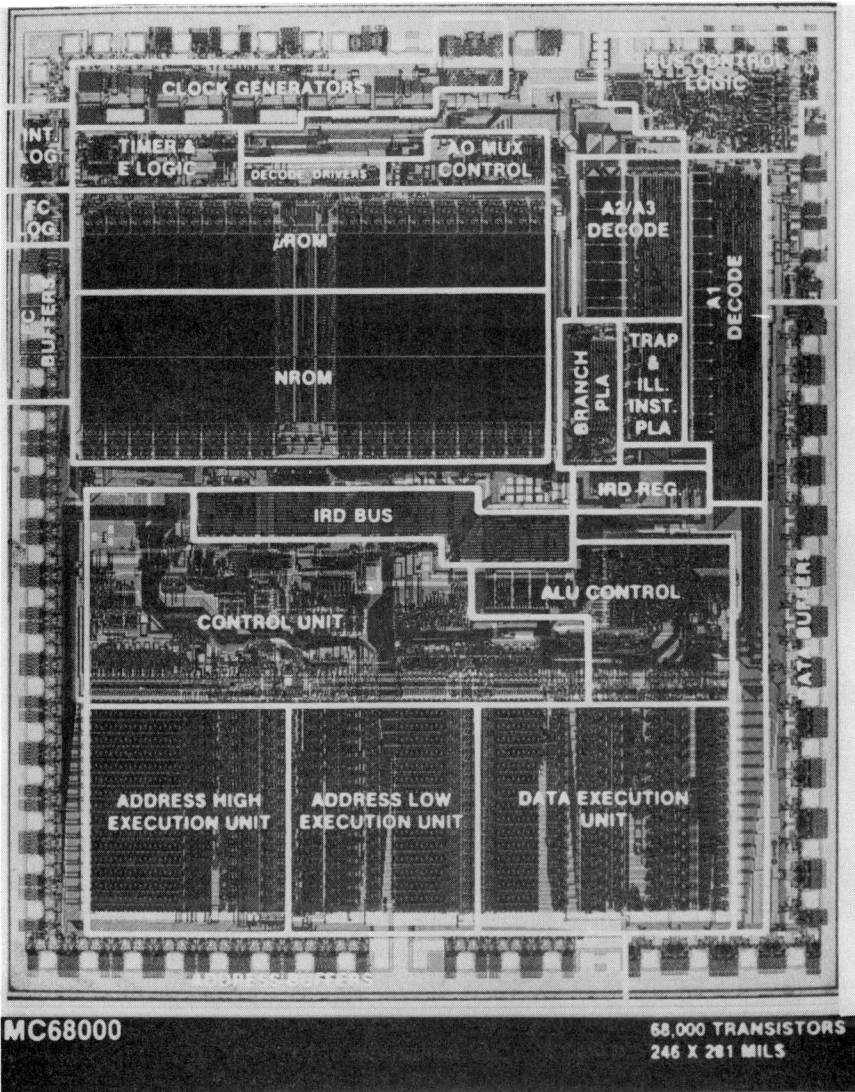

Figure 1.1   *The MC68000 microprocessor die*

A new register architecture

Figures 1.2 and 1.3 show the MC6800 and MC68000 programming models. Gone are the dedicated 8- and 16-bit registers, to be replaced by eight data registers and eight address registers each 32 bits wide.

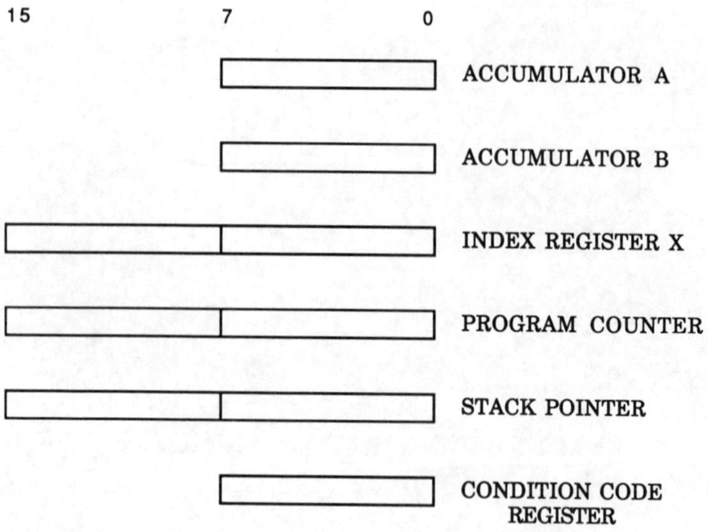

15	7	0

ACCUMULATOR A

ACCUMULATOR B

INDEX REGISTER X

PROGRAM COUNTER

STACK POINTER

CONDITION CODE
REGISTER

Figure 1.2   *MC6800 processor user programming model*

31   0

A0
A1
A2
A3
A4   ADDRESS REGISTERS
A5
A6
A7

D0
D1
D2
D3
D4   DATA REGISTERS
D5
D6
D7

PROGRAM COUNTER

CONDITION CODES

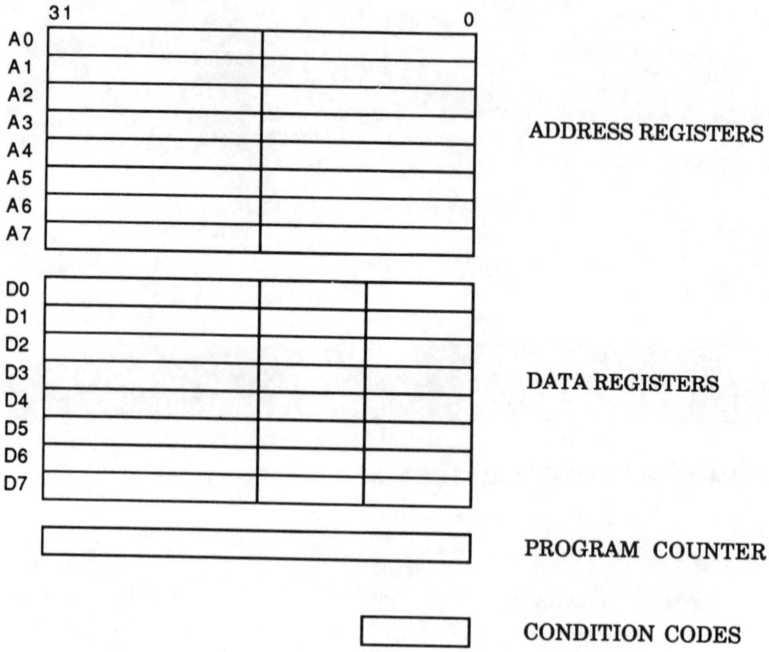

Figure 1.3   *MC68000 processor user programming model*

These registers are general purpose: any data register can be used for an arithmetic operation and all eight address registers can be used as stack pointers. This removes much of the data stacking and moving that high level language compilers generated for the 8-bit architectures and used either to preserve intermediate data or to ensure it was in the correct register, before execution of certain instructions.

The program counter has been expanded to a full 32 bits, although only 24 bits appear externally. This provides 16 Mbytes of direct addressable memory, in comparison with the 64 Kbytes of the MC6809. Microprocessor system software falls into two general categories:

A operating systems software, concerned with supervising the system, and
B application software which uses the facilities provided by the system software to perform the required system tasks.

Unfortunately, with the 8-bit microprocessor there was no simple way of preventing application software using the areas of memory accessed by the supervisory software. If an application program failed, it inevitably corrupted the supervisory software and caused a total system crash. No attempt was made to protect the supervisory resource or to provide a mechanism to isolate the cause and maintain system integrity. The MC68000 uses a SUPERVISOR/USER concept to solve this problem.

The MC68000 normally executes code in the USER state. However, if an exception occurs, such as a software or hardware interrupt, the processor will change into the SUPERVISOR state and has access to extra programming registers. This allows the use of a different stack pointer for example. Figure 1.4 shows the additional SUPERVISOR registers for the MC68000 microprocessor.

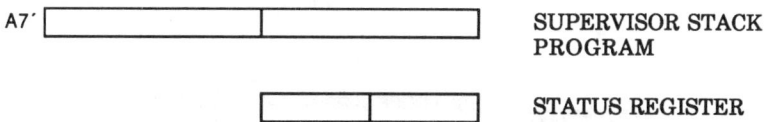

A7´ | [|] | SUPERVISOR STACK
                                                     PROGRAM

            [|]   STATUS REGISTER

Figure 1.4 *MC68000 processor supervisor programming model*

When the exception occurs, the processor builds external stack frames which hold data describing the cause of the exception, the state of the program counter and other internal information. Figure 1.5 shows a stack frame for a Bus Error exception. This is then used by the exception handling software routines running in the SUPERVISOR state. Each particular exception is allocated a vector which points to a specific or generic handler. On completion, control can be returned to the USER software, either by executing the RFE (Return From Exception) instruction or by changing the SUPERVISOR bit in the status register. Figure 1.6 shows a typical system partition and shows how both the SUPERVISOR and USER have their own stack areas and program code allocated to them. These resources can be hardware protected by the use of the *Function Code* outputs, as shown in Figure 1.7. The processor state, shown externally by the three Function Code outputs FC0–2, can be used in the external memory address equation to partition the external memory. As a result, different stacks and memory areas can be maintained and protected.

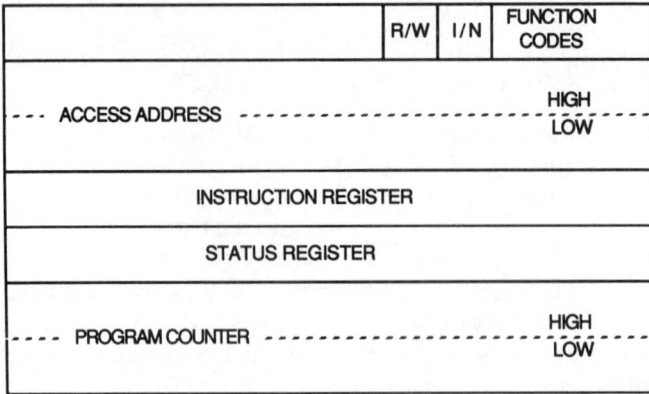

			R/W	I/N	FUNCTION CODES
--- ACCESS ADDRESS					HIGH
					LOW
INSTRUCTION REGISTER					
STATUS REGISTER					
--- PROGRAM COUNTER					HIGH
					LOW

R/W - READ or WRITE   I/N - INSTRUCTION or NOT

Figure 1.5 *MC68000 stack frame for bus error exceptions*

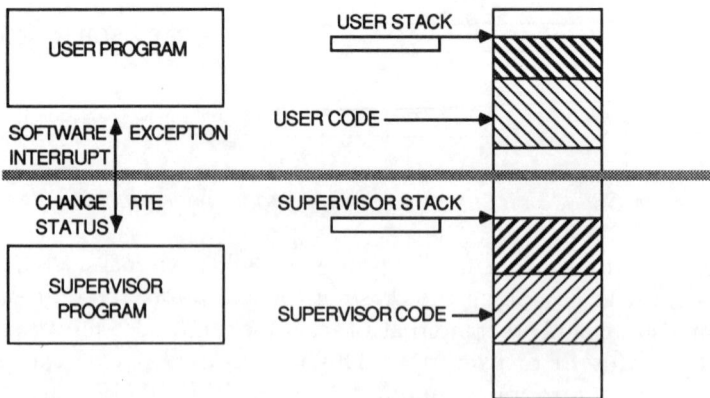

Figure 1.6 *User/supervisor partition with the MC680x0*

FUNCTION CODE OUTPUT			REFERENCE CLASS
FC0	FC1	FC2	
0	0	0	Reserved
0	0	1	User Data
0	1	0	User Program
0	1	1	Reserved
1	0	0	Reserved
1	0	1	Supervisor Data
1	1	0	Supervisor Program
1	1	1	Interrupt Acknowledge

Figure 1.7 *Function code outputs table*

New generation of hardware interface

The MC68000 hardware interface is radically different from its predecessors, in that it has both a 16-bit data port and a 24-bit address port combining to provide a non-multiplexed asynchronous bus. Although the external data bus is only 16 bits wide, the processor can deal with data from 1 to 32 bits in size: 32-bit accesses simply use two consecutive 16-bit accesses. The A0 address bit is fully decoded as a lower and upper data strobe to allow access to the odd and even bytes within the 16-bit word. The bus data and address ports are non-multiplexed to allow maximum throughput. (Multiplexing not only slows down the microprocessor internally but also requires external demultiplexing circuitry, which can insert delays into the memory access timing.)

An asynchronous bus is used to allow the processor to access any speed memory or peripheral. The processor does not discriminate between memory and I/O functions. Both appear as simple memory locations. The transfer relies on handshaking between the processor and the memory to indicate the completion of the various parts of the cycle. The handshaking allows the cycle to go as fast as the slowest partner in the cycle. There are three stages: first the processor acknowledges that a bus cycle has started and that valid address data are on the bus, then the peripheral responds with an acknowledgement that the data has been transferred, and finally the processor acknowledges the signal and terminates the cycle.

The basic operation is shown in Figure 1.8. A bus cycle is started by the address, function codes, read/write and data strobes being driven on the bus. These signals are then validated by the address strobe AS★. The peripheral will decode the signals and generate the correct chip select. It presents or latches data and will finally assert a data transfer acknowledge signal, DTACK★, back to the processor to indicate a successful transfer. If necessary, this signal can be delayed and 'wait states' inserted allowing more time to access the memory. The processor then negates the data and address strobes to acknowledge the peripheral. This bus is truly asynchronous: if no DTACK★ is returned, the processor will wait indefinitely or until a bus watchdog timer times out and asserts the bus error signal, BERR★.

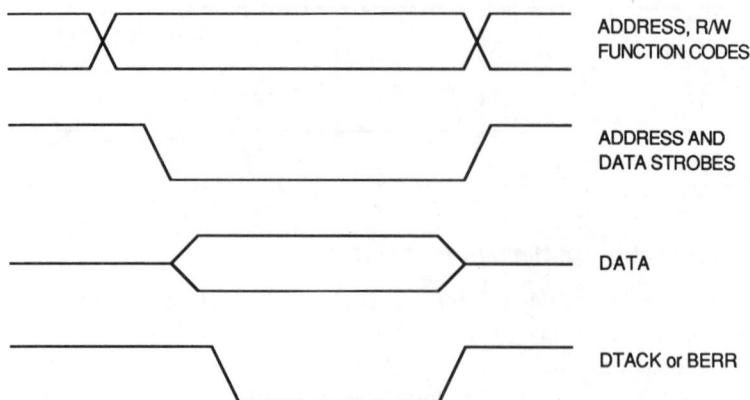

Figure 1.8   *Basic operation of the MC68000 asynchronous bus*

This ability to insert wait states dynamically provides two advantages: it allows slower memory or peripherals to be easily interfaced to the MC68000 and it allows processor speed upgrades to be performed with little or no circuit modification. Such upgrades do not require an upgrade of the system peripherals, as was the case with earlier microprocessors— changing from an MC68A09 1 MHz clock to an MC68B09 2 MHz part also required all peripherals to be uprated as well.

The BERR★ and HALT★ signals provide a mechanism for aborting the current bus cycle and either retrying automatically or causing an exception for software to handle. If the software resolution is chosen, the Bus Error stack frame contains the relevant processor information to allow the exception handler to determine exactly what went wrong and, more importantly, how to correct the situation. The BERR★ signal provides a simple mechanism to implement a bus watchdog timer to prevent pseudo 'system crashes' when the DTACK★ signal is not returned.

In addition, the retry mechanism allows external logic to resolve the 'deadly embrace' problem of two processors trying to access the same bus simultaneously. A typical solution is to abort the bus cycles of both processors and then to stagger the bus cycle retries. Figure 1.9 shows how this works.

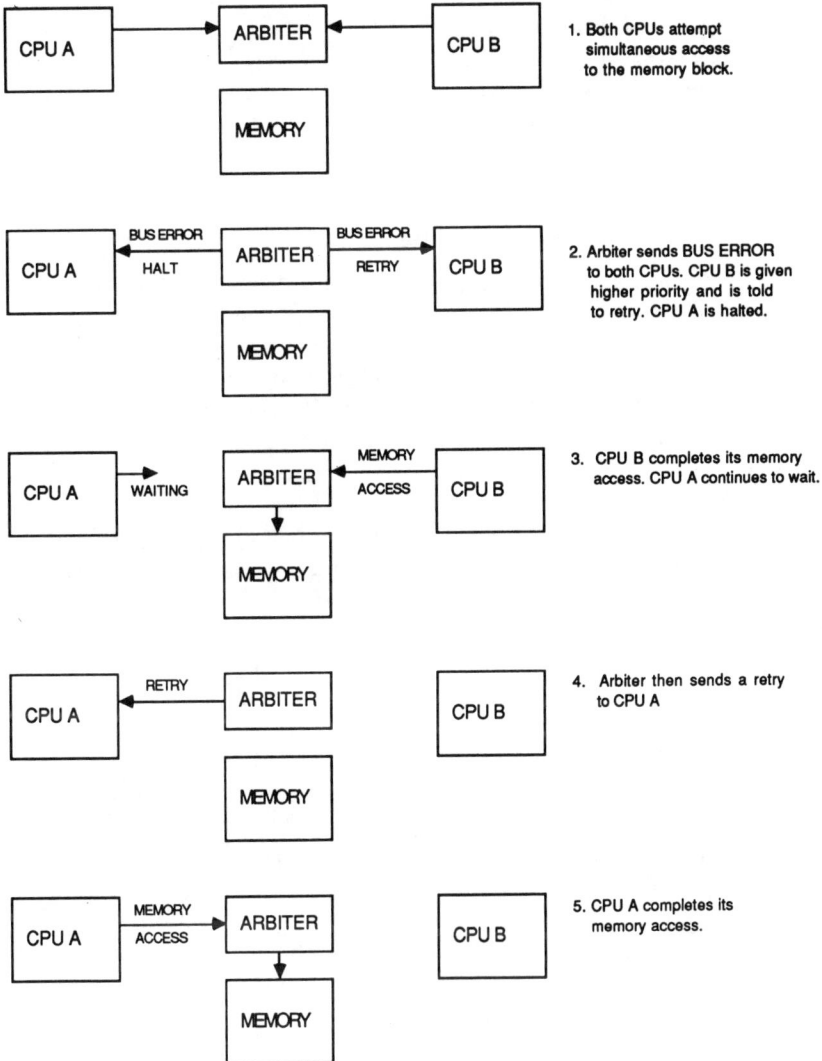

Figure 1.9 *Resolving a 'deadly embrace' between two competing processors*

Microcoded design

Another problem of the early generations of microprocessors was their response to invalid *op codes*. At best, they could be ignored or simply halt the processor and system. At the worst, it was possible for them to be put into undocumented test modes, which could cause the address bus to act as a free running counter with disasterous effects on the outside system. These characteristics often restricted the use of microprocessors in applications like process control.

The MC68000 family uses a design which pre-loads microcode into logic sequencers to provide the internal functions required. This technique means that illegal op codes can be recognized and prevented from putting the processor into an unknown state. Instead, an exception is caused allowing software to decide exactly what to do. This technique can also be used to execute user-defined instructions.

Multiprocessor communication support

In the late 1970s, an emerging trend in microprocessor system design was the use of multiple processors to increase system throughput. These techniques were initially quite primitive due to the lack of direct support available from the processor. Bus cycles and clocks were stretched, delayed or removed to allow other bus masters, such as direct memory controllers, other processors and intelligent peripherals, to access the main system bus. This involved extensive external logic—again, simpler, more efficient support was required.

Today, a three wire bus arbitration scheme is provided by the MC68000 processor to allow any bus master to ask for and receive the MC68000 bus. A request is made by asserting the Bus Request signal, BR★. When the current processor bus cycle has completed, a Bus Grant (BG★) output is asserted which tells the requester that the bus is available. The register then takes the bus and asserts the Bus Grant Acknowledge (BGACK★) which removes the bus request.

Seven levels of interrupt are supported and either a predefined vector for the interrupt level, or a peripheral supplied vector can be used to select one of 256 possible software handler routines. All but interrupt level 7 can be masked. Within the system, certain vectors can be defined for use with each peripheral, thereby removing the need for the software handler to interrogate the system in order to determine what action is required. These vectors are contained with all the other exception vectors in a vector table in the bottom 1024 bytes of memory starting at 000000. Figure 1.10 shows the vector table for an MC68000 and the exceptions that it handles.

MEMORY ADDRESS   VECTOR NUMBER   MEMORY ADDRESS   VECTOR NUMBER

Memory Address		Vector Number
0	RESET	0
8	Bus Error	2
C	Address Error	3
10	Illegal Instruction	4
14	Divide-by-Zero	5
18	CHECK Instruction	6
1C	TRAPV Instruction	7
20	Privilege Violation	8
24	Trace	9
28	Line 1010 Emulator	A
2C	Line 1111 Emulator	B
30	Unassigned - Reserved	C
3C	Uninitialised Interrupt	F
40	Unassigned - Reserved	10

Memory Address		Vector Number
60	Spurious Interrupt	18
64	Level 1 Autovector	19
68	Level 2 Autovector	2A
6C	Level 3 Autovector	1B
70	Level 4 Autovector	1C
74	Level 5 Autovector	1D
78	Level 6 Autovector	1E
7C	Level 7 Autovector	1F
80	16 TRAP Instructions	20
C0	Unassigned - Reserved	30
100	192 User-Definable Vector Locations	40
3FC		FF

Figure 1.10 *MC68000 vector table*

Future upgradeability

The MC68000 was designed to provide a platform for the arrival of the full 32-bit versions, the MC68020, MC68030 and MC68040. All these processors have the same User Programming model and are 100% compatible with the MC68000 user instruction set. This provides easy movement of software both up and down the family, allowing applications designers to choose the most appropriate hardware configuration.

Generated new bus requirements

With such a radical departure from the original microprocessor design, it became clear that a new bus standard was required to fully exploit the potential of this new family.

It would need to support:

A   8-, 16- and 32-bit micros and their respective data and address paths
B   shared memory access via a high speed bus interface
C   multiprocessor systems

D   multiple level interrupt structure
E   I/O facilities
F   future upgrades.

Motorola proposed VERSAbus to meet these requirements.

VERSAbus – the precursor

Electrically, this bus was very similar to the VMEbus, providing an asynchronous non–multiplexed data transfer bus with bus arbitration and multiple level interrupts. It supported 8, 16, 32–bit data and address paths with parity and defined a transmission line type backplane to provide optimum performance. It was extremely popular in the United States but never caught on in Europe.

The reason for this unpopularity appears to be the large form factor and the edge connectors it used to connect a board into the backplane. Although they provided large areas to realize high functionality, the boards were cumbersome in comparison with the Eurocard packaging scheme, based around the next generation of connectors, which had found favour in Europe.

The solution appeared to be obvious: take the VERSAbus electrical specification and adapt it to the Eurocard form factor and DIN pin and socket connectors. This was done by Motorola Microsystems in Munich, and VMEbus rev A was born.

VMEbus

The first VME rev A products from Motorola Munich were announced in 1981. These were an MC68000 based processor card running at 8 MHz called the VECPU100, and a 64/256 Kbyte dynamic RAM module, the VECPU200. However, it was not until the release of rev B in 1982, with the joint backing of Philips, Thompson, Mostek (now part of Thompson) and Motorola, that the specification stabilized and the VMEbus products started to appear in the marketplace in significant quantities.

Since then, feedback of customers, the electrical standardization authorities, the IEC and IEEE have revised the specification to revision level C.

This revision to the specification extended the functions by providing support for misalignment and by clarifying and recommending solutions and/or interpretations. Since then, the bus has been given IEC and IEEE recognition in the form of IEC–821BUS and IEEE–P1014. Further minor revisions have been incorporated into the current release revision C1.

For the user, the VMEbus has provided the fastest growing industry bus standard, with over 300 manufacturers producing products world-wide, many active Users' Groups and its own trade association, VITA (VMEbus International Trade Association).

But what does VME stand for?

This question is often asked, but the definitive answer appears to be lost in the mists of time. The VM stands for VersaModule, the name of the boards based around the VERSAbus specification. The E either stands for Europe, where the initial idea originated, or from the Eurocard packaging it used.

2
VMEbus primer

VMEbus—its design concepts

The VMEbus is designed as a global parallel interconnect supporting 8, 16 and 32-bit processors and data paths. Data transfers are based on a non-multiplexed asynchronous protocol which allows transfers between bus masters and slaves (e.g. processor and memory card) to be performed at the highest speed that the slowest card will allow. This asynchronous communication allows speed upgrades to be performed without having to modify the entire system.

Multiprocessor support is essential for any bus to be accepted and this is an integral part of the VMEbus specification. Such support requires:

A a mechanism to prevent simultaneous bus accesses and to prioritize bus usage by multiple masters,

B a method of organizing and directing interrupt handling and system resource partitioning, and

C a protocol to reconcile different processor data and address bus widths.

The signal groups

The signals are best divided into four functional groups:

A the data transfer bus (DTB),
B DTB arbitration,
C interrupt bus, and
D utility bus.

The DTB performs the actual data transfers, providing protocols to cope with access times, misalignment and different address and data paths.

The DTB arbitration group deals with multiprocessor applications and provides an arbitration scheme to prevent catastrophic simultaneous bus accesses.

The interrupt bus provides the interrupt and vectoring mechanisms. System clocks, voltage supplies, system and power failure signals form the utility bus.

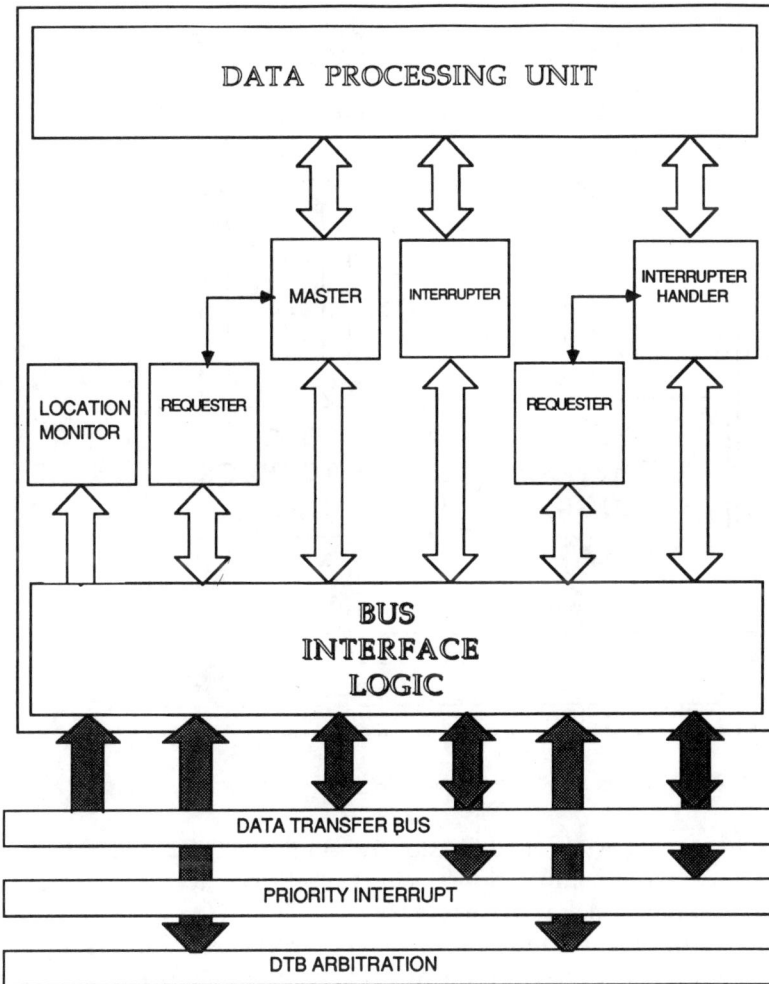

Figure 2.1 *VMEbus MASTER functional blocks*

The data transfer bus (DTB)

The data transfer bus provides the interface between a VMEbus MASTER and SLAVE. Their functional block diagrams are shown in Figures 2.1 and 2.2.

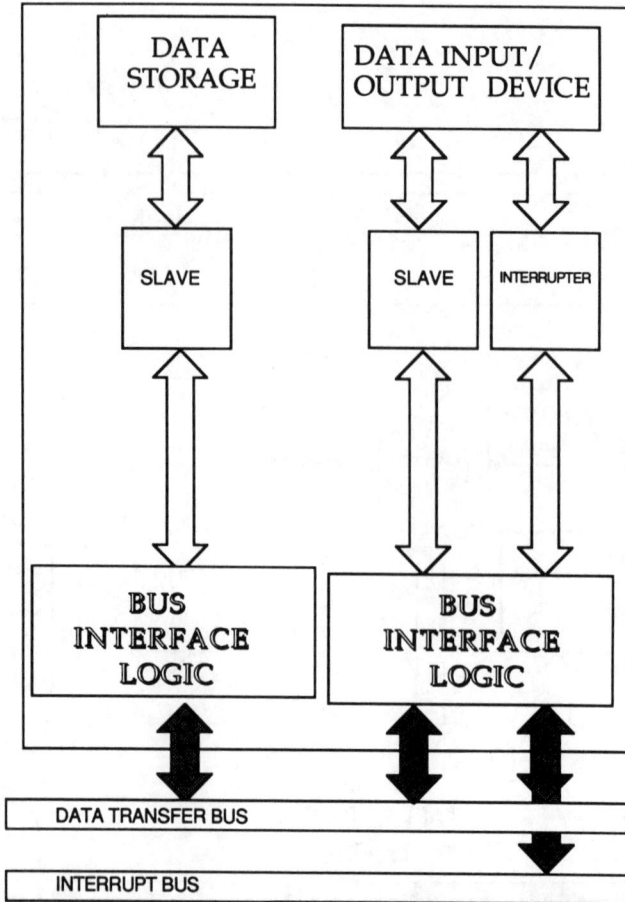

Figure 2.2 *VMEbus SLAVE and INTERRUPTER functional blocks*

A *system controller* located in slot 1, monitors DTB transfers and arbitrates between competing MASTERS for access to the bus. Figure 2.3 shows a functional diagram.

A MASTER initiates and controls any data transactions across the bus where memory is accessed on a SLAVE board. The SLAVE plays a purely passive role and can only respond to a MASTER; it cannot initiate a transfer.

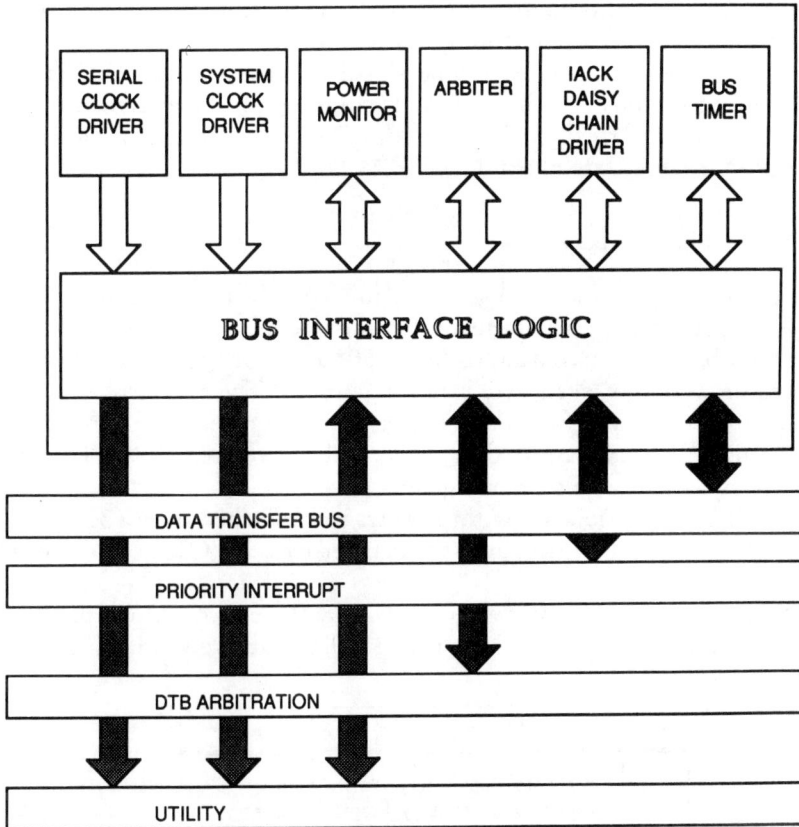

Figure 2.3 *VMEbus system controller functional blocks.*

A processor board may house both MASTER and SLAVE interfaces. The MASTER interface is used when the processor accesses VMEbus memory and the SLAVE interface allows other MASTERS to access onboard VMEbus memory. Only one transaction can be conducted on the bus at any one time.

The DTB comprises a non-multiplexed 32-bit address bus and a 32-bit data bus. Address bits 24–31 and data bits 16–31 are connected via the second P2 connector.

For systems using only 24-bit addressing and 16-bit data paths, the P2 connector is not required but is often fitted to provide greater mechanical strength and robustness. Six address modifier bits are used to specify the address width and the type of access being performed and 16 are available for the user to define and use as needed.

Address bit 0 is decoded as two data strobe signals, DS0★ and DS1★, which are used with the LWORD★ signal to identify the data width for the transfer. In addition, there are signals to indicate if the cycle is a read or write operation or an interrupt acknowledgement.

The bus uses an address strobe signal to indicate that valid data is present on the bus and that a cycle is commencing. The asynchronous handshaking returned by the slave uses DTACK★ to reply a successful transfer or BERR★ to abort the cycle.

DTB read and write cycles

The VMEbus supports the use of any mix of 8, 16 and 32-bit processors by using bus signals to indicate the data bus size and addressing, on a cycle by cycle basis. The two data strobes (DS0★ and DS1★) indicate whether a word or an odd or even byte is being accessed. The two strobes are, in fact, a decoded address line A0. For 32-bit transfers, the long word (LWORD★) signal is asserted. If a mismatch in size occurs, e.g. accessing a byte as a word, a bus error is generated.

Unaligned transfers allow three bytes to be fetched over a 32-bit bus and are supported by decoding the data strobes, LWORD★ and the A1 address bit.

Different address widths are indicated by the use of address modifier codes to inform the system how many address bits are valid. Three sizes

Code	Function
3 f	Standard Supervisory Block Transfer
3e	Standard Supervisory Program Access
3d	Standard Supervisory Data Access
3b	Standard Non Privileged Block Transfer
3a	Standard Non Privileged Program Access
3 9	Standard Non Privileged Data Access
2d	Short Supervisory Access
2 9	Short Non Privileged Access
0 f	Extended Supervisory Block Transfer
0e	Extended Supervisory Program Access
0d	Extended Supervisory Data Access
0b	Extended Non Privileged Block Transfer
0a	Extended Non Privileged Program Access
0 9	Extended Non Privileged Data Access

n.b. 1. Codes 10 to 1F are User Defined.
      2. All other codes are reserved.

Figure 2.4 *Address modifier codes and their function*

are supported: 16, 24 and 32 bit, giving 64 Kbyte, 16 Mbyte and 4 Gbyte addressing, respectively. The address modifiers also indicate whether data/program, user/supervisor, block transfer or other user-defined access is taking place.

These modifiers allow hierarchical system partitioning, memory bank switching and similar schemes. Their use also provides fault tolerance, in respect of failures of address generating components. Figure 2.4 shows the defined address modifier codes and their meaning. The only difference between op code fetches, data accesses, etc. are the contents of the address modifiers.

The transfer mechanism is very similar to that used by the MC68000

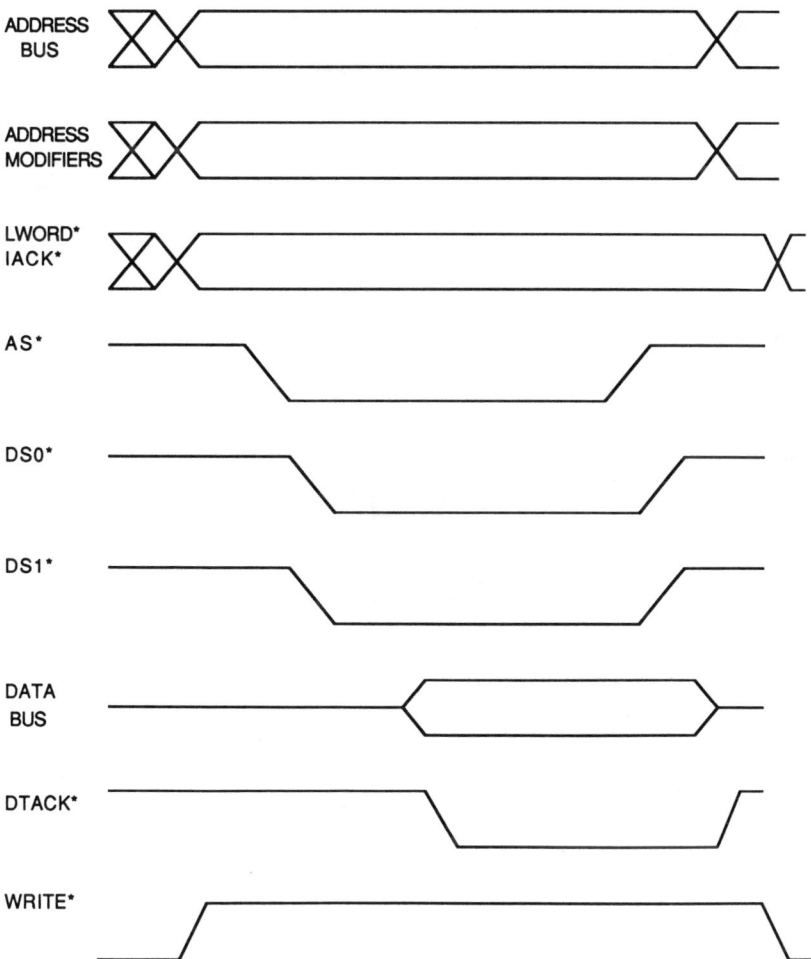

Figure 2.5 *VMEbus data transfer READ cycle*

microprocessor. The MASTER that currently owns the bus initiates a data transfer by driving the address modifiers, the address bus, IACK★, WRITE★ and LWORD★ as required. The address strobe, AS★, is then asserted to start the cycle. If the transaction is a write, the MASTER must supply the valid data before driving the data strobes DS0★ and DS1★ to indicate the data width. The SLAVE responds to the data strobes by either receiving the data in a write cycle or supplying data in a read cycle. The SLAVE acknowledges the transfer by asserting the DTACK★ signal. The MASTER responds by releasing the address and data strobes, which the SLAVE acknowledges by releasing DTACK★, and the cycle is completed.

If there is an error, the cycle is aborted by asserting BERR★ instead of

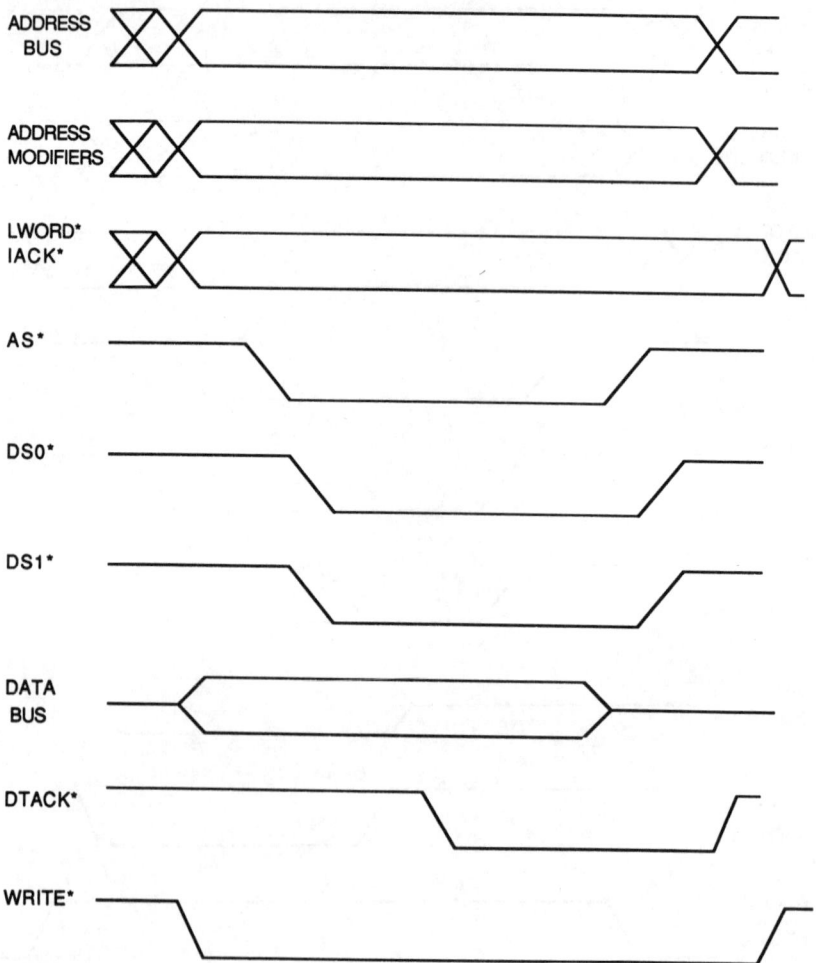

Figure 2.6   VMEbus data transfer WRITE cycle

driving DTACK★. The interface is truly asynchronous: if no DTACK★ or BERR★ is received, the MASTER waits indefinitely, locking up the bus and the system. Most systems implement at least one bus watchdog timer to assert BERR★ if the cycle is not completed within a specified time period. Figures 2.5–2.8 show typical timing diagrams for both successful and aborted read and write cycles.

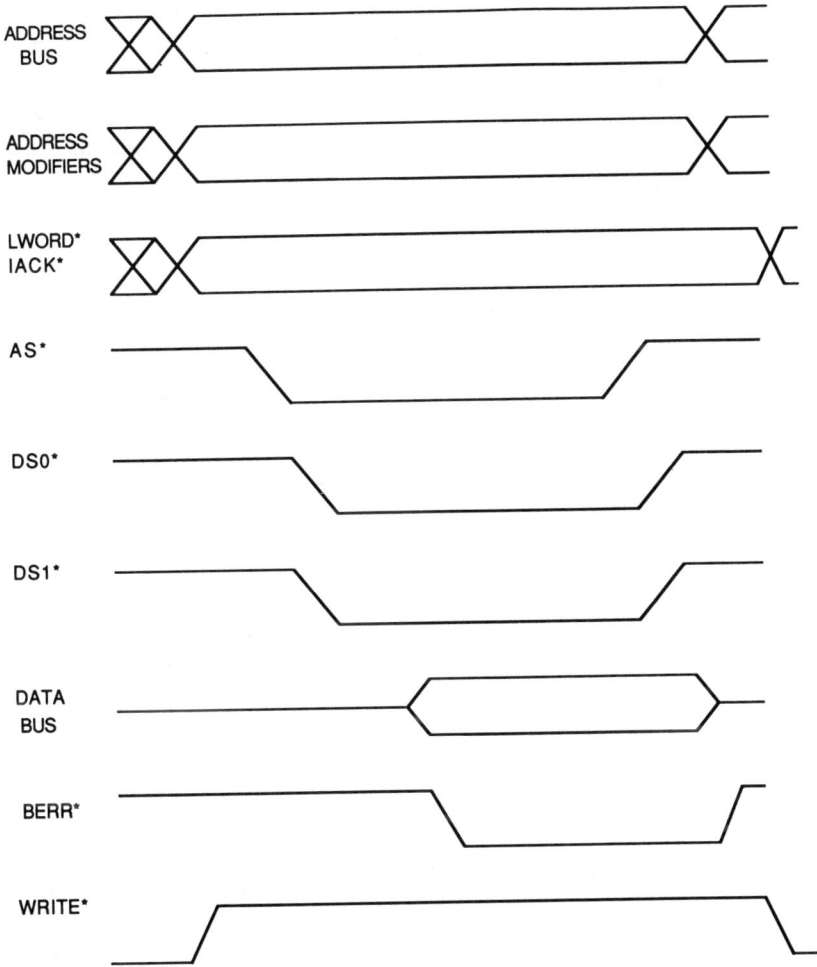

Figure 2.7 *VMEbus data transfer aborted READ cycle*

Read—modify—write cycles

The MC68000 microprocessor family supports software semaphores by providing a test and set instruction which reads data, modifies it and

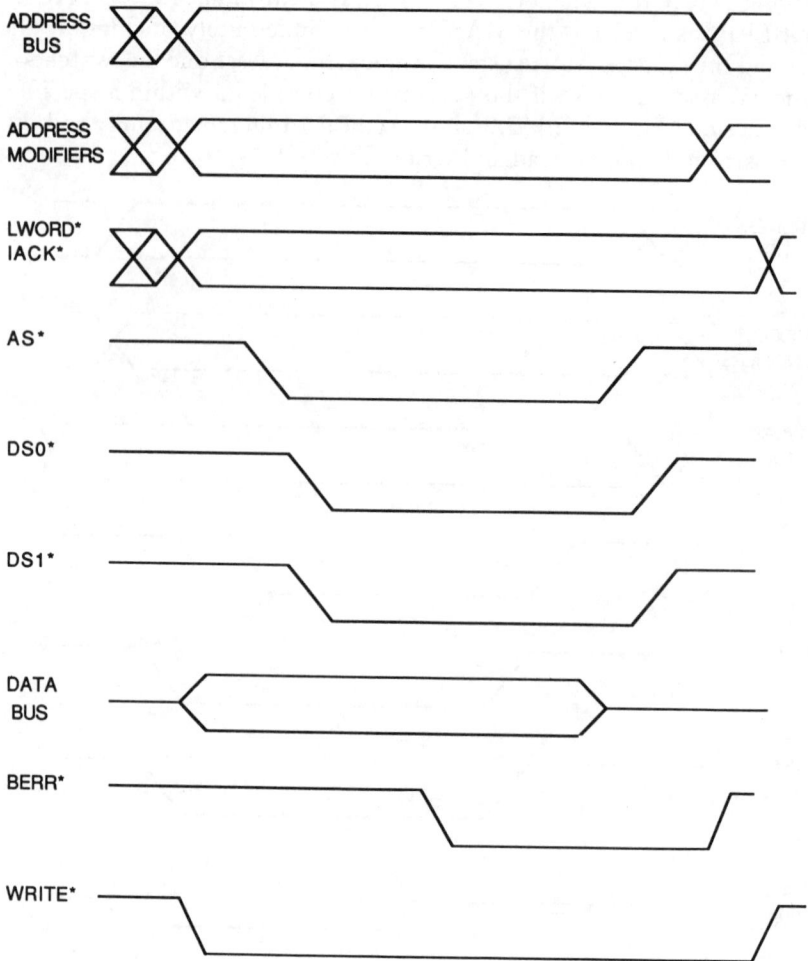

Figure 2.8   VMEbus data transfer aborted WRITE cycle

writes it out again. This whole operation is indivisible, thus preventing possible semaphore corruption. The DTB supports this type of operation.

The read part of the cycle is exactly the same as a normal cycle. When the DTACK★ has been sent by the SLAVE, the MASTER only releases the data strobes. The address strobe remains asserted, indicating that this is a read—modify—write cycle. When DTACK★ is released, the MASTER drives WRITE★ low and places the modified data on the bus. The data strobes are then toggled and the data received by the SLAVE: the cycle is terminated as for a normal write operation.

Block transfers

By specifying a special address modifier code, large blocks of data can be transferred over the bus without having to continually drive the address bus.

The start of the block transfer is the same as a standard data transfer: the address and qualifying signals, including the address modifier code, are placed on the bus. The data strobes are then toggled and acknowledged by the SLAVE to complete the first transfer. The data strobes are then driven high and toggled again to start the next transfer. The address and other qualifiers remain constant and it is the SLAVE's responsibility to increment the address of the location being accessed. The size of this increment will depend on the number of bytes transferred on each cycle. At the end of the block transfer, the address bus and qualifying signals are released.

The VMEbus specification supports address pipelining. This is where the address of the next location is placed on the address bus while the data of the preceding transaction is still on the bus.

Address only cycles

This is the only cycle that never transfers any data. The cycle starts as normal, but the data strobes are not asserted and the MASTER finishes the cycle without DTACK* or BERR* being driven. It is used to speed up accesses across the VMEbus.

A processor starts a memory cycle which may access either a VMEbus SLAVE or some local memory. The address only cycle allows the VMEbus address decoding to start in parallel with the onboard decoding instead of waiting. This removes the delay before starting a VMEbus access caused by checking for a local access first.

Location monitoring

Location monitors simply monitor the VMEbus cycles and generate onboard signals if accesses are performed. This provides a mechanism for global message passing and interrupts.

The DTB arbitration bus

The VMEbus is a multiMASTER system and therefore has to be controlled so only one MASTER accesses the DTB at any one time. The mechanism for deciding which MASTER should have the DTB and how the ownership should be transferred is provided by the DTB arbitration bus.

There are two cases to consider:

1   arbitrating for the bus when it is not in use, and
2   arbitrating for the bus when another MASTER is using it.

In both cases, before a MASTER can use the bus, it must request it by asserting one of the four bus request lines (BR0* to BR3*) and waiting for the system bus arbiter (located in slot 1) to reply.

If the request is the highest pending and the bus is vacant, it will be acknowledged by asserting the appropriate bus grant signal for that level.

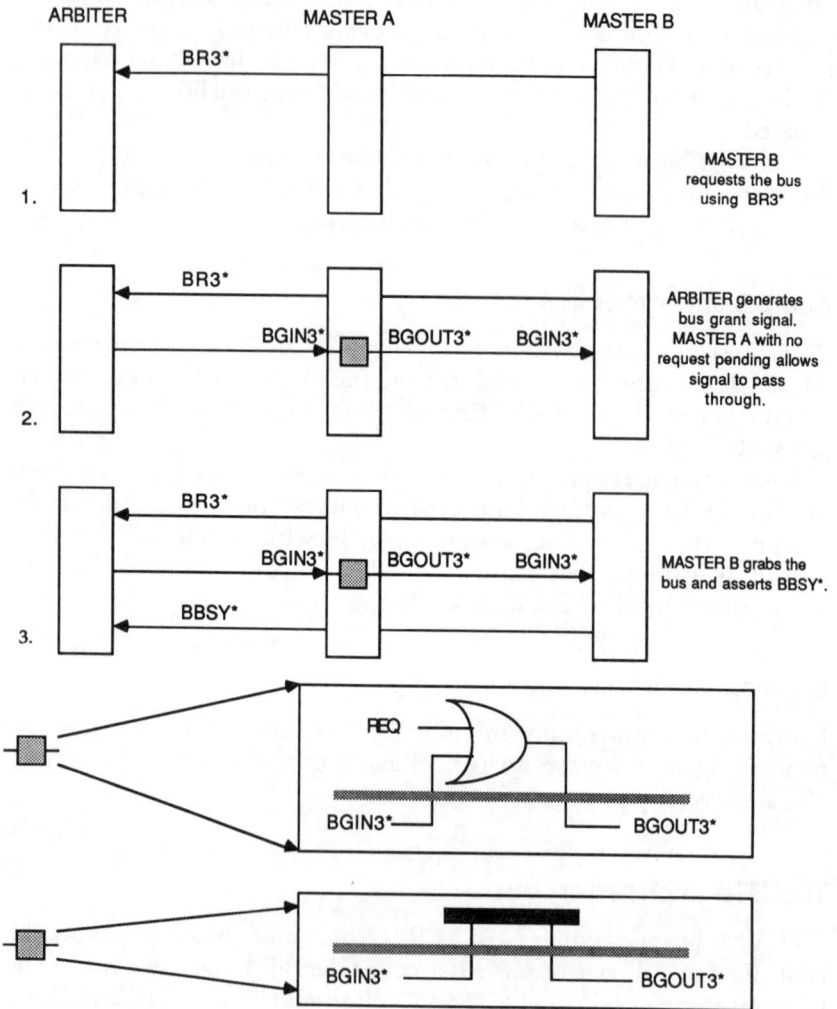

Figure 2.9   *VMEbus DTB arbitration slot priority*

These signals are daisy-chained down the backplane using the BGIN*
and BGOUT* signals.

This means that, for a particular arbitration level, there is a hierarchy
based on slot position. Figure 2.9 shows the operation: if a MASTER
does not require the bus, the bus grant signal is passed through to the next
adjacent board. If the MASTER does require the bus, the bus grant signal
is received and prevented from being passed further down the daisy-
chain. It asserts the bus busy signal, BBSY*, and relinquishes the bus
request. The arbiter sees the BBSY* signal and releases the bus grant
signal. The MASTER continues to assert the BBSY* signal during its use
of the DTB; when control is relinquished, the BBSY* signal is pulled
high by termination resistors, indicating that the bus is free. It is
extremely important for this mechanism to work that the daisy-chain is
unbroken: backplane jumpers must be used to link empty slots or boards
without such links.

In addition to this priority arbitration, single level and round robin
schemes are also supported. The bus arbiter, located on the system
controller in slot 1, can request a MASTER to relinquish the bus after
completion of its usage (Release on Request, ROR) or the present bus
cycle (Release On Demand, ROD). The latter is very important for a
real-time response. Bus arbitration is concurrent with data transfer to
maximize throughput.

If a MASTER is already using the bus, and it is of a lower priority than
the requester, then the bus has to be given up. The release of the bus
follows either a ROR (where the MASTER will monitor the request
lines and release them when another request is made) or RWD (Release
When Done, where the MASTER will relinquish the bus when it has no
further use for it).

The choice of release mechanism is important in determining the
overall system characteristics. RWD suits a MASTER that frequently
uses the bus and does not want to continually arbitrate. The disadvantage
is that it can result in 'bus hogging', which increases interrupt latency and
decreases response times. The ROR is more suitable for less frequent
users, where the arbitration waiting time is decreased and interrupt
latency reduced; however, it can increase arbitration delays during
periods of heavy VMEbus traffic.

Requester modules can monitor either the BCLR* or ACFAIL*
signals so that they can relinquish the bus if either of the signals becomes
active. This is extremely important for the ACFAIL* line because it
signals an impending power failure for which the system may only have a
few microseconds to prepare.

This specification only refers to the three arbitration schemes
mentioned so far. Many more sophisticated VMEbus boards allow
alternative algorithms to be implemented, often under software control.

This permits fairer implementations and hierarchies to be used.

Interrupt handling

VMEbus boards do not have to use the interrupt structure at all; however, if a system does, a handler must be assigned to each one of the seven interrupt priority levels. This can either be centralized and handled by a single MASTER or distributed throughout the system, as shown in Figure 2.10. Distributed configurations will have two or more MASTERS handling interrupts between them. Only one handler should be assigned to each level.

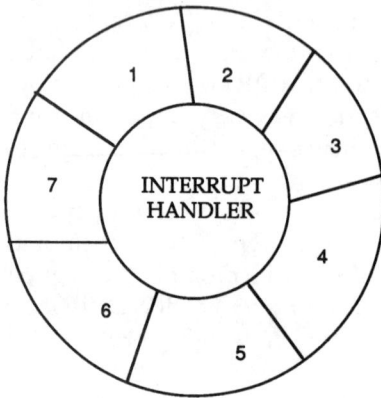

CENTRAL INTERRUPT HANDLING

One handler for all 7 interrupt levels.

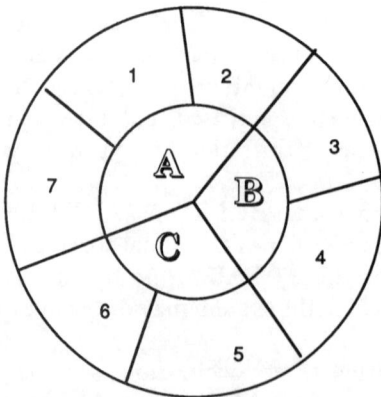

DISTRIBUTED INTERRUPT HANDLING

A handles levels 1,2,7
B   "   "   3,4
C   "   "   5,6

Figure 2.10 *VMEbus interrupt handling schemes*

An interrupt is started by asserting one of the interrupt request lines, IRQ1★ to IRQ7★. IRQ7★ is the highest priority and IRQ1★ the lowest. The interrupt handler for that level receives the request and immediately requests control of the DTB.

Once the bus has been granted, the handler starts an acknowledgement cycle: a 3-bit code which identifies the interrupt level being acknowledged is placed on address bits 1–3 and the IACK★ and AS★ signals driven low. The handler drives the data strobes low to indicate the status data size, i.e. 8, 16, or 32 bits. The daisy-chain driver in slot 1 then drives IACKIN★, providing it is not the interrupter board, and this signal is propagated down the IACKIN★ and IACKOUT★ daisy-chain. This is shown in Figure 2.11. Each board receives this signal and when the interrupter sees the signal it checks the 3-bit code and passes the signal down if it does not correspond to its pending interrupt level. If it does, the IACKOUT★ signal is not passed on and the status data are placed on the bus. The interrupter drives DTACK★ low, the handler reads the data and

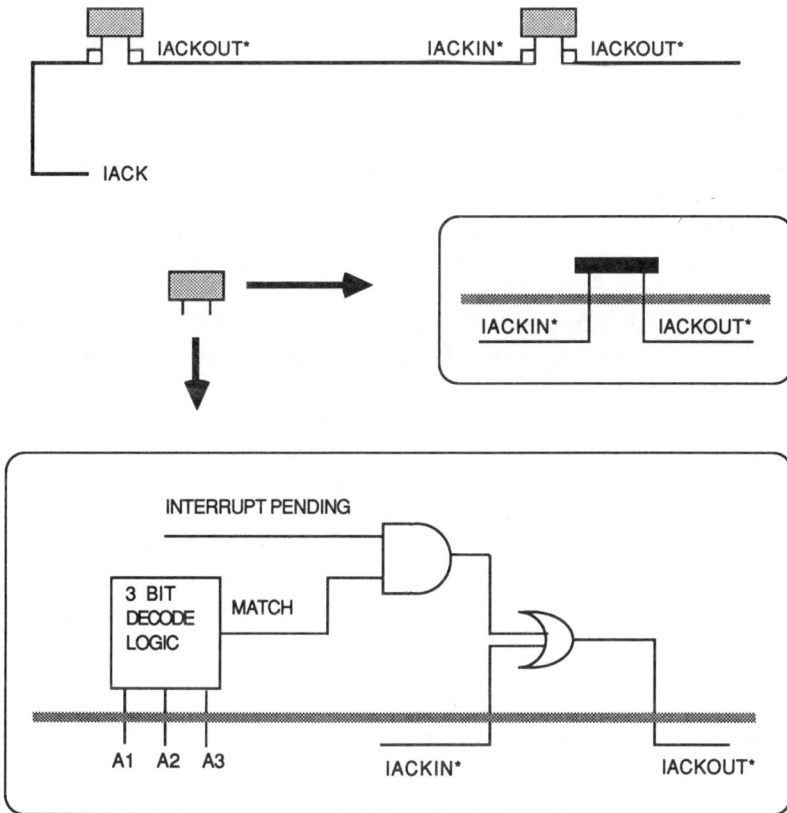

Figure 2.11 *VMEbus interrupt priority daisy-chaining*

releases the bus. The interrupter removes the DTACK⋆ signal and the acknowledgement cycle is complete. The daisy-chaining provides an additional priority scheme to the seven levels based on a slot position. The nearer slot 1, the higher priority within a level. It is important to have an unbroken chain to ensure that the IACK signals are not stopped prematurely.

The interrupt request can be released in one of two ways:

1   The termination of a successful interrupt acknowledgement cycle is used by a 'release on acknowledgement' interrupter.

2   A 'release on register access' interrupter only removes the request after an onboard register has been accessed from the VMEbus. This is usually performed by the handler's interrupt routine and therefore may incur delays in the complete system.

There is no relationship between the interrupt level and bus request level, although for maximum interrupt response, high priority interrupts should be handled by handlers with high priority bus request levels.

The utility bus

The utility bus comprises the power rails, the system reset and clock, the system and power fail signals and the I/O pins.

The VMEbus specifies the supply of +5V, +12V, −12V and a standby + 5V rails. In practice, the backplane distributes the power from central connectors.

A 16 MHz clock signal is available from the SYSCLK⋆ signal. This is supplied from the system controller function located in slot 1, although many boards do not use it, preferring to generate their own signals onboard. It does not have any timing relationship with the bus signals or timings. It is mainly used for the VMEbus serial bus, VMS.

The SYSFAIL⋆ signal allows any board to indicate its own failure by asserting the line. The ACFAIL⋆ signal is generated by a separate power supply monitor and indicates an imminent power supply failure. Both these signals are routed through to a supervisor processor board, where they generate a non-maskable interrupt so that a fast system response can be obtained.

The SYSRESET⋆ resets all the boards in the system when asserted. It can be used at any time either by a VMEbus board or by some external hardware to reset the system. On most VMEbus processor boards the reset button can be set to generate a global reset as well as a local one.

Mechanical specifications

VMEbus boards come in three main sizes. The two most common are the single and double Eurocard form factors which measure 160 mm by 233.35 mm and 100 mm by 160 mm respectively. The third type extends the depth of the Eurocard to give a larger board area. Such extensions do cause difficulties with racks and subassemblies if other

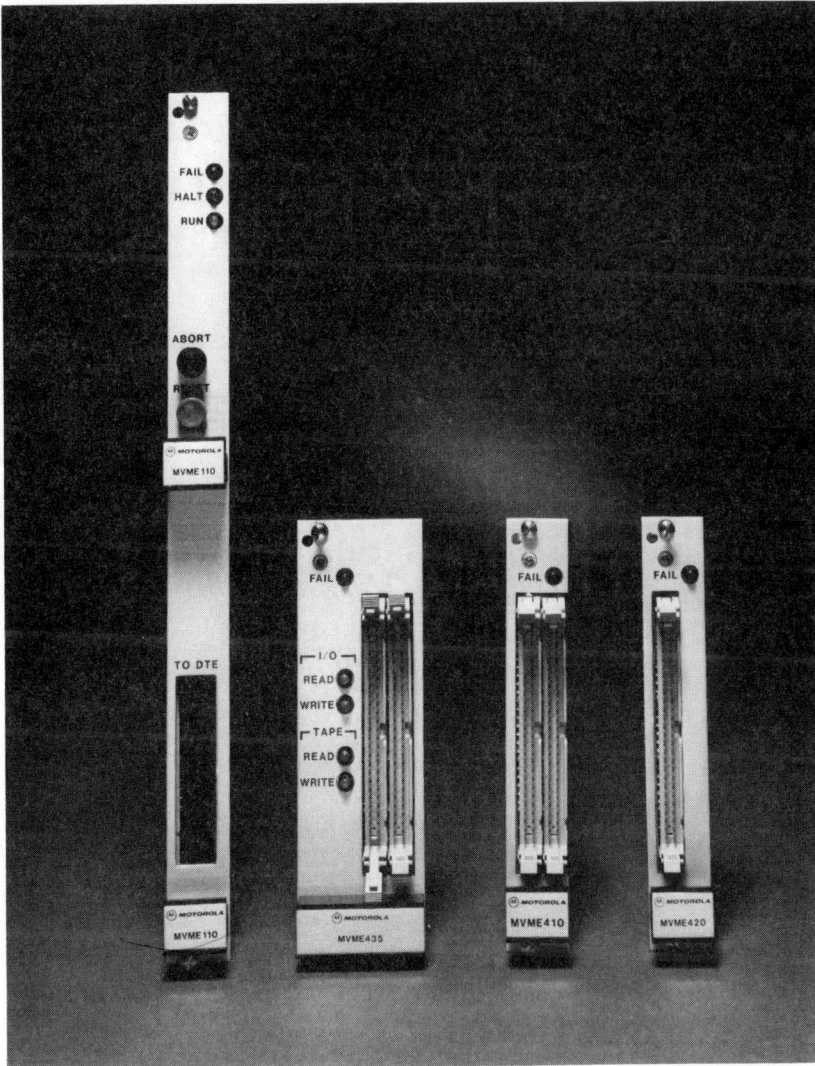

Figure 2.12 *Example single and double height Eurocards*

normal sized boards are used as well. The specification prescribes standards for the complete mechanics of the system ranging from screw thread sizes to panel thicknesses. Figure 2.12 shows a double height Eurocard vmebus board with single and double width, single height Eurocard I/O channel boards. Figure 2.13 shows a VMEbus rack with a mixture of such boards installed. A large plug-in power supply is located on the right of the rack. The VMEbus backplane can be seen on the back.

The connector pin outs are shown in appendix D.

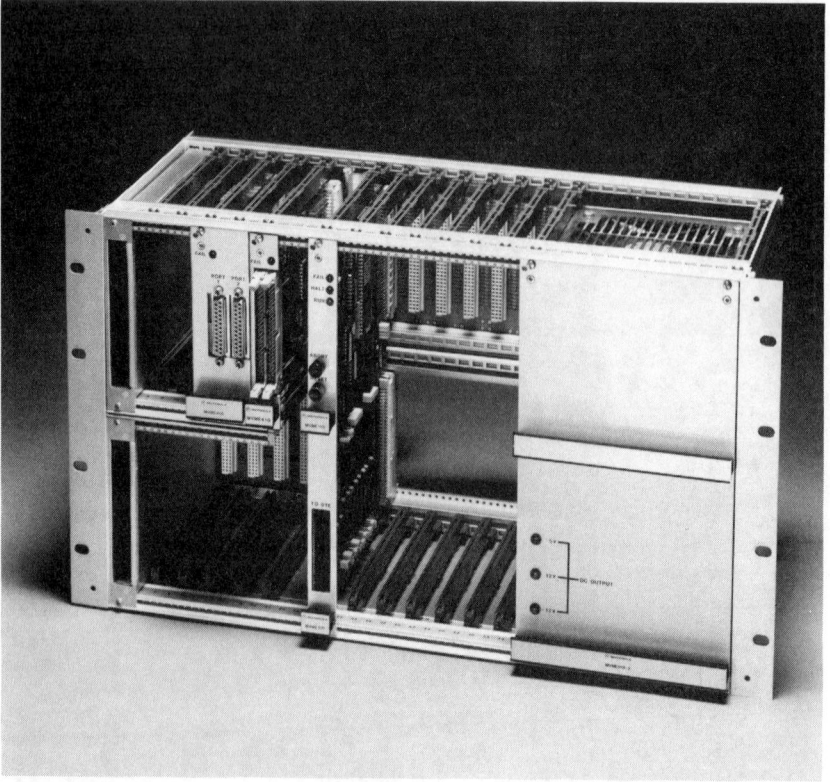

Figure 2.13 *A VMEbus rack*

3
VSB and other secondary buses

This chapter describes the following associated buses:

- VSB, the VME subsystem bus
- VMS, serial communications bus
- VXI, the instrumentation subsystem bus
- VIC, the intercrate bus

VMX – the first subsystem bus

Many early VMEbus documents make reference to a VMX memory extension bus and not to VSB. VMX was proposed before VSB and before the advent of the 32-bit MC68020 microprocessor in 1984. It specifies a local memory extension bus using the user defined I/O pin on the second P2 connector with a 32-bit data path and a 24-bit addressing capability. It was this restriction that contributed to its rejection by the VMEbus community. Although it provided a simple extension suitable for MC68000 based systems that needed the additional highway to improve multiprocessor designs, it failed to cater for the new bus needs of the MC68020.

With the arrival of the MC68020 and its 32-bit data and address widths, caches and dynamic bus sizing, the inadequacy of VMX became apparent. It did not support any of these features. The biggest problem was with the 24-bit address range: many of the applications that became possible with the power provided by the MC68020 needed in excess of the 16 Mbytes provided by 24-bit addressing. A further potential concern was the multiple mapping that could occur with a mixed system. Figure 3.1 shows the problem. The partial addressing within a 32-bit system could result in the VMX memory being multiple mapped within the system, thus fooling any memory sizing system into believing that the system had more memory than it had in reality. As a result, VMX was not deemed suitable for many applications where an extension bus is most beneficial. Motorola implemented a different bus called VMX32, which had a full 32-bit address range and support for the MC68020 bus features. This first appeared on its MVME130/1 processor boards and was rapidly accepted as a better solution. It also formed a subset of the VSB specification.

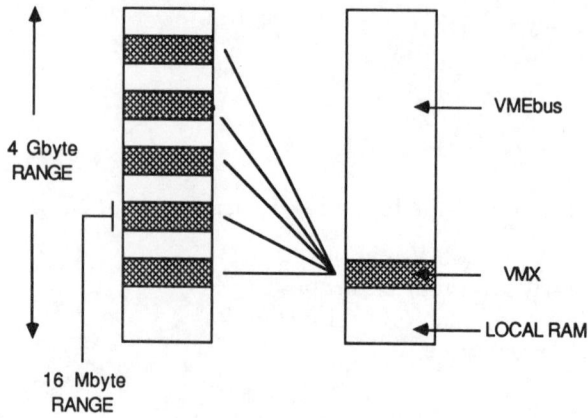

Figure 3.1 *Multiple memory mapping of the VMXbus through partial address decoding*

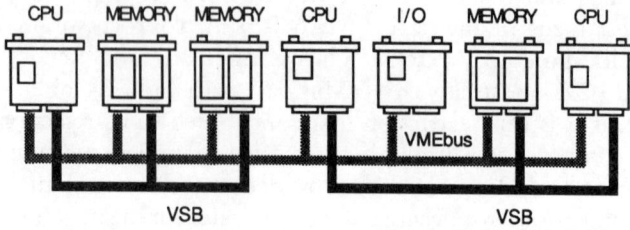

A dual VSB sub system.

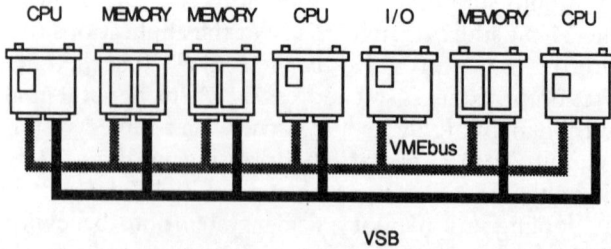

A single VSB sub system with the maximum number of boards.

Figure 3.2 *Typical VSB configurations*

VSB—the VMEbus subsystem bus

The VSB uses the user-defined I/O pins available on the P2 connector. Like the VMEbus, it has data transfer, bus arbitration and interrupt handling facilities and much of the terminology is similar: transfers are initiated by a MASTER and responded to by a SLAVE. Prior to such transfers, the bus is arbitrated for and there is a interrupt mechanism. It supports up to six boards, each one being assigned a unique, geographic address depending on slot position. Within a VMEbus system, there may be more than one VSB system. Typical configurations are depicted in Figure 3.2.

Figure 3.3 describes the signals and their functions.

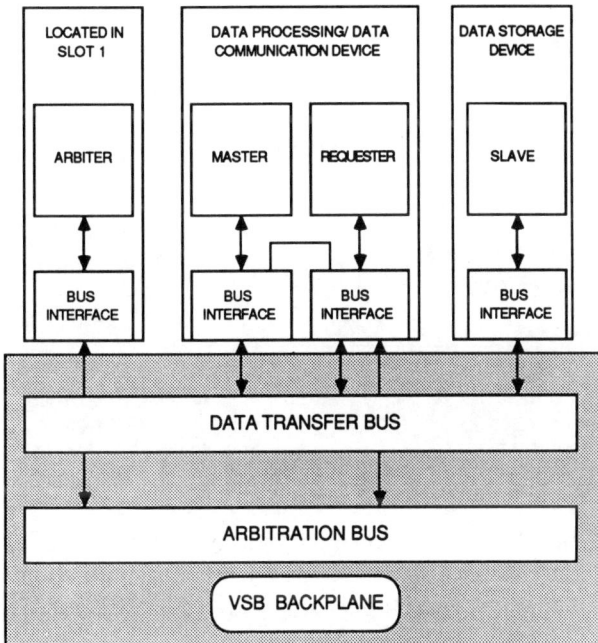

Figure 3.3 *Functional modules and sub-buses defined by VSB*

The VSB data transfer bus

The basic functional blocks involved in data transfers are shown in Figure 3.4. VSB has a similar concept to that of VMEbus involving MASTERS, SLAVES and a System Controller located in slot 1.

MASTER   SLAVE

ACQUIRE DATA TRANSFER BUS
INITIATE ADDRESS BROADCAST

ACKNOWLEDGE ADDRESS
BROADCAST

TERMINATE ADDRESS BROADCAST

INITIATE DATA TRANSFER

ACKNOWLEDGE DATA
TRANSFER

TERMINATE DATA TRANSFER

TERMINATE CYCLE

ACKOWLEDGE CYCLE
TERMINATION

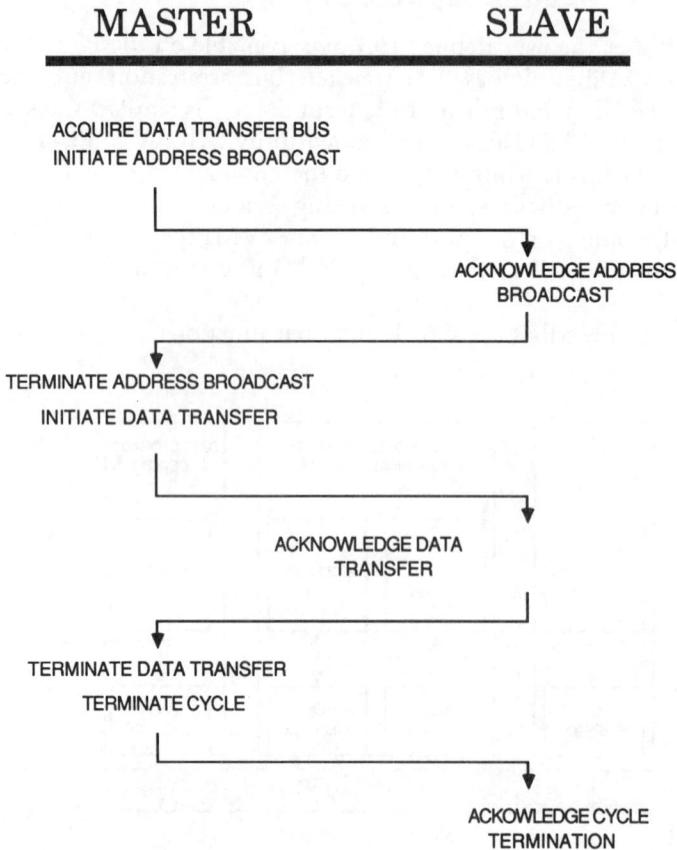

Figure 3.4   *General flow of a VSB data transfer cycle*

Due to the limited number of signal pins available, the 32-bit address and data buses are multiplexed on to 32 AD00–AD31 address data lines. During the first part of a data transfer cycle, the address is issued on these lines, followed by the data. The address is further qualified and can be in one of three address spaces:

1   the System Address Space,
2   the I/O Address Space, or
3   the Alternate Address Space.

These spaces are defined by two space pins SPACE0 and SPACE1. In addition, their fourth state indicates an INTERRUPT-ACKNOW-LEDGE or an ARBITRATION cycle. the WR★ and LOCK★ signals define read/write cycles and indivisible cycles.

Once a MASTER has arbitrated and obtained the bus, it can commence a data transfer. Such a transfer is shown in Figure 3.4. The first part is the address broadcast phase, where the address and its space information, read/write status and the bus lock information are driven on to the bus. This information is decoded by the VSB SLAVES when PAS* is driven low. The number of bytes that the MASTER needs to transfer is given by the SIZE0 and SIZE1 pins and forms part of the address decoding performed by the SLAVE.

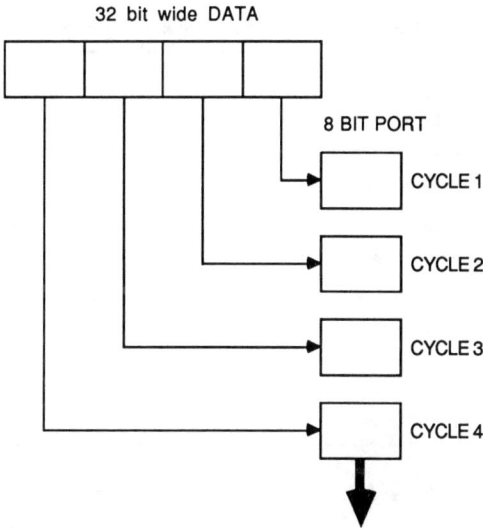

32 bit wide DATA

8 BIT PORT

CYCLE 1

CYCLE 2

CYCLE 3

CYCLE 4

Transfering a 32 Bit Word to a 8 Bit Port via VSB

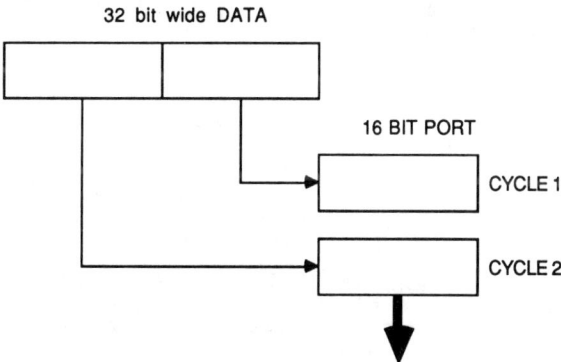

32 bit wide DATA

16 BIT PORT

CYCLE 1

CYCLE 2

Transfering a 32 Bit Word to a 16 Bit Port via VSB

Figure 3.5 *Dynamic bus sizing for VSB*

When the SLAVE has completed the decode, it asserts a code on the ASACK0 and ASACK1 pins, which also indicate the maximum number of bytes that the SLAVE can accept. This mechanism provides a dynamic bus sizing mechanism which tells the MASTER how many cycles will be required to complete the data transfer; for example, if the SLAVE has an 8-bit port, four cycles will be required to transfer 32 bits. The mechanism is shown in Figure 3.5. If the SLAVE needs more time, it will assert WAIT★ and force the MASTER to wait until the SLAVE releases AC★.

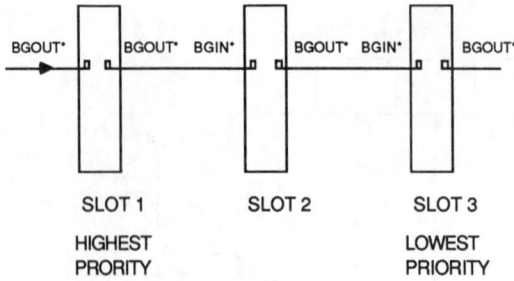

Figure 3.6   *Serial arbitration for VSB*

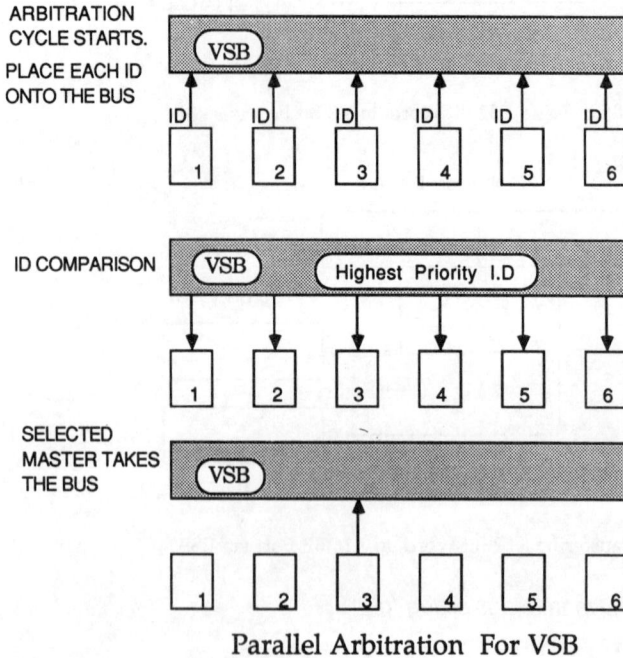

Parallel Arbitration For VSB

Figure 3.7   *Parallel arbitration for VSB*

When the address phase is complete, the AD00–31 lines are used to transfer the data. This is indicated by the MASTER by asserting the DS★ signal. Once the data have been transferred, the responding SLAVE drives ACK★ to indicate a successful completion or ERR★ if there is a failure such as a parity error. In addition, the SLAVE can indicate if the data can be cached via the CACHE★ pin.

The data transfer bus supports single and block transfers as well as address only transfers. In addition, there is a broadcast/broadcall facility for global message passing and cache coherency mechanisms.

VSB arbitration

VSB has two types of arbitration mechanism: both serial and parallel schemes are supported. Figures 3.6 and 3.7 show how they work.

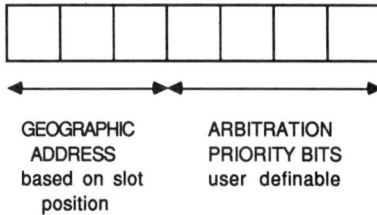

GEOGRAPHIC   ARBITRATION
ADDRESS   PRIORITY BITS
based on slot   user definable
position

Figure 3.8 *VSB arbitration ID*

The serial mechanism is similar to that of the single level VMEbus arbiter. Priority is simply based on slot position and using a daisy-chain mechanism. Two protocols are supported: Release When Done (RWD) and Release On Request (ROR). The RWD bus requester will release the bus when its MASTER no longer requires the bus, while ROR will only do so if there is another request pending. This latter scheme reduces the number of arbitrations required. If a MASTER needs the bus, its requester asserts BREQ★ and waits for a low level on BGIN★ to indicate that the bus is available. This signal is daisy-chained down the backplane through the BGIN★ and BGOUT★ signals in a similar way to that of the VMEbus. If a MASTER does not require the bus, the bus grant signal is passed on to the next board.

An alternative scheme uses a parallel arbitration method, where all MASTERS in the system participate simultaneously to select a new bus MASTER. The mechanism starts when the current active MASTER sees a bus request on the BREQ★ line. When the active MASTER no longer requires the bus, it starts an ARBITRATION cycle. This is denoted by the unique code on the two SPACE0–1 pins. During this cycle, the requesters negotiate for the bus. After detecting a high level on the

WAIT★ signal, they drive their ARBITRATION ID on to pins AD24–30 of the address data bus. After this has happened and their own selection logic has settled, each requester releases its contribution to the AC★ signal. When the last requester does this, the AC★ goes false, and the ARBITRATION ID on the bus is that of the requester with the highest priority. Each requester now compares this ID with its own, and the requester which matches takes control of the bus by driving BUSY★ low. The unsuccessful requesters then release AD24–30, the original active MASTER terminates the ARBITRATION cycle and the new MASTER can start transferring data.

The ARBITRATION ID, Figure 3.8, is a 7-bit value which comprises user-defined priority bits from AD27–AD30 and a geographical address on bits AD24–AD26. The geographical address is a unique code associated with each slot position and ensures that no ambiguous IDs are issued which would cause two MASTERS to assume the bus simultaneously.

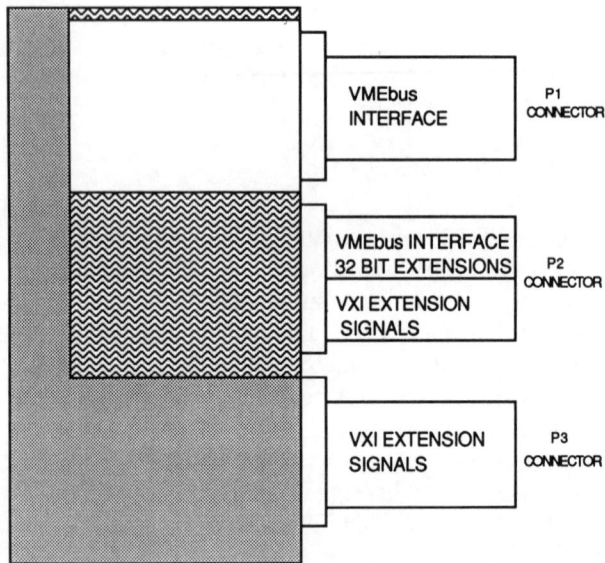

Figure 3.9   *VXI board sizes and extension signals*

Only one arbitration scheme can be employed at any one time. The selection of either serial or parallel arbitration is performed during power up. If parallel arbitration is chosen, the first active bus MASTER is also selected. This is essential as the arbitration mechanism requires an active bus MASTER at all times to initiate the arbitration cycles. If there is no active MASTER, no arbitration can take place and the system deadlocks and collapses.

VSB interrupts

The VSB defines two basic interrupt mechanisms for handling interrupts. The first uses a similar mechanism to parallel arbitration to decide which SLAVE interrupt request will be serviced next. The second is a simple polling mechanism, where the handling MASTER polls each SLAVE STATUS/ID register to determine which SLAVE needs servicing.

Both mechanisms start when an interrupting SLAVE generates an interrupt request by driving IRQ★ low. If the polling mechanism is used, the handling MASTER reads each SLAVE's STATUS/ID register by accessing a pre-arranged memory location. On each access, the SLAVE drives IRQ★ high so that when the requesting SLAVE is accessed in this way, the interrupt request is removed. The MASTER then must decide how to handle this interrupt within its own software. Usually the STATUS/ID register has a bit to indicate if it is asserting IRQ★. This system is simple but does place most of the selection responsibility in the hands of the software engineer and also requires the cooperation of the hardware engineer. The STATUS/ID register address must be unique for each board. An obvious solution is to use the geographical address bits, which are determined by slot position, to select a unique address in a memory block.

The second system uses an INTERRUPT–ACKNOWLEDGE cycle which is initiated by the handling MASTER. During this cycle, each participating SLAVE drives a 7-bit interrupt ID code on to AD24–AD30. This comprises the three geographical address bits and a user-defined 4-bit priority code. As with the parallel arbitration scheme, once this is complete, the INTERRUPT ID on the bus is used to select the SLAVE, by comparing it with the onboard value. If there is a match, the SLAVE supplies the STATUS/ID information to the MASTER, which then services the interrupt request. The MASTER may access the SLAVE many times to obtain the information required.

VMSbus serial bus interface

This is a serial bus which transfers data at 3.2 Mbits per second, decreasing to 363 Kbits with the two communication points 25 m apart. It uses a three-wire system: SERCLK is a high current signal obtained from the serial clock module located usually on the system controller. SYSRESET★ is used to initialize all the modules on the serial bus and

SERDAT★ is a wired OR line which can be driven by any open collector module on the bus. The system uses a token-passing mechanism to control access to the bus. Up to 1024 tokens can be created and passed from board to board. Control and data are obtained by sending various frames down the bus. There are eleven possible frames available: six associated with different size frames for data transfer while the remainder have controlling functions. Its main advantage is that it can pass data, events and semaphores from board to board and can provide similar communication to that offered by the VMEbus itself. This makes it eminently suitable for fault tolerant designs or where a lower cost, lower performance alternative to the VMEbus can be used.

The VMSbus has been talked about for many years, but it has not seen the adoption within the industry that was hoped. The only boards that support it are available from Philips, who also manufacture the silicon support chips. The main reason has been the delay in the availability of silicon support for it, which has prevented its use and forced designers to consider other communication links such as Ethernet, X25 and MAP. The silicon support chips, the SCC68173 VMSbus controller, talker and listener and SCC68171 SYSCLK monitor are now available and therefore only time will tell if this bus becomes better adopted.

Its main use is to provide communication between VMEbus systems and for fault tolerant systems that require a secondary communication path between modules. In this latter mode it can pass data, interrupts, etc. to provide similar functionality to the VMEbus, although at a greatly reduced rate.

VXI—the VMEbus eXtensions for Instrumentation

The VXIbus is a superset of the VMEbus specification, designed for instrumentation applications like automatic test equipment, which require high speed data communications and special signals present on a single backplane. It was pioneered by five instrumentation companies: CDS, Hewlett-Packard, Racal-Dana, Tektronix and Wavetek, who realized that the new generation of instrumentation systems would need backplane communications to improve performance. If a standard specification is used, systems can be built and expanded using standard 'instrument on a card' modules. The specification uses the existing VMEbus to provide a data transfer channel, and supplements the existing user-defined I/O pins of the second P2 connector with a third connector for extra signals. In addition, the modules can specify different form-factors ranging from the normal VMEbus half and double height size A and B Eurocards to the larger size C and D. This larger formfactor allows design layouts to be optimized to reduce crosstalk and interference while making precise analogue measurements. Figure 3.9 shows the relative size differences in board sizes and the connector relationships.

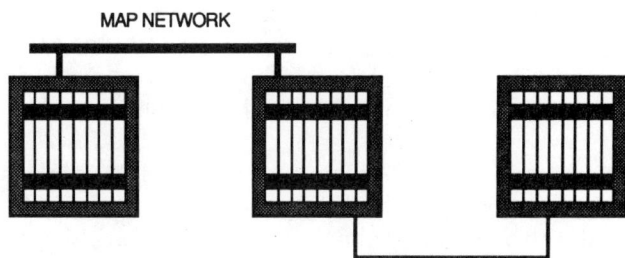

MAP NETWORK

SERIAL LINK

Using networks to link VMEbus systems

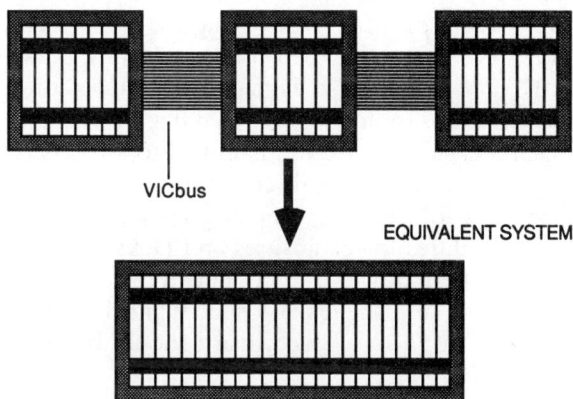

VICbus

EQUIVALENT SYSTEM

Using VICbus to link VMEbus systems

Figure 3.10 *Linking separate VMEbus systems*

The VMEbus provides a data communication channel between 'commander' and 'servant' modules for the VXIbus. There are no modifications to the VMEbus specification at all. The communication protocols that are used across the VMEbus are user-defined and can be, for example, the IEEE–488.2 GPIB bus, already used in many instrumentation applications, or a test orientated language such as CIIL. It is expected that the initial systems will use a VXIbus–IEEE 488 adaptor so that VXIbus systems will simply plug into existing designs. The system is self configuring with each servant module having registers identifying its manufacturer, function and system requirements. The manufacturer code is simply obtained by completing a simple form; a general breadboard code has already been defined for custom modules.

There are several types of servant boards: dumb boards which have no intelligence and are controlled by registers, memory devices and smart devices with onboard intelligence where control is by message-passing.

The new extension defines the user-defined pins of the P2 connector and the P3 connector for other functions: it adds a 10 MHz emitter coupled logic (ECL) clock, logic and analogue power supply lines, ECL and TTL logic trigger lines and a daisy-chained bus structure using 24 pins.

The TTL triggering capability is in excess of 10 MHz, while that of the ECL is greater than 50 MHz. The triggering can either be synchronous, where a module drives a single line, semi-synchronous, where accepter modules will handshake on the same line, or asynchronous, using a pair of lines. Communication between existing instrumentation racks will commonly use this last method. The P3 provides extra pins for even faster communication protocols approaching 1 Gbyte per second. The local bus allows transfer of many types of signals along it and therefore the VXIbus modules must define their use to prevent ECL signals from appearing on a TTL interface and so damage the modules concerned. The VXIbus has classifications for low, medium and high analogue levels and for TTL and ECL. Each classification is linked to a mechanical keying system, which prevents the wrong insertion of a module.

The specification also covers power and cooling requirements for boards and the capabilities for enclosures and racks. This is extremely important due to the high power often used and the cooling restrictions placed by RF screening and shields. By specifying these levels, system integrators can easily decide if a given board should be used in a given enclosure or configuration.

VICbus—Vertical Intercrate Bus

This is a proposed bus to allow communication between VMEbus crates so the complete system appears as a single large VMEbus system with transparent links. It supports all the VMEbus cycles in a completely transparent way. For example, a CPU in crate A could access a memory board in crate B across the VMEbus by simply starting a VMEbus cycle. Simple single point architectures are very simple to build, as shown in Figure 3.10, but the more complicated multipoint systems have several difficulties associated with them in terms of arbitration mechanisms etc. For instance, if a VMEbus crate is connected to a multipoint system, would all the bus transfers need to be transmitted to all other crates in the network? If they do, what effect does that have on bus bandwidth, transfer speeds and real-time response? How does a round robin arbiter cope with bus requests from a priority system? An obvious solution is to restrict such interconnects to simple linear architectures, but this may place artificial barriers to further development. The whole project is very much in its early development.

At the present time, the VICbus specification is being considered by a technical subcommittee at CERN in Geneva. Until the VICbus is defined and products are available, the more costly methods of serial communication will be used to fulfil this function.

4
VMEbus I/O systems

All computer systems have to interface with the outside world: VMEbus is no exception and provides many ways of achieving this. Input and output (I/O) requires both a physical interface, in the form of a connector, and an electrical interface, to define how the data are received or sent to the system. Such is the diversity of I/O requirements that the majority of VMEbus boards currently available are designed to cover interface requirements such as simple serial and parallel links to isolated high voltage breakdown I/O lines.

Physical connections

Many I/O boards available today offer at least two choices as to the location of the physical I/O connections.

The obvious choice is to place connectors either directly on the front panel or directly on the board, where they can be cabled via a front panel slot. This option is cheap and robust but can lead to a wiring spaghetti on the front panels which obstructs other, more important, front panel switches. Subsequent board removal can also be complicated.

An alternative is to use the 60 pins reserved on the P2 connector for user-defined I/O. This removes the wiring to the rear of the chassis, providing an unobstructed front access, and allows the use of transition boards. However, this assumes the pins are not being used for other user-defined purposes like the VSB memory extension bus.

The MVME 332 8-channel serial communications board either provides eight subminiature connectors for front panel connection or uses an MVME700 series transition board and a ribbon connection to the P2 connector to provide a subpanel with eight standard D-type connectors. Such transition boards can fit into empty Eurocard slots and be positioned anywhere in the system. They can also provide additional jumpering space and level conversion. TTL compatible levels can be buffered and converted to meet the required electrical specification without consuming valuable space on the VMEbus board. Figure 4.1 shows a rear mounted transition board in a VMEbus system.

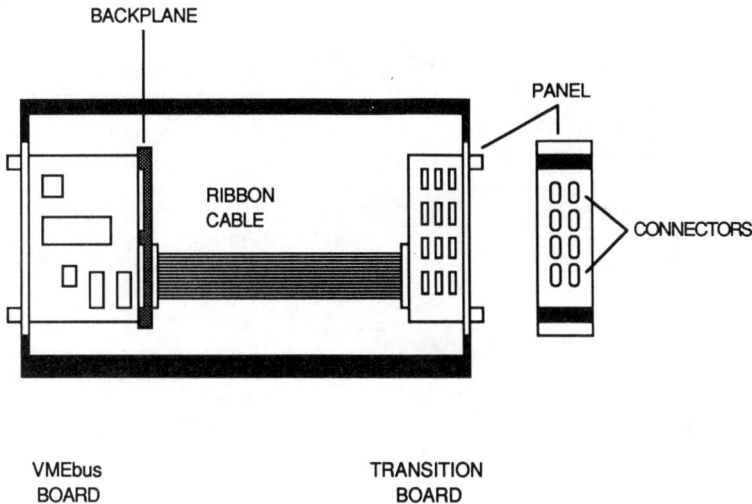

Figure 4.1 *VMEbus I/O transition board*

The Dutch based VMEbus board manufacturer, Compcontrol, have taken a slightly different approach but use the same basic concept: their RS232 transition board plugs directly on to the backplane and uses ribbon cable connections to the sockets. The principle remains the same: the plug-in board has all the signal buffering and jumper networks required to take TTL levels and convert them to either RS232 or RS422 levels suitable for serial communication.

Intelligent and non-intelligent boards

When implementing I/O functions on the VMEbus, a decision has to be made concerning the overheads that the board will place on the VMEbus traffic and its processors.

The simplest method of providing I/O functions is to interface the peripherals via a simple SLAVE interface such that they appear within the VMEbus memory map and are thus available to any MASTER within the system. This interface may be direct to the peripherals or via a dual port mechanism.

I/O interrupt structures can be connected to the VMEbus, allowing both polling and interrupt-driven software techniques to be used. Such dumb I/O implementations place overheads both on the bus traffic and on designated processors which service their needs. All this occurs across the VMEbus, and therefore contradicts the original design intent of a global message-passing bus.

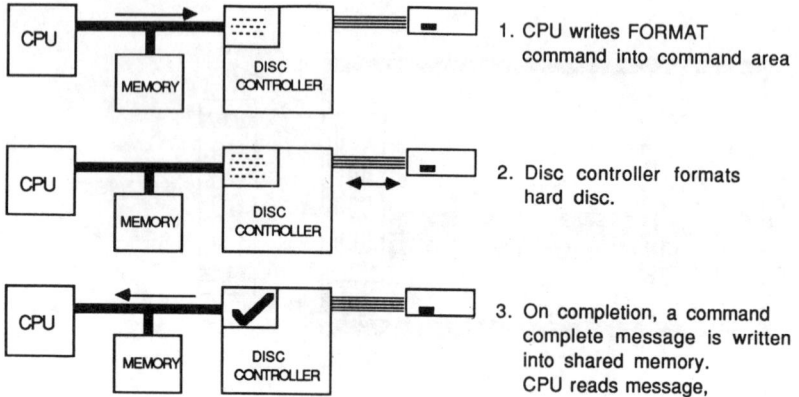

1. CPU writes FORMAT command into command area

2. Disc controller formats hard disc.

3. On completion, a command complete message is written into shared memory. CPU reads message,

FORMAT command:

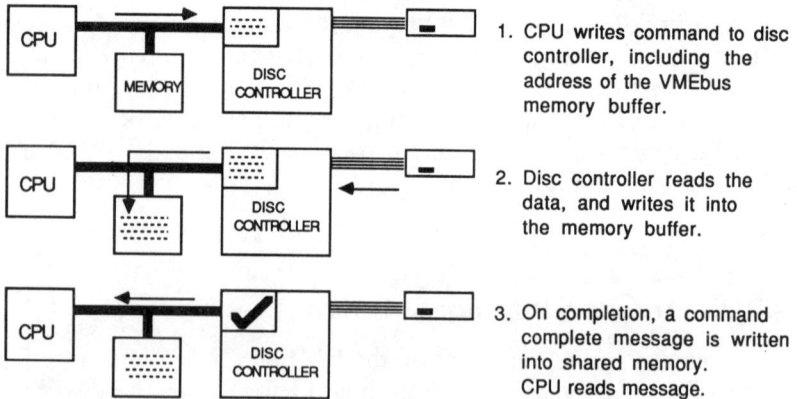

1. CPU writes command to disc controller, including the address of the VMEbus memory buffer.

2. Disc controller reads the data, and writes it into the memory buffer.

3. On completion, a command complete message is written into shared memory. CPU reads message.

READ SECTOR command:

Figure 4.2   *Using an intelligent disc controller*

This may be acceptable for single processor systems, but can restrict further development. The obvious solution is to provide some local intelligence allowing the routine peripheral requirements to be handled locally and the communication with the other VMEbus MASTERS to be performed at a higher message-passing level.

A dumb controller requires many VMEbus accesses to perform even a simple task such as reading a sector from disc. The controller needs to be programmed to select the right disc drive, check it is ready, find the required track and, finally, read or write the data, byte by byte. All these accesses severely cripple a system if they are performed over the VMEbus. Onboard intelligence performs these tasks and communicates with other processors, using messages passed over the VMEbus. Such commands may simply comprise a command, drive selection and a buffer pointer. The MVME319 disc controller only needs a simple 7-byte message to format a complete disc and just 22 bytes to read or write

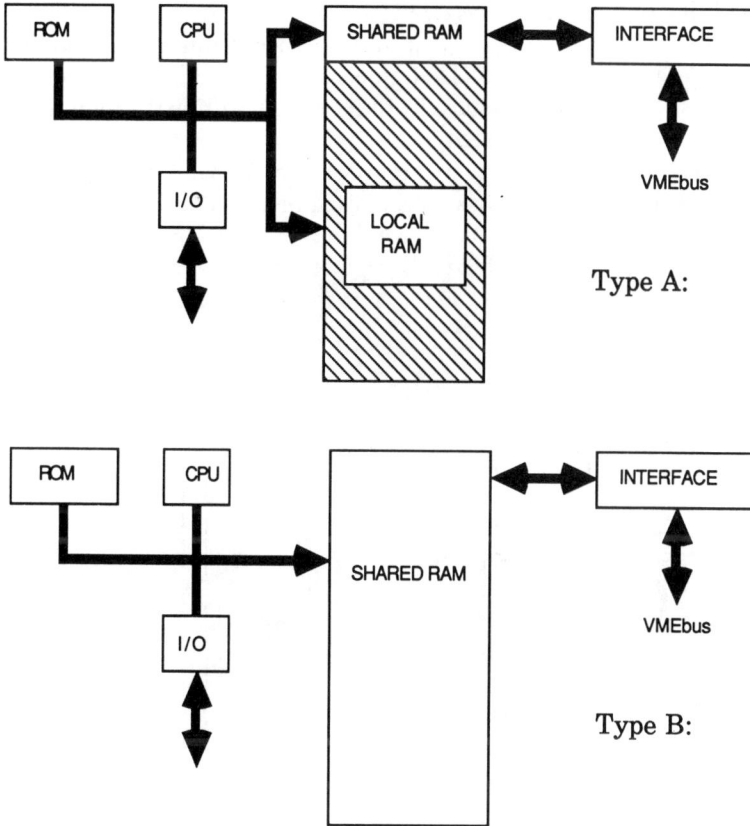

Figure 4.3 *Two types of intelligent I/O VMEbus boards*

to any sector. Information, like disc sector contents, is passed or received using memory buffers stored in the VMEbus global memory. Figure 4.2 shows a typical command sequence and the resulting accesses for formatting and reading a sector from a hard disc using an intelligent disc controller.

To access such information, intelligent boards must have a MASTER interface, and their use immediately turns a single CPU system into a multiprocessor system. Their use requires the same design methodology and considerations as are used for a multiple CPU design.

Intelligent I/O boards

Intelligent I/O boards share a common functionality with VMEbus processor boards. They have an onboard processor, peripherals, a VMEbus MASTER interface and memory. Figure 4.3 shows how difficult it can be to differentiate between them.

The memory is usually organized differently from normal processor designs, depending on which engineering trade-offs are made. Most designs use one of two schemes. Both schemes partition the memory into two or more areas, designated local or global.

The first scheme, shown in Figure 4.4, designates the bulk of the memory as local and only has a very small memory area accessible from the VMEbus. This area, similar to a mailbox, allows command packets to be sent to the board and effectively replaces the conventional register set found in many peripherals. These command packets contain memory

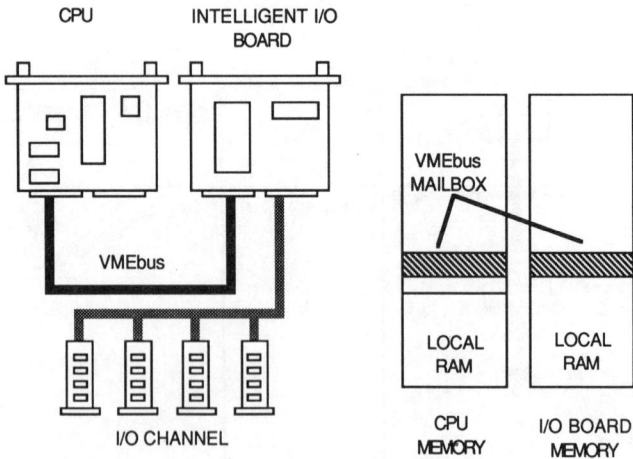

Figure 4.4   *Intelligent I/O with a VMEbus mailbox*

pointers to the data buffers in global VMEbus memory. The advantage this scheme has is that it simplifies the hardware design and allows the onboard processor uninterrupted access to the local memory, maximizing the onboard processor performance. This scheme is implemented in many processor-intensive I/O applications like serial communications and disc controllers such as the MVME332 communications controller mentioned previously. The disadvantage of the scheme is the increase in VMEbus traffic which occurs when the I/O board has to continually access the buffers located in VMEbus memory. Many accesses may need to be performed during the execution of a command.

The second scheme, Figure 4.5, extends the amount of dual port memory so the whole of the onboard memory is shared between the VMEbus and the local processor. The buffers are allocated to this area of global memory and are now only accessed once by the VMEbus for the CPU board to either write the output data or read the incoming data. All the I/O processor accesses are performed as local accesses thus reducing the VMEbus overheads. The main disadvantage with this scheme is that the local processor can be delayed in accessing the local memory while a VMEbus MASTER is accessing the memory from the VMEbus side. This can cause serious problems during, for example, interrupt handling. In addition, the hardware design is more complex and the dual ported memory is not protected.

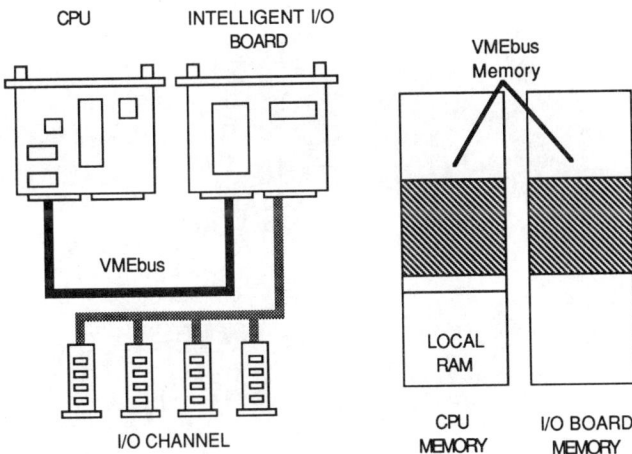

Figure 4.5 *Intelligent I/O with shared memory*

The first scheme trades off VMEbus overheads for maximizing local performance while the second exchanges local performance for reduced VMEbus overheads.

Using a dedicated I/O bus

Interfacing I/O directly on to the VMEbus places additional limitations on system design. The I/O cannot be remote from the VMEbus system, as is often required in factory automation applications where one VMEbus based processing unit controls multiple I/O subsystems.

The full capability of the VMEbus is not used with many peripheral chips which use 8-bit data buses and 1–2 MHz bus speeds. These types of chips, like the MC6821 Parallel Interface Adaptor and the Z8035 Serial Communications Controller, have been available for many years and are now very inexpensive.

The cost of adding a VMEbus interface to a VMEbus I/O board using these chips comprises about 90% of the total building cost because its advanced performance requires more expensive chips. This is why similar functionality I/O boards for VMEbus are more expensive than for an older, lower performing bus. An obvious solution is to use a simpler dedicated bus for I/O which either simplifies and reduces the cost of the bus interface, or allows a direct interface to the other simpler bus standards, allowing the designer access to more off-the-shelf components.

Figure 4.6 *A MVME410 I/O channel board*

The I/O channel

The I/O channel was first used with VERSAbus boards to provide a low cost interface for I/O. It has an 8-bit wide data bus and a 12-bit wide address range. It supports transfers up to 2 Mbytes per second and has up to four interrupt levels. The interface is asynchronous in nature and is designed to support a single MASTER communicating to multiple SLAVE I/O boards. There is no bus arbitration or multiprocessing support. Figure 4.6 shows an MVME410 dual parallel port I/O channel board. The parallel ports are provided by the two MC68B21P devices. The rest of the board is the simple logic needed to implement the bus interface.

Each I/O card on the bus is given a memory block between 256 bytes to 4 Kbytes in size within the addressing range. The peripheral control registers are located within this block and accessed as memory locations.

The I/O channel does not require any backplane and uses ribbon cable to carry the signals. This cable can be up to 20 feet in length, allowing remote stations to be connected. I/O channel boards are of single Eurocard format and are compatible with VMEbus racking systems.

A typical I/O channel configuration comprises a controlling processor which communicates with the SLAVE I/O boards on the bus. In this respect, it operates as a replacement for the native processor bus. The I/O channel address space is memory mapped into the processor's address map, allowing it to be accessed simply as memory, and the actual interface is transparent to the user.

For VMEbus applications, there are two ways of adding the I/O channel interface to the VMEbus. The first provides a dumb interface which maps the I/O channel into the VMEbus memory space. The I/O channel boards then simply act as VMEbus SLAVES and are globally available. The interrupt is interfaced to one of the VMEbus interrupt lines. The MVME316 I/O channel interface from Motorola can provide this simple connection. The MVME316 provides a simple solution but it suffers from the same disadvantages as a dumb VMEbus I/O board. In its defence, it does facilitate remote I/O stations and allows the designer to mix and match the I/O requirements from off-the-shelf boards. For custom designs, the bus interface only requires a few logic packs to implement, thus reducing cost and complexity.

The second solution is to use a VMEbus processor board which has the I/O channel interface. This removes the I/O channel connection from the VMEbus and access to the I/O boards is made via the local processor. This removes the loading from the VMEbus, and allows intelligent I/O clusters to be built.

As stated previously, there is no functional difference between a VMEbus processor and an intelligent I/O board. Controlling software can either be downloaded or present in onboard firmware, allowing the easy design and configuration of such a cluster. Typically, the processor handles both servicing of the I/O and pre-processing the data. Such systems can form the basis of sophisticated distributed multiprocessor systems. Designs using these techniques are described later in the book. This solution provides a modular approach to building intelligent I/O boards and allows the designer to implement exactly what is needed, in terms of interface protocols, I/O facilities, etc.

Alternatives

The I/O channel used as an example of a low cost I/O bus is not the only protocol available on the market. Nearly every major manufacturer has their own implementation of such a bus. They are, unfortunately, generally incompatible with each other and this defeats one of the main advantages of a standard interface.

There are many low cost 8-bit bus standards which are eminently suitable for this purpose and have the advantage of standard hardware and multiple sources. A good example of this is the G64 bus, which uses Eurocard formats and provides a good 8-bit bus structure. GSM-Syntel have an MC68020 based processor board with onboard G64 and VMEbus interface. It can be used to provide an intelligent gateway for G64 I/O boards on to the VMEbus, or can be used to upgrade existing G64 systems, where additional processing power and/or memory addressing is required. This provides a convenient stepping stone between the 8-bit world and the VMEbus. The use of dual interface processor boards acting as gateways is increasing within the VMEbus world.

For higher performance systems, the VSB can be used to provide a similar role to that of the I/O channel. Its 32-bit data and address paths provide transfer rates similar to that of the VMEbus, and its support of two MASTERS allows intelligent processor-to-processor communication using similar techniques to the VMEbus. Although limited to only six Eurocard slots, it does allow high speed intelligent I/O clusters to be designed without loading the VMEbus. Candidates for such applications include high speed graphics, disc controllers and video processors. Providing the VMEbus racks are close enough, VSB can also be used to provide rack-to-rack communications.

Again, Compcontrol have provided a different solution based around their CC103 processor board for I/O. The basic board uses an MC68020 32-bit processor with a floating point coprocessor accessing 1 Mbyte of local memory. In addition there is 128 Kbyte of dual ported memory. The onboard processor data and address bus are brought out to onboard connectors which allow a single daughter I/O module to be connected directly to the processor board. The resulting combination is two slots wide but provides a very fast bus interface with versatile interrupt capability, a mailbox using dual ported memory and vast DMA (direct memory access) facilities. This board can provide extremely fast and efficient I/O for VMEbus systems while still allowing the ability to change the I/O modules. This offers users the choice of designing their own interface boards or buying an off-the-shelf module. Currently, Compcontrol can supply an IBM token ring I/O module for networks. The basic principles of token ring networks are explained in Chapter 15.

5
Operating systems

What do operating systems provide?

Operating systems are software environments that provide a buffer between the user and the low level interfaces to the hardware within a system. They provide a constant interface and a set of utilities to enable users to utilize the system quickly and efficiently. They allow software to be moved from one system to another and therefore can make application programs hardware independent as shown in Figure 5.1. Program debugging tools are usually included which speed up the testing process. Many applications do not require any operating system support at all and run direct on the hardware. Such software includes its own I/O routines, for example, to drive serial and parallel ports. However, with the addition of mass storage and the complexities of disc access and file structures, most applications immediately delegate these tasks to an operating system.

Such delegation decreases software development time by providing system calls to enable application software access to any of the I/O system facilities. These calls are made by building a parameter block, loading a specified register with its location and then executing some form of TRAP instruction as depicted in Figure 5.2. This instruction is the MC68000 family equivalent of the software interrupt and switches the processor into supervisor mode to execute the required function. It effectively provides a communication path between the application and the operating system kernel. The kernel is the heart of the operating system which controls the hardware and deals with interrupts, memory usage, I/O systems, etc. It locates a parameter block by using an address pointer stored in a predetermined address register. It takes the commands stored in a parameter block and executes them. In doing so, it is the kernel that drives the hardware, interpreting the commands passed to it through a parameter block. After the command is completed, status information

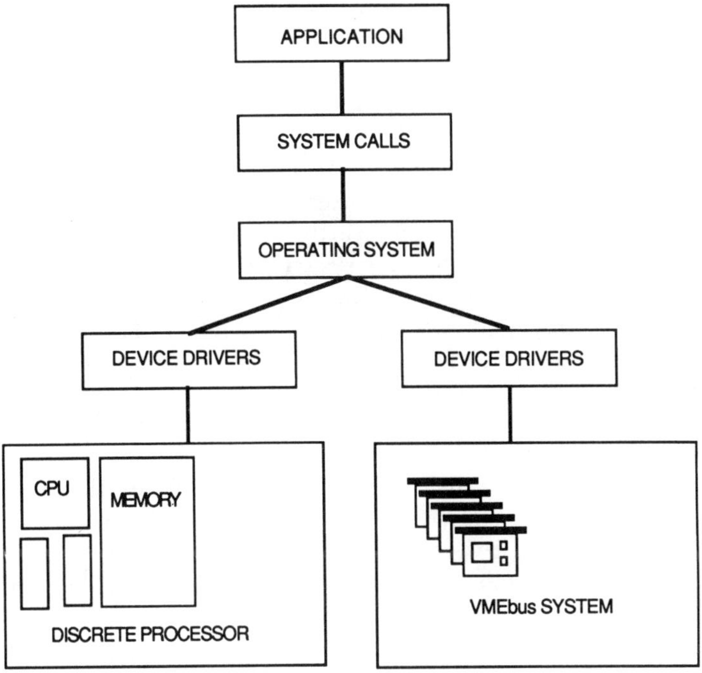

Figure 5.1 *Hardware independence through the use of an operating system*

is written back into the parameter block, and the kernel passes control
back to the application, which continues running in USER mode. The
application will find the I/O function completed with the data and status

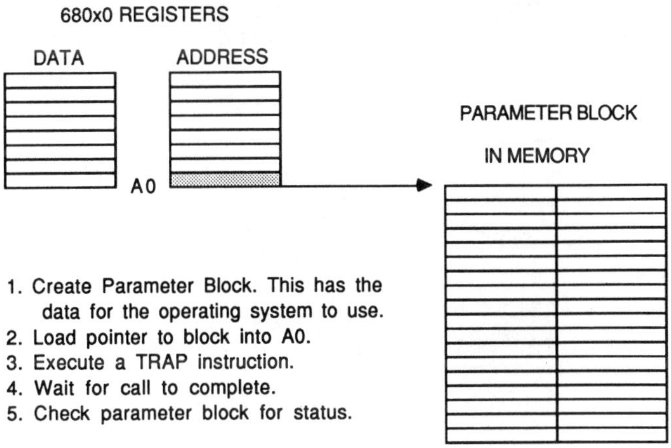

Figure 5.2 *Typical mechanism for executing a system for the 680x0 range of microprocessors*

information written into the parameter block. The application has had no direct access to the memory or hardware whatsoever.

These parameter blocks are standard throughout the operating system and are not dependent on the actual hardware performing the physical tasks. It does not matter if the system uses an MC68901 multifunction peripheral or an 8530 serial communication controller to provide the serial ports: the operating system driver software takes care of the dependencies. If the parameter blocks are general enough in their definition, data can be supplied from almost any source within the system; for example, a COPY utility could use the same blocks to get data from a serial port and copy it to a parallel port as copying data from one file to another. This idea of device independence and unified I/O allows software to be reused rather than rewritten. Software can be easily moved from one system to another. This is important for VMEbus designs, where system hardware can easily be upgraded and/or expanded.

The use of memory management usually implies the use of an operating system to remove the time consuming job of defining and writing the driver software. This software controls the translation of logical addresses to different physical addresses as shown in Figure 5.3. In this example, the processor thinks that it is accessing memory at the bottom of its memory map, while in reality it is being fetched from different locations in the main memory map. The memory does not even need to be contiguous: the processor's single block or memory can be split into smaller blocks, each with a different translation address.

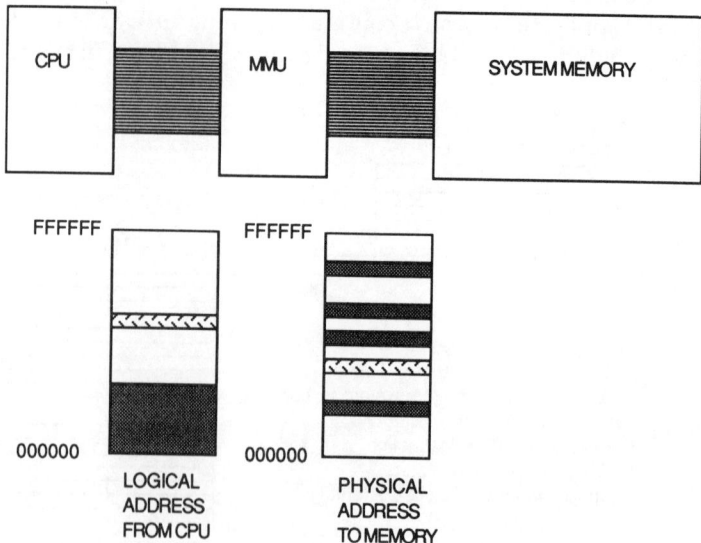

Figure 5.3   *The basic principles of memory management*

If no memory management hardware is present, most operating systems can replace it with a software based scheme, providing that the code is written to be position independent and relocatable. This is necessary in order to execute programs in different locations from that in which they were generated. If the operating system program loader cannot allocate the original memory, the program is relocated into the next available block and the program allowed to execute. Relocatable code does not have any immediate addressing values and makes extensive use

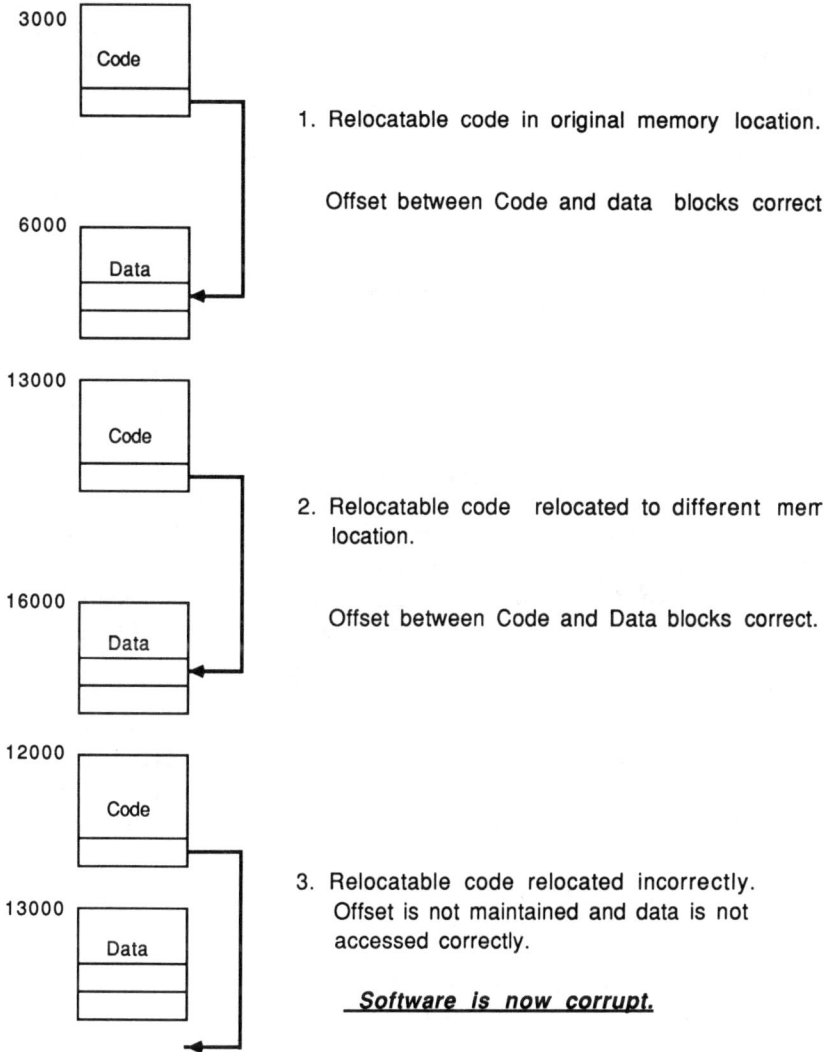

3000

Code

1. Relocatable code in original memory location.

Offset between Code and data blocks correct

6000

Data

13000

Code

2. Relocatable code relocated to different merr location.

16000

Data

Offset between Code and Data blocks correct.

12000

Code

3. Relocatable code relocated incorrectly. Offset is not maintained and data is not accessed correctly.

13000

Data

Software is now corrupt.

Figure 5.4 *An example of relocatable code*

of program relative addressing. Data areas or software subroutines are not referenced explicitly but are located by relative addressing modes using offsets; for example:

- Explicit addressing
  Branch to subroutine at address $0F04FF
- Relative addressing
  Branch to subroutine which is offset from here by $50 bytes.

Providing the offsets are maintained, then the relative addressing will locate data and code wherever the blocks are located in memory as shown in Figure 5.4. Most modern compilers will use these techniques but do not assume that all of them do.

The simulation of hardware is quite common within operating systems: many system clocks are performed in software rather than in a real-time clock chip.

Single tasking operating systems

The first widely used operating system was CP/M, developed for the Intel 8080 microprocessor and 8 inch floppy disc systems. It supported I/O calls by two jump tables—BDOS (basic disc operating system) and BIOS (basic I/O system). It quickly became a standard within the industry and a large amount of application software became available for it. Many of the micro-based business machines of the late 1970s and early 1980s were based on CP/M. Its ideas even formed the basis of MSDOS, chosen by IBM for its personal computers.

CP/M is a good example of a single tasking operating system. Only one task or application can be executed at any one time and therefore it only supports one user at a time. When an application is loaded, it provides the user-definer part of the total 'CP/M program'.

Any application program has to be complete and therefore the available memory often becomes the limiting factor. Program overlays are often used to solve this problem (Figure 5.5). Parts of the complete program are stored separately on disc and retrieved and loaded over an unused code area when needed. This allows applications larger than the available memory to run, but it places the control responsibility on the application. This is similar to virtual memory schemes where the operating system divides a task's memory into pages and swops them between memory and mass storage. However, the operating system assumes complete control and such schemes are totally transparent to the user.

With a single tasking operating system, it is not possible to run multiple tasks simultaneously. Large applications have to be run sequentially and cannot support concurrent operations. There is no support for message-

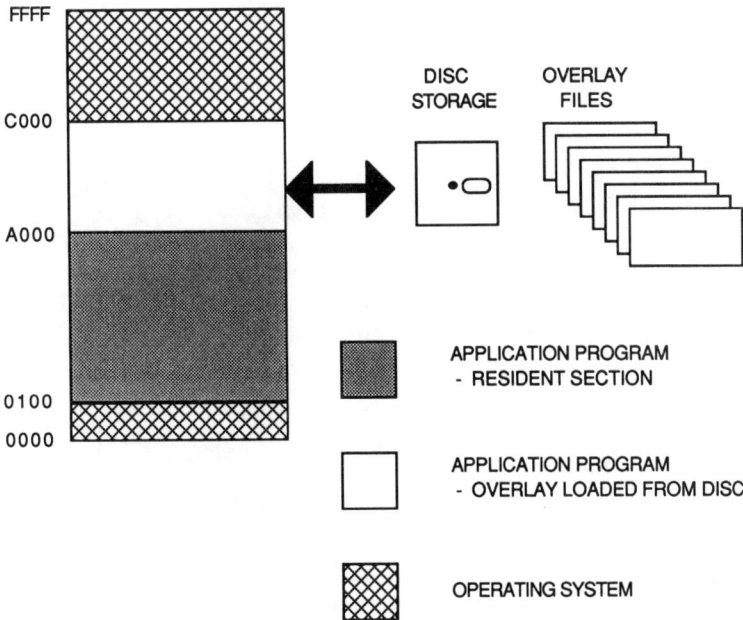

Figure 5.5 *Program overlays*

passing or task control, which would enable applications to be divided into separate entities. If a system needs to take log data and store it on disc and, at the same time, allow a user to process that data using an on-line database package, a single tasking operating system would need everything to be integrated. With a multitasking operating system, the data logging task can run at the same time as the database. Data can be passed between each element by a common file on disc, and neither task needs have any direct knowledge of the other. With a single tasking system, it is likely that the database program would have to be written from scratch. With the multitasking system, a commercially available program can be used, and the logging software interfaced to it.

These restrictions forced many applications to interface directly with the hardware and therefore lose the hardware independence that the operating system offered. Such software would need extensive modification to port it to another configuration.

Multitasking operating systems

For the majority of VMEbus applications, a single tasking operating system is too restrictive. What is required is an operating system that can run multiple applications simultaneously and provide intertask control and communication. The facilities once only available to mini and mainframe computer users are now required by 16/32 bit microprocessor users.

A multitasking operating system works by dividing the processor's time into discrete time slices (Figure 5.6). Each application or task requires a certain number of time slices to complete its execution. The operating system kernel decides which task can have the next slice, so instead of a task executing continuously until completion, its execution is interleaved with other tasks. This sharing of processor time between tasks gives the illusion to each user that he is the only one using the system.

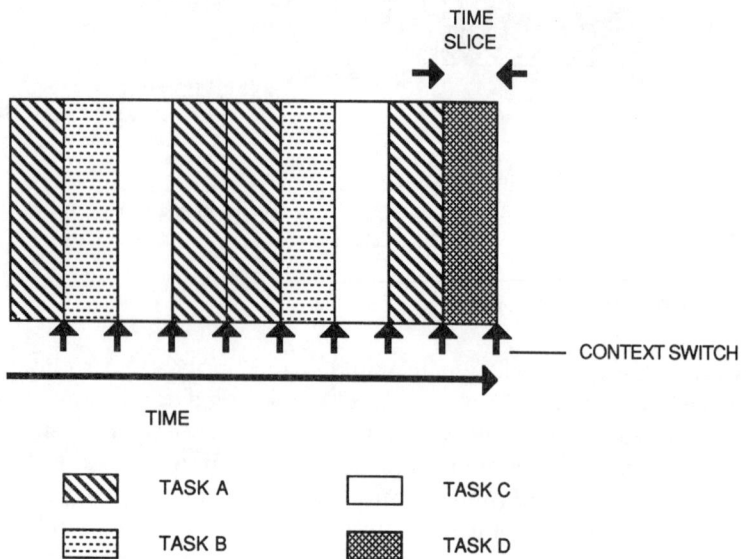

Figure 5.6   *Time slice mechanism for multitasking operating systems*

Context switching, task tables and kernels

Multitasking operating systems are based around a multitasking kernel which controls the time slicing mechanisms. A time slice is the time period each task has for execution before it is stopped and replaced during a context switch. This is periodically triggered by a hardware interrupt from the system timer. This interrupt may provide the system clock and several interrupts may be executed and counted before a context switch is performed.

When a context switch is performed, as shown in Figure 5.7, the current task is interrupted, the processor's registers are saved in a special table for that particular task and the task is placed back on the 'ready' list to await another time slice. Special tables, often called task control blocks, store all the information the system requires about the task, for example, its memory usage, its priority level within the system and its error handling. It is this context information that is switched when one task is replaced by another.

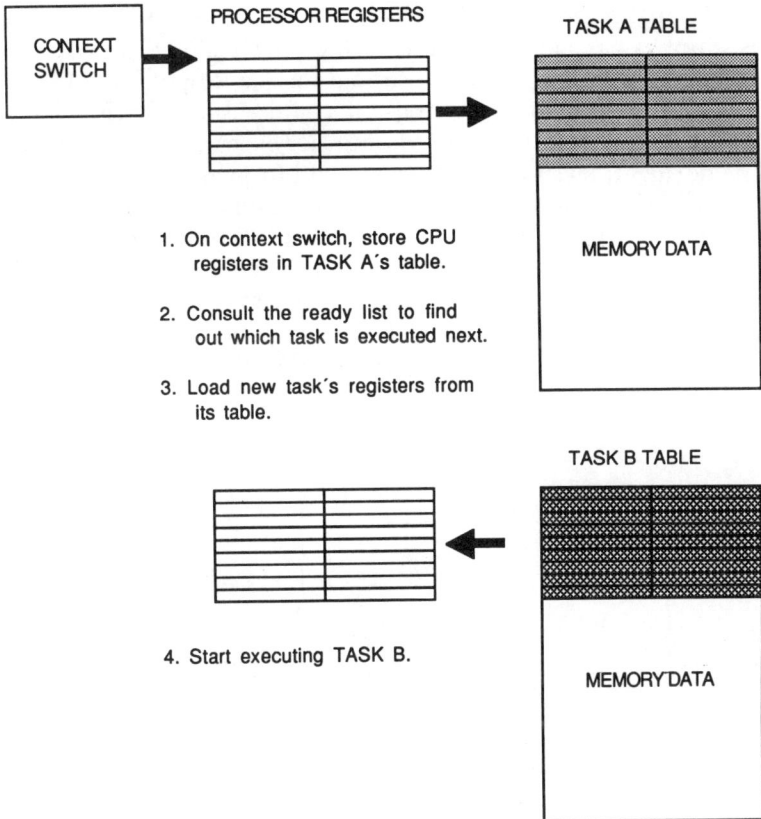

PROCESSOR REGISTERS

CONTEXT SWITCH

TASK A TABLE

1. On context switch, store CPU registers in TASK A's table.

2. Consult the ready list to find out which task is executed next.

3. Load new task's registers from its table.

MEMORY DATA

TASK B TABLE

4. Start executing TASK B.

MEMORY DATA

Figure 5.7 *The mechanism of a context switch*

The 'ready' list contains all the tasks and their status and is used by the scheduler to decide which task is allocated the next time slice. The scheduling algorithm determines the sequence and takes into account a task's priority and present status. If a task is waiting for an I/O call to complete, it will be held in limbo until the call is complete.

Once a task is selected, the processor registers and status at the time of its last context switch are loaded back into the processor and the processor is started. The new task carries on as if nothing had happened until the next context switch takes place. This is the basic method behind all multitasking operating systems.

Figure 5.8 shows a simplified state diagram for RMS68K, a real–time kernel which forms the basis of Motorola's VERSAdos operating system which uses this time slice mechanism. On each context switch, a task is selected by the kernel's scheduler from the 'ready' list and is put into the run state. It is then executed until another context switch occurs. This is normally signalled by a periodic interrupt from a timer. In such cases the task is simply switched out and put back on the 'ready' list, awaiting its next slot. Alternatively, the execution can be stopped by the task executing certain kernel commands. It could suspend itself, where it remains present in the system but no further execution occurs. It could become dormant, awaiting a start command from another task, or even simply waiting for a server task within the operating system to perform a special function for it. A typical example of a server task is a driver performing special screen graphics functions. The most common reason for a task to come out of the run state, is to wait for a message or command, or delay itself for a certain time period. The various wait directives allow tasks to synchronize and control each other within the system. This state diagram is typical of many real–time operating systems.

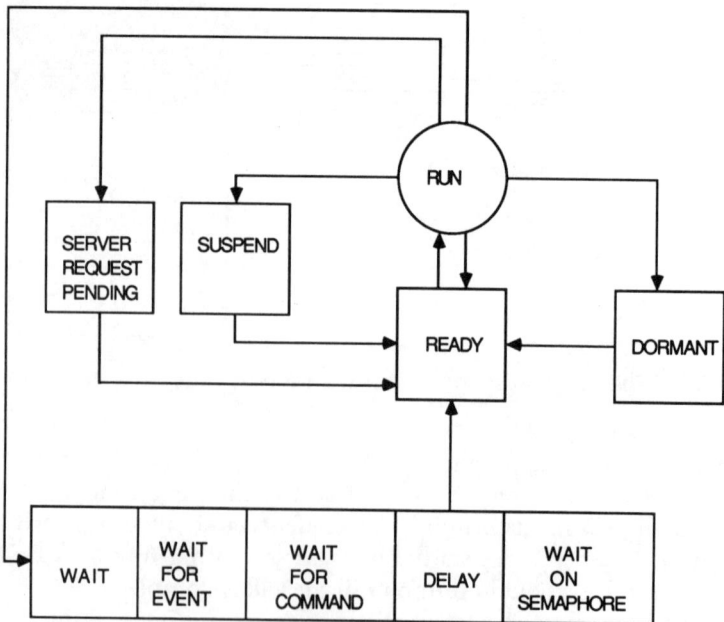

Figure 5.8 *State diagram for RMS68K real-time kernel*

EVENT MANAGER

GTASQ	Allocate Asq
SETASQ	Change Asq/Asr Status
QEVNT	Queue Event To Task Asq
GTEVNT	Get An Event
RDEVNT	Read An Event From Asq
WTEVENT	Wait For Event
RTEVNT	Return After Servicing Event
DEASQ	Detach Asq

MEMORY MANAGER

GTSEG	Allocate A Memory Segment
DESEG	Detach A Segment
DCLSHR	Declare A Segment Sharable
ATTSEG	Attach To A Sharable Segment
SHRSEG	Grant Shared Segment Access
TRSEG	Transfer A Segment
RCVSA	Receive Segment Attributes
MOVELL	Move From Logical Address
MOVEPL	Move From Physical Address
FLUSHC	Flush User Cache

EXCEPTION MONITOR MANAGER

EXMON	Attach Exception Monitor
EXMMSK	Set Exception Monitor Mask
REXMON	Run Task Under Monitor Control
RSTATE	Receive Task State
PSTATE	Modify Task State
DEXMON	Detach Exception Monitor
CEXMSK	Set Coprocessor Exmon Mask
CPSTAT	Put Coprocessor Task State
CRSTAT	Get Coprocessor Task State

TASK MANGER

CRTCB	Create Tcb
CRXTCB	Create Tcb Using Coprocessor
START	Task Goes From Dormant To Ready
SETPRI	Change Priority Of A Task
STOP	Task Goes To Dormant State
TERM	Task Terminates Itself
TERMT	Target Task Is Terminated
ABORT	Task Aborts Itself
ABORTC	Critical Task Aborts Itself
WAIT	Task Moves To Wait State
WAKEUP	Target Task Moves To Ready From Wait
SUSPND	Task Suspends Itself
RESUME	Target Task Moves To Ready From Suspend
RELINQ	Task Moves From Run To Ready
TSKATTR	Receive Task Attributes
TSKINFO	Receive A Copy Of Tcb
GTTASKID	Get A Task Id
GTTASKNM	Get A Task Name And Session

EXCEPTION MANAGER

CISR	Configure Isr
SINT	Simulate Interrupt
RTE	Return From Isr Execution
EXPVCT	Announce Exception Vectors
TRPVCT	Announce Trap Vectors
RESVCT	Claim Reserved Vectors
CDIR	Configure A New Directive
SNPTRC	Snapshot Of System Trace
SUPER	Temporary Transfer To Supervisor

TIME MANAGER

DELAY	Task Moves To Delay State
DELAYW	Delay And Wait Task
RQSTPA	Periodically Run Task
STDTIM	Set Date And Time
GTDTIM	Get Date And Time

SEMAPHORE MANAGER

CRSEM	Create Semaphore
ATSEM	Attach To Semaphore
WTSEM	Wait On Semaphore
SGSEM	Signal Semaphore
DESEM	Detach From Semaphore
DESEMA	Detach From All Semaphores

TRAPSERVER MANAGER

SERVER	Task Is Made A Server Task
AKRQST	Server Acknowledge Request
DERQST	Set User/Server Status
DSERVE	Detach Server Function

ASQ - Asynchronous Service Queue
ISR - Interrupt Service Routine

Figure 5.9 *Command list for RMS68K real-time kernel*

The kernel controls memory usage and prevents tasks from corrupting each other. If required, it also controls memory sharing between tasks, allowing them to share common program modules, such as high level language run time libraries. A set of memory tables is maintained, which is used to decide if a request is accepted or rejected. This means that resources, such as physical memory and peripheral devices, can be protected from users without using hardware memory management providing the task is moral enough to use the operating system and not access the resources directly. This is essential to maintain the system's integrity.

Message-passing and control can be implemented in such systems by using the kernel to act as a message-passer and controller between tasks. If task A wants to stop task B, then by executing a call to the kernel, the status of task B can be changed and its execution halted. Alternatively, task B can be delayed for a set time period or forced to wait for a message.

With VERSAdos, there are two types of messages that the kernel will deal with:

1   semaphores, which are simply flags that can control but cannot carry any implicit information, and
2   events, which can carry information and control tasks.

The kernel maintains the tables required to store this information and is responsible for ensuring that tasks are controlled and receive the information. Figure 5.9 shows the basic RMS68K kernel commands available. They provide the facilities that have been described above.

With the facility for tasks to communicate between each other, system call support for accessing I/O, loading tasks from disc, etc., can be achieved by running additional tasks, with a special system status. These system tasks provide additional facilities and can be included as required.

To turn the RMS68K kernel into VERSAdos requires the addition of several such tasks to perform I/O services, file handling and file management services, task loading, user interface and driver software. What was about a 16-Kbyte sized kernel grows into a 120-Kbyte operating system. These extra facilities are built up as layers surrounding the kernel. Application tasks then fit around the outside. The VERSAdos structure is shown as an example in Figure 5.10.

Due to the modular construction, applications can generally access any level directly if required. Therefore, application tasks that just require services provided by the kernel can be developed and debugged under the full environment, and stripped down for integration on to the target hardware.

In a typical system, all these service tasks and applications are controlled, scheduled and executed by the kernel. If an application wishes to write some data to a hard disc in the system, the process starts with the

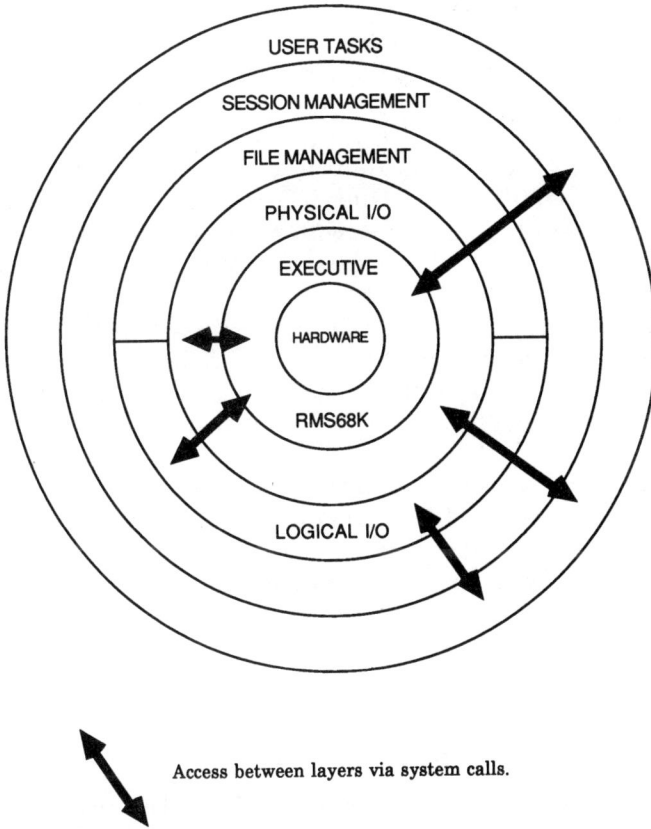

Access between layers via system calls.

Figure 5.10 *VERSAdos structure*

application creating a parameter block and asking the file manager to open the file. This system call is normally executed by a TRAP instruction. The kernel then places the task on its 'waiting' list until the file manager has finished and passed the status information back to the application task. Once this event has been received, it wakes up and is placed on the 'ready' list awaiting a time slot.

These actions are performed by the kernel. The next application command requests the file handling services to assign a logical unit number (LUN) to the file prior to the actual access. This is needed later for the I/O services call. Again, another parameter block is created and the file handler is requested to assign the LUN. The calling task is placed on the 'waiting' list until this request is completed and the LUN returned by the file handler. The LUN identifies a particular I/O resource such as a serial port or a file without actually knowing its physical characteristics. The device is therefore described as logical rather than physical.

With the LUN, the task can create another parameter block, containing the data, and ask the I/O services to write the data to the file. This may require the I/O services to make system calls of its own. It may need to call the file services for more data or to pass further information on. The data are then supplied to the device driver which actually executes the instructions to physically write the data to the disc. It is generally at this level that the logical nature of the I/O request is translated into the physical characteristics associated with the hardware. This translation lies in the domain of the device driver software. The user application is unaware of these characteristics.

A complex system call can cause many calls between the system tasks. A program loader that is requested by an application task to load another task from memory needs to call the file services and I/O services to obtain the file from disc, and the kernel to allocate memory for the task to be physically loaded.

The technique of using standard names, files, and/or logical unit numbers to access system I/O makes the porting of application software from one system to another very easy. Such accesses are independent of the hardware the system is running on, and allows applications to treat data received or sent in the same way, irrespective of their source.

What is a real-time operating system?

Many multitasking operating systems available today are also described as 'real-time'. These operating systems provide additional facilities allowing applications that would normally interface directly with the microprocessor architecture to use interrupts and drive peripherals to do so without the operating system blocking such activities. Many multi-tasking operating systems prevent the user from accessing such sensitive resources. This overzealous caring can prevent many operating systems from being used in applications such as industrial control.

A characteristic of a real-time operating system is its defined response time to external stimuli. If a peripheral generates an interrupt, a real-time system will acknowledge and start to service it within a maximum defined time. Such response times vary from system to system, but the maximum time specified is the worst case figure, and will not be exceeded due to changes in factors such as system workload.

Any system meeting this requirement can be described as real-time, irrespective of the actual value, but typical industry accepted figures for context switches and interrupt response times are about 100 μs

The consequences to industrial control of not having a real-time characteristic can be disasterous. If a system is controlling an automatic assembly line, and does not respond in time to a request from a conveyor belt limit switch to stop the belt, the results are easy to imagine (Figure 5.11). The response does not need to be instantaneous – if the limit switch is set so that there are 3 s to stop the belt, any system with a guaranteed worst case response of less than 3 s can meet this real-time requirement.

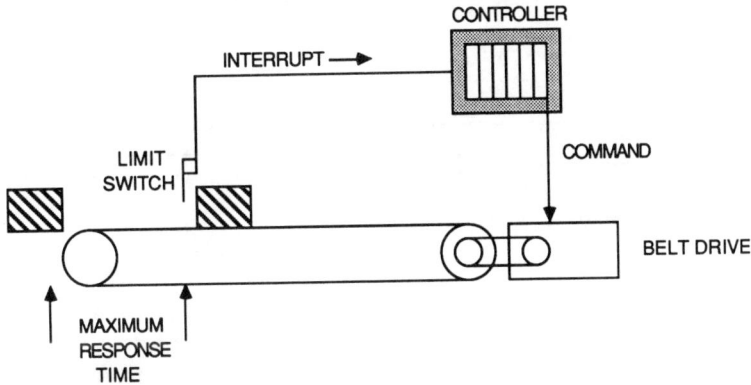

Figure 5.11 *Definition of real-time response*

For an operating system to be real-time, its internal mechanisms need to show real-time characteristics so that the internal processes sequentially respond to external interrupts, in guaranteed times.

When an interrupt is generated, the current task is interrupted to allow the kernel to acknowledge the interrupt and obtain the vector number that it needs to determine how to handle it. A typical technique is to use the kernel's interrupt handler to update a linked list which contains information on all the tasks that need to be notified of the interrupt.

If a task is attached to a vector used by the operating system, the system actions its own requirements prior to any further response by the task. The handler then sends an event message to the tasks attached to the vector, which may change their status and completely change the priorities of the task ready list. The scheduler analyses the list, and dispatches the highest priority task to run. If the interrupt and task priorities are high enough, this may be the next time slice.

Figure 5.12 depicts such a mechanism: the interrupt handler and linked list searches are performed by the kernel. The first priority is to service the interrupt. This may be from a disc controller indicating that it has completed a data transfer. Once the kernel has satisfied its own needs, the handler will start a linked list search. The list comprises blocks of data identifying tasks that have their own service routines. Each block will contain a reference to the next block, hence the linked list terminology. Each identified task is then sent a special message. This will start the task's service routine when it receives its next time slice. The kernel's interrupt handler will finally execute an RTE return from exception instruction which will restore the processor state prior to the interrupt. In such arrangements the task service routines execute in USER mode. The only SUPERVISOR operation is that of the kernel and its own interrupt handler. As can be imagined, this processing can increase the interrupt latency seen by the task quite dramatically. A ten fold increase is not uncommon.

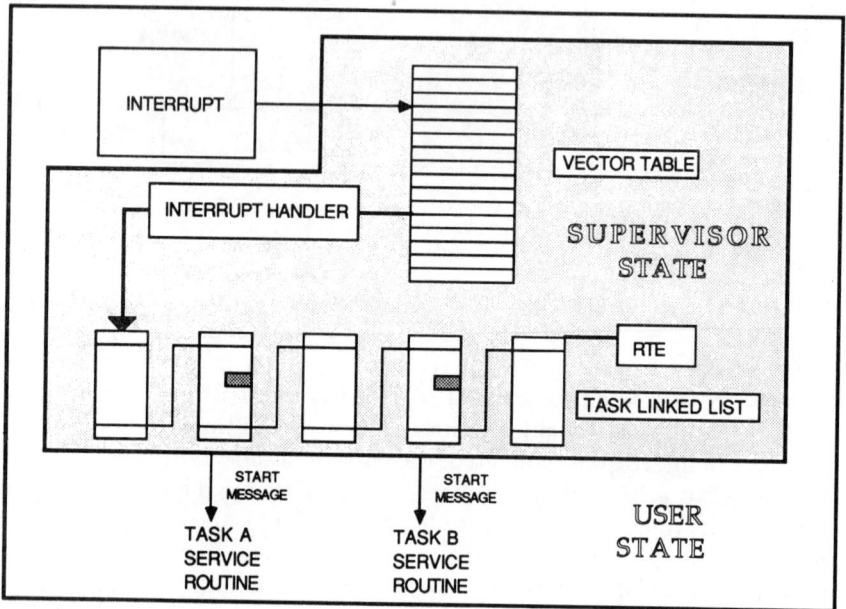

Figure 5.12   *How to allow tasks to handle interrupt routines within an operating system*

To be practical, a real-time operating system has to guarantee maximum response times for its interrupt handler, event-passing mechanisms and scheduler algorithm, and provide system calls to allow tasks to attach and handle interrupts.

As with the previous example of a conveyor belt, a typical software configuration would dedicate a task to controlling the conveyor belt. This task would make several system calls on start-up to access the parallel I/O peripheral that interfaces the system to components such as the drive motors and limit switches and tells the kernel that certain interrupt vectors are attached to the task and are handled by its own interrupt handling routine.

Once the task has set everything up, it remains dormant until an event is sent by other tasks to switch the belt on or off. If a limit switch is triggered, it sets off an interrupt which forces the kernel to handle it. The currently executing task stops, the kernel handler searches the task interrupt attachment linked list, and places the controller task on the ready list, with its own handler ready to execute. At its appropriate time slice, the handler runs, accesses the peripheral and switches off the belt. This result may not be normal, and so the task also sends event messages to the others, informing them that it has acted independently and may force other actions. Once this has been done, the task goes back to its dormant state awaiting further commands.

Real-time operating systems have other advantages: to prevent a system from power failure usually needs a guaranteed response time so that the short time between the recognition of and the actual power failure can be used to store vital data and bring the system down in a controlled manner. The VERSAdos operating system actually has a power fail module built into the kernel so that no time is lost in executing the module code.

Real-time operating systems and UNIX

UNIX has probably established itself as the most well known multi-tasking operating system within the microprocessor and minicomputer environment. It was originally developed for the DEC PDP–11 mini-computer at Bell Laboratories in the early 1970s. Its popularity became established within the academic community, which had ready access to the source, and later spread, as graduates moved into industry.

UNIX is a non-real-time, multitasking operating system with a hierarchical file system (Figure 5.13), which takes a basic root directory and divides it into subdirectories. The system revolves around its file

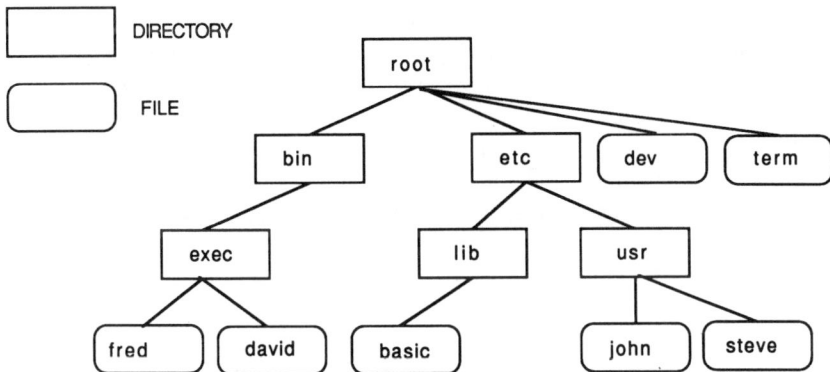

Figure 5.13 *A hierarchical file system*

structure and all physical resources are accessed as files. Tasks running under UNIX are called processes. Processes can duplicate themselves, via a fork system call, creating a 'parent' and 'child'.

Processes have three standard files associated with them: stdin, stdout and stderr which are the default input, output and error message files. Other files or devices can be reassigned to these files to either receive or provide data for active process. Data can be fed from one process directly into another using a 'pipe'.

A process to print a file on to the screen can be piped into another process which converts all lower-case characters to upper-case and then pipes its data output into another process, which pages it automatically before displaying it. This command line can be written as a data file or 'shell script', which provides the commands to the user interface or shell. Shell scripts form a programming language in their own right and allow complex commands to be constructed from simple ones. If the user does not like the particular way a process presents information, a shell script can be written that executes it, edits and reformats the data and then presents it. There are two commonly used shell interfaces: the standard Bourne shell and the 'C' shell. Many application programs provide their own shell which hides the UNIX operating system completely from the user.

The UNIX operating system is written almost entirely in the high level language 'C' and has been ported to many architectures and machines. The earlier versions, 6 and 7, have been superceded by System V from AT&T and the BSD 4.2 version available from the University of California at Berkeley. These variations will eventually be united in the System V release 4 from AT&T. UNIX has become the dominant operating system for engineering workstations and office automation systems.

What distinguishes UNIX from other operating systems is its wealth of application software and its determination in keeping the user away from the physical system resources. There are many compilers, editors, text processors, compiler construction aids and communication packages supplied with the basic release. In addition, packages providing anything from complete CAD and system modelling to integrated business office suites are available.

Unfortunately, UNIX is not the utopian operating system for all applications: its need for memory management, many megabytes of RAM and large mass storage (>40 Mbytes) immediately limits the range of systems it can successfully run on. Mass storage is not only used for holding file data, but also provides, via its virtual operating system and management scheme, overflow storage for applications which are too big to fit in the system RAM at one time. Such applications are divided into pages and unused pages are stored on disc. When the processor wishes to access a page which is not resident in memory, the memory management asserts a page fault, selects the least used page in memory and swaps it with the wanted page stored on disc (Figure 5.14). Therefore, to reduce the system overheads, fast mass storage and large amounts of RAM are normally required.

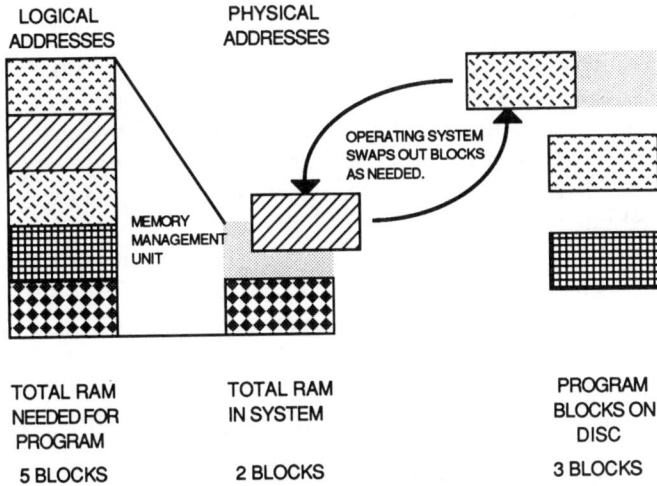

Figure 5.14 *An operating system virtual memory scheme*

Its use of a non–real-time scheduler, where there is no guarantee when a task will complete, further excludes UNIX from many VMEbus applications. Through its use of memory management to protect its resources, the simple method of writing an application task which drives a VMEbus board directly via its physical memory is rendered almost impossible. Physical memory can be accessed via the slow '/dev/mem' file technique or by incorporating a shared memory driver, but these techniques are either very slow or restrictive. There is no straightforward method of using or accessing the system interrupts and this forces the user to adopt polling techniques.

In addition, the system makes extensive use of disc cacheing techniques, which use RAM buffers to hold recent data in memory for faster access. This helps to reduce the system degradation experienced, particularly with a combination of external page swapping and slow mass storage. The system does not write data immediately to disc but stores it in the buffer. If a power failure occurs, the data may only be memory resident and therefore lost. As this can include directory structures from the superblock, it can corrupt or destroy files, directories or even entire systems! Such systems cannot be treated with the contempt other more resilient operating systems can tolerate – UNIX systems have to be carefully started, shut down, administered and backed up.

While there are developments under way to generate a real–time resilient UNIX, its use in many applications must be carefully considered. Its biggest restriction is the lack of real–time characteristics and easy access to the physical resource.

Real-time UNIX?

A possible method of providing a UNIX environment with a real–time characteristic is to use two processors—one running UNIX and the other running a real–time kernel. The two systems use shared global VMEbus memory to communicate, but have no real knowledge of each other. The real–time processor has VMEbus interrupts assigned to it, can access VMEbus memory and provides the real–time characteristics. The UNIX processor has its own resource and simply accepts data from processing from the shared memory area. Figure 5.15 shows a typical configuration. Real–time operating systems such as VRTX, VMEPROM

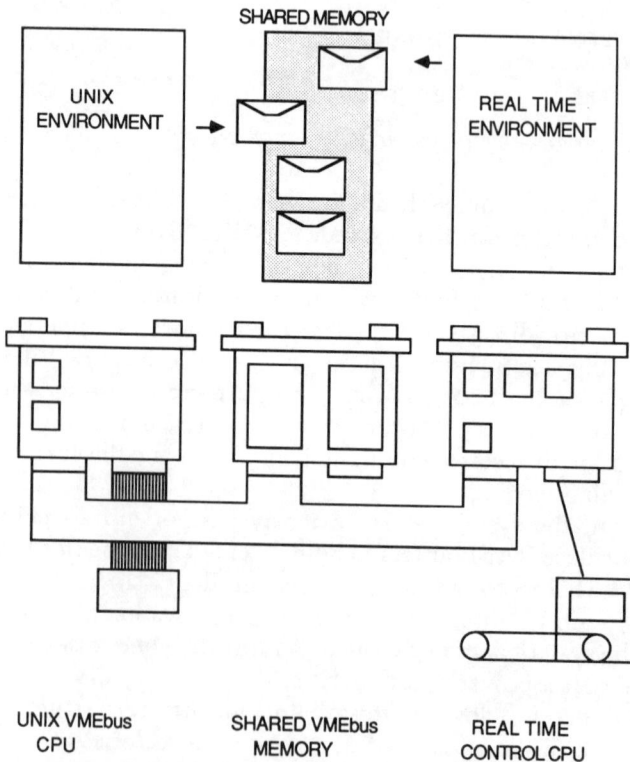

Figure 5.15 *A multiprocessor UNIX with real-time control*

and VMEexec are now available for such configurations, along with the communication software for the UNIX side.

VMEPROM and VMEexec—the ways forward?

With operating systems becoming more and more complex and software becoming increasingly expensive to develop and maintain, it is not surprising to see developments that try and use software as efficiently as possible. VMEPROM and VMEexec have taken two different approaches to solving the same problem.

FORCE Computers have taken the idea of an onboard monitor and the pDOS ROM resident real-time kernel and have combined the two into a VMEPROM. This provides a complete environment which is available, tested, and off the shelf. It removes many of the problems of porting operating systems and establishes an environment where complete system software can be programmed into ROM and run as an embedded system. With its predefined, tested interface, it provides a relatively easy interface to a UNIX environment, allowing the combination of both real-time and UNIX operating systems to be used either for ease of software development or as a true multiprocessor target system. For example, software can be generated within a UNIX environment and then downloaded to a FORCE processor in the system for debugging and testing. Once tested, the board can be run. Alternatively, the processor can remain within the UNIX environment to provide real-time functions using supplied communication software.

VMEexec takes the hardware advantages of a standard bus, and applies them to the software environment. It refers to a family of standard software interfaces covering real-time, UNIX system calls and environmental support, device drivers and networking products as shown in Figure 5.16. For example, the different libraries would allow UNIX applications to be transferred directly over to a real-time environment and vice versa. The software can even be developed under a UNIX environment and then run on other processor target boards within the system. It has direct support for memory management, shared memory communication and multiprocessor configurations.

It takes the approach that designers require a common software interface for applications which would allow them to run a different configuration with any complient kernel. This would allow system characteristics to be altered by changing the kernel, rather than rewriting the application. Each operating system kernel has different characteristics in terms of context switch speed, resource protection and interrupt handling. By defining a common interface, designers can reuse software without having to standardize on one kernel and its characteristics. The designer can choose complient kernels to get the most applicable for his/her

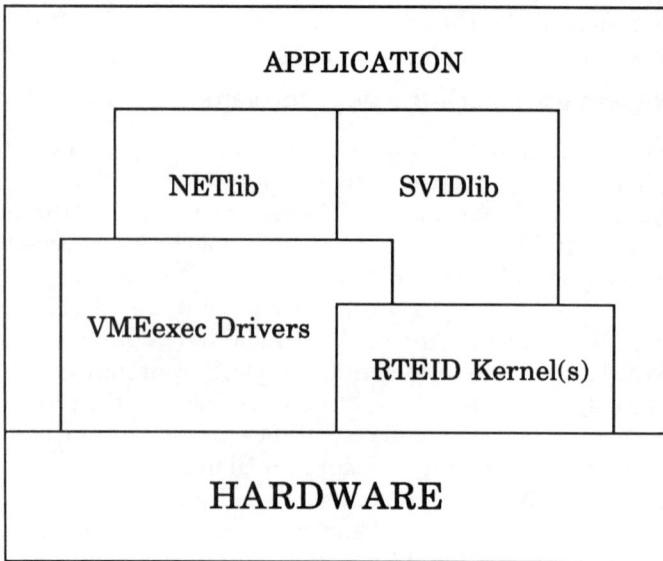

NETlib:	Network Interface Definition.
SVIDlib:	System V Interface Definition.
VMEexec Drivers:	I/O & Pseudo Device Driver Interface Definition.
RTEID Kernel(s):	Real Time Executive Interface Definition

Figure 5.16 *The VMEexec operating system structure and definitions*

application. For example, speed of operation may be the dominant requirement for application A, while resource protection is needed for application B. These two requirements tend to be mutually exclusive and using a single kernel would impose performance trade-offs for both applications. The first releases of VMEexec were imminent at the time of writing.

It will be interesting to see if these differing approaches are accepted in the market place.

Multiprocessing operating systems

Most currently implemented multiprocessing systems actually use multiple copies of real-time kernels to implement multiprocessing. Each processor runs independently under the control of a master processor which allows events and messages to be routed through it. This type of scheme is not too efficient and often requires the addition of new system facilities to the kernels. They do not require major surgery to be performed on the kernel internals, which allows their rapid development and easier testing.

The true multiprocessing operating system which has one kernel and allocates tasks to be run on the next available processor, in a similar way to post offices and banks which serve one queue with multiple windows, is just beginning to appear. Figure 5.17 shows the principle involved: as each window or CPU becomes free, the dispatcher allocates the next task to it. A UNIX software house called Unisoft have developed an implementation of UNIX which allows it to run with multiple MC68030 based processor boards, giving performances up to 100 MIPS (million instructions per second). These performance ratings are aggregate: the system can run ten processes which consume 10 MIPS each, not one process at 100 MIPS. The granularity of the multiprocessing is at process level. A list of currently available operating systems is given in appendix H.

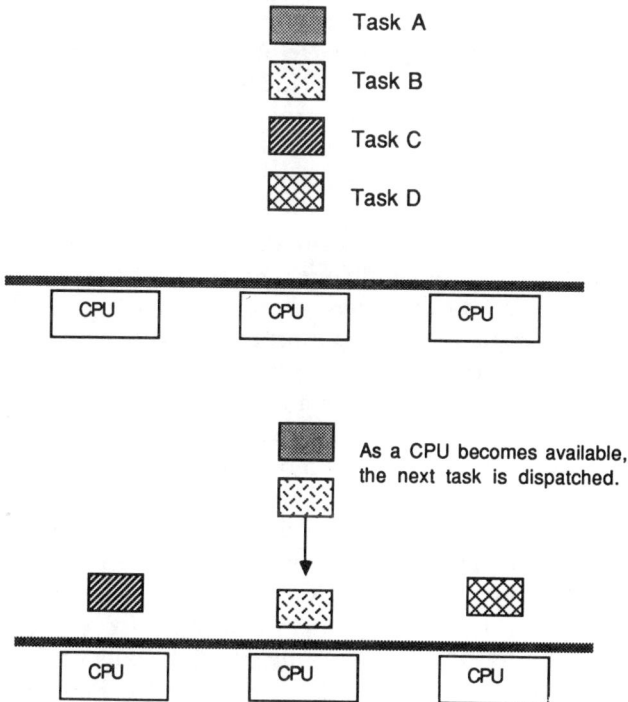

Figure 5.17 *Dispatching tasks to multiple processors*

6
Single processor systems

Controllers and MASTERS

While single processor VMEbus systems are extremely common, single VMEbus MASTER systems are extremely rare. Many applications are based on a processor board, some memory and some I/O. Usually included in the I/O is a disc controller, which is often intelligent. Intelligent controllers transfer data to and from the processor via globally available VMEbus memory and using either a DMA controller or a processor.

As stated previously, there is no functional difference between a processor board MASTER and an intelligent controller MASTER from a VMEbus standpoint. Both request the bus and access it. This makes many single processor systems multiprocessor, in reality, although this characteristic is often well hidden by the VMEbus and software interfaces. It is only when the system is expanded that this may impose limitations and restrict configurations. The intelligent controller is preprogrammed and therefore there is often little that a designer can do to change its characteristics as would be the case with a true multi-CPU system. Such boards must be treated as complete standalone entities.

Many applications use the VMEbus interface to act on an electronic cement binding processor and I/O building blocks together. The VMEbus interface is used in the same way as the native processor bus: it becomes the main traffic highway, supporting the bulk of the processor accesses. For such applications, only parts of the VMEbus specification need be supported. Therefore, before deciding which board to use or design, consideration has to be given as to the minimum system requirements.

Anatomy of a processor card

A typical VMEbus processor board can be divided into two sections: the first is the normal memory and I/O facilities that any microprocessor requires; the second is the logic needed for the VMEbus interface.

Most commercially available boards provide various amounts of RAM and ROM for the processor, and a couple of serial ports so that a terminal and a host computer can be connected, allowing the use of an onboard

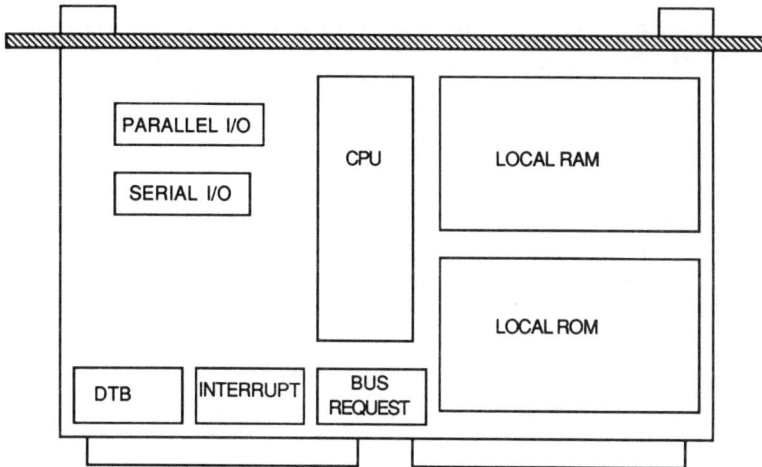

A typical VMEbus processor board.

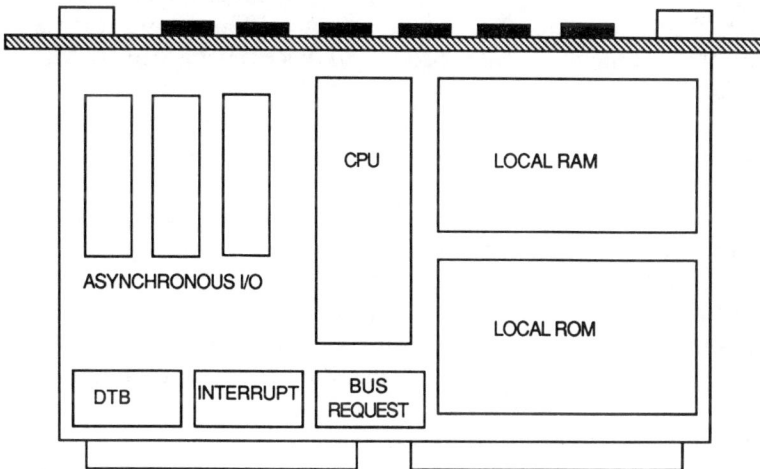

A typical intelligent comms controller

Figure 6.1   *Example of VMEbus MASTER boards*

debugger/monitor. A typical block diagram for a Motorola MC68000 processor is shown in Figure 6.1. The interface logic needed totally depends on the functions supported by the processor board.

The absolute minimum: MASTER DTB interface

The minimum VMEbus support is a MASTER DTB interface, allowing the processor to access memory and peripherals across the VMEbus. In the simplest designs, where the onboard memory is not available from the VMEbus, part of the processor memory map is assigned to VMEbus accesses. The address decode circuitry starts a VMEbus access when the processor's requested address falls into this range. The standard decode logic requires modification to generate the address modifiers that the VMEbus requires. This usually involves decoding the processor function codes to determine the type of access.

The function codes differentiate between SUPERVISOR and USER data, program accesses and interrupt acknowledgements. The usual method of generating the address modifiers is to use the function codes and higher order address bits to act as an address for a bipolar PROM which contains the address modifiers. Reprogramming the PROM allows any modifier code to be issued with the VMEbus address. This is very advantageous in multiprocessor configurations, where the system can be partitioned.

More sophisticated designs often use a control register to generate the extra bits that the function codes do not provide. This allows software to dynamically change the modifier codes. In this case, it is usually prudent to have a bus watchdog timer to assert the BERR* signal to abort any access not completed within a set time period. Although this facility may be provided elsewhere in the system, it is safer to assume it is not. Extra watchdogs are better than no watchdogs.

The other essential part of the DTB MASTER interface is a bus requester. This uses the VMEbus arbitration signals and requests the bus if the onboard processor needs to access a memory location via the VMEbus prior to the actual access. If the bus is unavailable, the interface logic requests the bus and inserts wait states in the processor cycle until the bus is granted; until the bus is granted, the interface must not drive the bus. Once the bus is received, the address is put on to the VMEbus.

The minimum requirement is a single level requester which only issues level 3 requests. More sophisticated bus requesters allow the board to issue requests on any of the four priority levels. The actual level used is determined by either a control register or a jumper configuration. Watchdog timers are often employed to trap overlong delays in obtaining the bus, or the processor bus watchdog is used, providing its delay is not too short.

Adding system controller functions

With the MASTER DTB interface and bus requester, a processor board can access other VMEbus slaves, but all its memory and I/O remain local to the processor and the system requires a system controller to implement the bus arbiter function and provide the SYSCLK signal.

The arbiter must support at least one of the arbitration schemes supported by the VMEbus, i.e. single level, priority or round robin. Most processor boards include these functions onboard so that the board can be placed in slot 1 and act as the system controller. With single processor systems, the choice of arbitration scheme is not crucial. As a result, the simpler single level arbiter is usually implemented, with only more sophisticated designs supporting the other schemes. The system controller functions should have a disable facility to allow their use with discrete system controllers or in multiple processor systems.

Interrupt handling

With all the functions described so far, single processor systems can be constructed. The onboard resources can be expanded by using the VMEbus as a type of electronic construction kit, where additional memory and peripherals are simply placed in the rack and the VMEbus on both the processor MASTER and the SLAVE boards provide a transparent VMEbus access. For software writers, the new resource just appears within the memory map and is accessed. In such simple systems, there is only any impact on the software if the new boards have control registers which may need setting.

The configuration described above does have one restriction in that VMEbus interrupts are not supported. For simple, single processor systems, this may not be a major problem. Instead of waiting for a peripheral to interrupt a processor so it can perform some type of service, the processor can periodically check the peripheral status to see if it needs to do something. However, this polling technique can consume processor time quite dramatically. For a VMEbus board to accept VMEbus interrupts and service them requires the addition of an interrupt handler module. This handler requires ownership of the bus so that it can start an interrupt acknowledgement cycle. Interrupt handlers are therefore only found on DTB MASTERS. Figure 6.2 shows a VMEbus MASTER with its full complement of VMEbus functions.

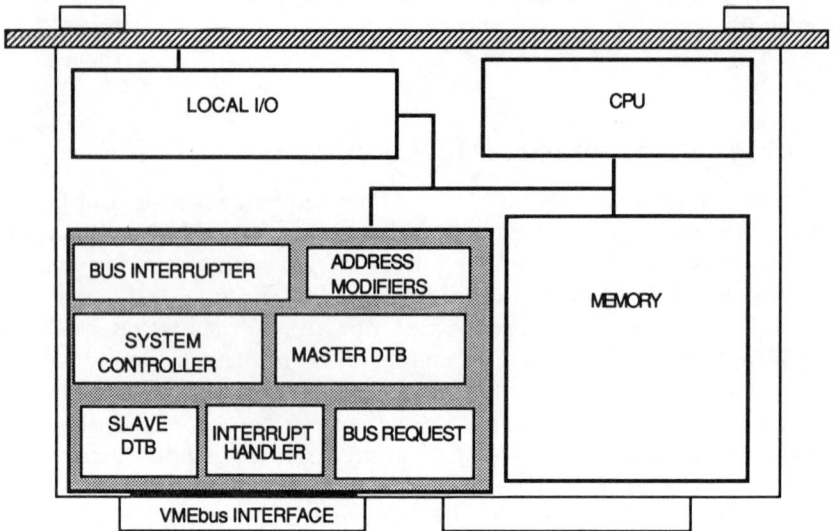

Figure 6.2   *VMEbus requirements for a processor board*

SLAVE VMEbus card

The VMEbus requirements for SLAVE boards are simpler than for MASTERS and basically require decoding logic for the address bus, address modifiers and byte strobes. The logic also needs to take into account the data and address bus widths. If the SLAVE cannot support 32-bit transfers, it needs to terminate a cycle with BERR★ when the LWORD★ signal is asserted.

This type of interface is straightforward to design but can be complicated if the memory is shared between local buses and the VMEbus. A memory board may support accesses between both VMEbus and VSB or a processor board may share its onboard memory with the VMEbus. The difficulty with these types of boards is in solving the 'deadly embrace' problem, where two MASTERS access the same memory location and either corrupt data or cause both MASTERS to wait and therefore lock up the bus.

There are two commonly used techniques for sharing memory as shown in Figure 6.3. The first uses special dual ported memory chips which have additional logic to provide simultaneous access to the same memory location via two different ports and to resolve possible contention problems. Their main restriction is the relatively small memory densities available and their slower access times. They are frequently used to provide the interface for intelligent I/O boards, where only small amounts of RAM are required. These boards tend to use the dual port RAM as a set of control registers which point and control memory structures in the global VMEbus memory.

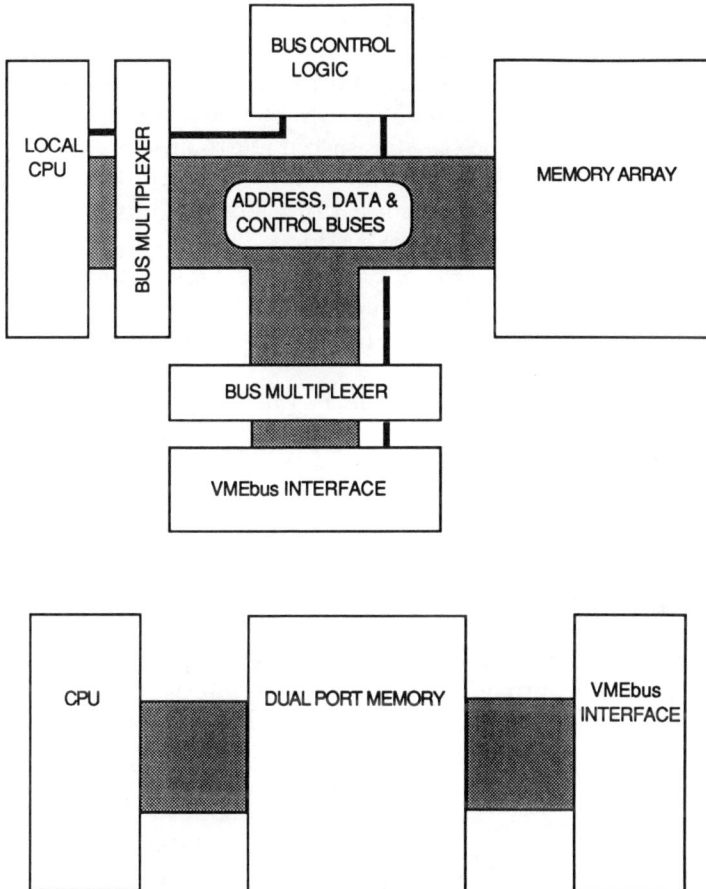

Figure 6.3 *Two methods of dual access memory for VMEbus*

The second technique involves sharing the memory with other MASTERS by using the same bus. This supports normal memory chips and therefore allows very large amounts of memory to be used. This technique uses external logic to force a second MASTER to wait for the first MASTER to finish accessing the memory. This can be done by arbitrating the bus away or by buffering the second MASTER signals and forcing wait states. Another method is to abort the bus cycle, force a retry and then arbitrate the bus away so that the MASTER waits for the bus to be granted. The problem with this technique is that the VMEbus interface is predefined, so the onboard processor has to be flexible and, inevitably, has to come second place in the priority scheme. The additional logic places additional wait states in to the access from the VMEbus, and while the VMEbus MASTER is accessing the shared memory, the onboard processor is held off and not able to do anything.

With microprocessors such as the MC68000 and the 80X86 families, which have very high bus bandwidth requirements, processing stops until the bus is returned. Devices like the MC68020 and MC68030, which have internal on-chip caches, are less susceptible to this restriction due to their reduced use of external bus bandwidth. It is therefore a good policy to consider the impact on processor performance when large amounts of data are being transferred across the VMEbus by another MASTER. This typically happens when a disc controller is performing read/write operations. In such cases, it may be better to use a separate VMEbus memory board to act as the transfer area between the controller and processor.

While earlier VMEbus processor boards often had no VMEbus accessable onboard memory, it has now become a standard requirement in any processor design.

Error handling

The main hardware mechanism used to detect system errors is the watchdog timer. It provides finite periods in which to complete tasks such as bus requests, accesses and interrupt acknowledgements; without them, system errors, such as incomplete bus cycles, hang up the system without crashing or locking up the bus. The bus is functioning correctly but waiting.

Sanity or COPs (Computer Operating Properly) timers are often used to check system software integrity. If the software fails to reset the timer, it times out and either resets the processor or generates a non-maskable reset. These timers can either reset a local resource or can be connected to the VMEbus allowing the entire system to be reset.

Parity protection is often used on the memory subsystems, but its use inevitably inserts a wait state into the memory cycles. Most commercially available boards allow parity to be disabled to remove this wait state. For most applications, the chance of a parity error is so remote, compared to other failure modes, that it can be ignored. For very critical systems, error detection and correction (EDC) may be a better choice.

Example configurations

Printer buffer

In this example, Figure 6.4, a processor, serial and parallel I/O and a large amount of memory (in the order of 1 to 2 Mbytes) were required. It needed to take raw data from a computer serial port, buffer it and send it to a parallel printer. The data could also be interpreted to emulate different printer configurations. The configuration used was not critical and was based more on availability, cost and short design time than anything else.

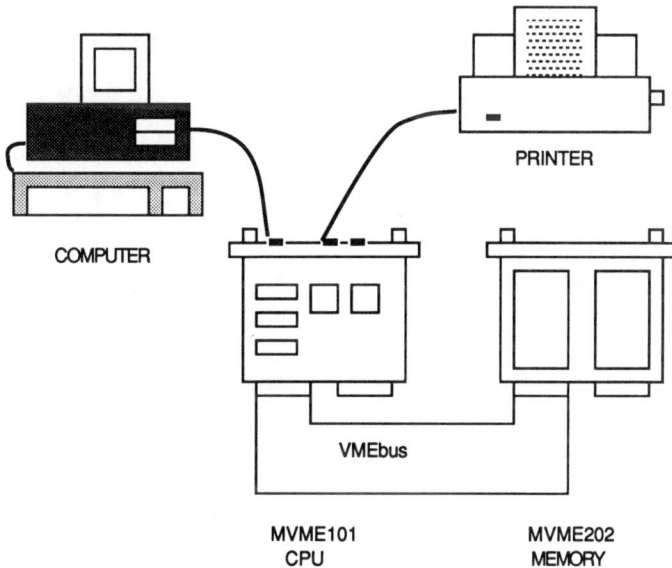

Figure 6.4 *Printer buffer using VMEbus*

The cheapest solution was to build the buffer using discrete components. This reduced the hardware costs dramatically, but would increase the engineering time to debug the hardware and software. Using standard off-the-shelf modules reduced the total engineering time.

A Motorola MVME101 processor board and an MVME202-2 2 Mbyte RAM board were used.

The MVME101 has onboard serial and parallel ports and 8 × 28 pin JEDEC RAM/ROM sockets. Two were used to provide RAM for the vector table and local stack area for the 8 MHz MC68000 processor and the remainder were populated with 256-Kbit EPROMs. The program and printer conversion tables were stored in the EPROMs and the RAM provided by the MVME202 via the VMEbus were used to buffer the data.

This type of system could easily have been built as a discrete design or using another standard bus interface. All that was being used was the DTB interface to provide a data highway. I/O interrupts were generated and handled locally on the processor board. However, using the VMEbus as the module cement allowed future upgrades. Buffer memory could be increased and, by using a software routine to access memory until a bus error, allowed the system to determine, on power-up, how much system memory was installed. A later configuration added more memory and supported data transfer from two serial ports to one printer. The system maintained two separate buffer areas, so files were printed as separate entities. This allowed two independent computers to share one printer, as well as providing the spooler facilities.

Computer system

The Motorola SYS319 VMEbus system, Figure 6.5, is a good example of a single processor multiMASTER system. It uses the same configuration as that of the printer buffer described above, but has an MVME319 disc controller to provide disc storage. The system runs the VERSAdos multitasking real-time operating system from the MVME202 VMEbus memory. The MVME101 performs the system controller functions, provides a single level arbiter, and has the highest bus priority. Its onboard memory is only used for the onboard debugger. The

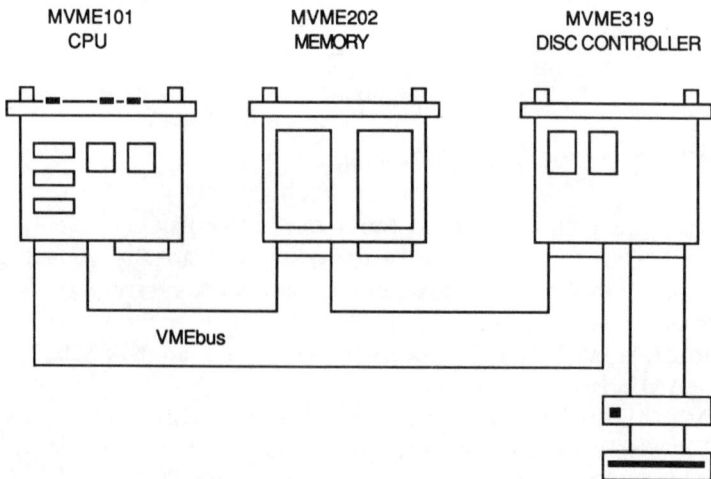

Figure 6.5 *Block diagram of the MVME319 system*

MVME319 disc controller is a VMEbus MASTER and uses VMEbus memory for data storage. Command packets are written into its dual port memory in the VMEbus short I/O address range by the processor board.

This system demonstrates the performance trade-off made when the VMEbus is used to replace the native processor bus. Running code offboard can typically increase performance times by about 20%. This is further compounded when disc access is required. If the MVME101 has the bus, which it does the majority of the time when all code and data are offboard, the MVME319 disc controller has to arbitrate for the bus for every access. When it gets the bus, the MVME101 processor is effectively stopped until it receives the bus again and can start fetching instructions. If the two MASTERS have to arbitrate continually for the bus, most of the processing time available is wasted. In an effort to reduce this overhead, the MVME319 only relinquishes the bus after it has completed eight transfers. This technique is common with disc controllers, where data are transferred a sector at a time. However, if the watchdog timers are not set to take this into account, bus error timeouts occur, causing further system problems. The software receives an error trying to access valid memory. This will often cause many operating systems to shut down with a system crash. The solution is to ensure that time out periods are long enough for all such block transfers to complete before expiry.

The MVME319 generates interrupts to inform the processor that it has completed its last command. The MVME101 and the backplane must be jumpered correctly to accept them. When the MVME319 has completed executing a command packet, it generates an interrupt on the VMEbus to inform the processor board that it needs to check the status area to find out which packet has been completed and the resulting status. The interrupt is routed through to the MC68000 processor which is then interrupted and control is passed to the interrupt handler.

7
Multiprocessor techniques

What is multiprocessing?

If a single processor system does not have enough processing power, an obvious method of increasing processing power is to add more processors and have a multiprocessing system.

The earlier 8-bit microprocessors, such as the MC6802 from Motorola, had a very high memory bus bandwidth requirement, which meant that placing more than two processors directly on the same bus was not practical in a tightly coupled system design. Two processors could be synchronized on one bus by generating two system clocks 180 degrees out of phase and driving a processor with each one. While one processor would be disabled during its dead time, the other would be operational and vice versa. With no timing penalty, both processors could operate simultaneously, giving twice the performance with only one data bus. As both processors used the same memory and I/O, communication between them would be straightforward. These types of implementations required careful matching of processors, and careful design of the clock generation circuitry to minimize clock skew, as shown in Figures 7.1 and 7.2.

This method was not practical for next generation processors, such as the MC68000 family. Their bus cycles require multiple system clock cycles to complete and therefore there is no system deadtime to allocate to another processor. However, their instructions are more complex and require more system clocks to execute than are needed to fetch the instruction in the first place. This results in time slots being available on the external bus, enabling other processors to access it. The MC68000 has an on-chip arbitration scheme to allow other MASTERS to use the bus. The problem with this scheme comes with the pre-fetch and pipeline mechanisms, which are used to maintain the instruction flow for the processor execution unit. They consume bus bandwidth and typical

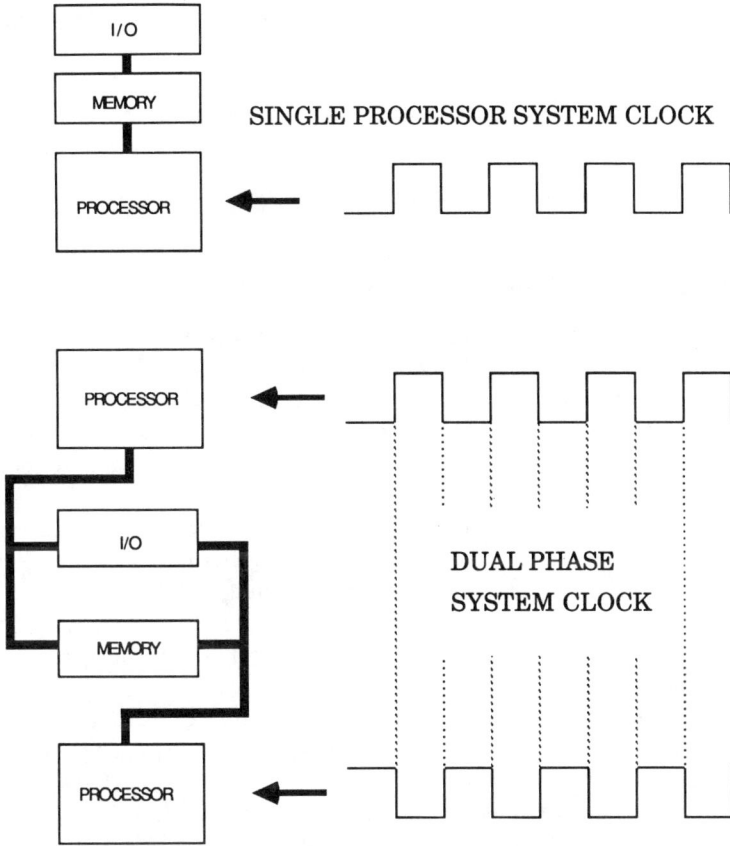

Figure 7.1 *A dual processor system using dual phase clocks*

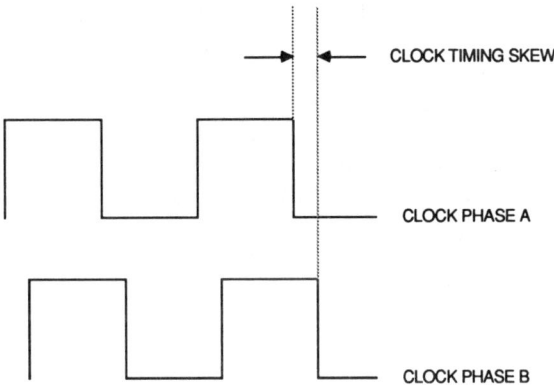

Figure 7.2 *Clock skewing with dual clocks*

utilization figures in excess of 80% are not uncommon. The remaining bandwidth may be suitable for data DMA but seriously reduces the performance of a second processor that has to share the single bus. The tightly coupled scheme of connecting processors is replaced by the loosely coupled method.

Loosely coupled multiprocessing systems

Loosely coupled systems use some form of shared resource to act as a communications bridge between the processors in the system. Each processor is ignorant of the others' existence and simply communicates to the bridge via a protocol. This bridge may appear as a set of registers or simply as a memory area, commonly called a mailbox. Data are sent and received via these bridges.

The most critical area in this type of arrangement is the synchronizing and controlling of the resource. With a shared memory system, all reads and writes to the area must be performed as discrete, complete operations. A second processor must be prevented from reading partially updated information or modifying the data while another processor is reading it.

Either semaphore flags, which are tested and set prior to access, or some form of negotiation protocol are used to solve this problem. A typical protocol for serial communications uses a unique token which is passed around the various processor links. Ownership of the token is a prerequisite for any message-passing. This effectively prevents two processors trying to use the link at the same time. The semaphore flag is a memory bit that is stored in shared memory. The mechanism is shown in Figure 7.3. Prior to an access, the processor checks the semaphore and will only access the mailbox if it is clear. On finding it clear, the bit is immediately set to force other processors to wait until the current processor has finished using the mailbox, and clears the bit. The semaphore is acting in a similar way to the token.

The problem with semaphores comes with multiple processors: it is possible that, between the checking and setting of the semaphore bit, another processor checks the access to the mailbox and finds it erroneously clear. The two processors will then access the mailbox simultaneously and cause its corruption as shown in Figure 7.4. To prevent this, the checking and setting of the semaphore must be an indivisible operation. Such operations are performed using the MC68000 family TEST and SET instruction which performs a read-modify-write operation as two consecutive indivisible cycles.

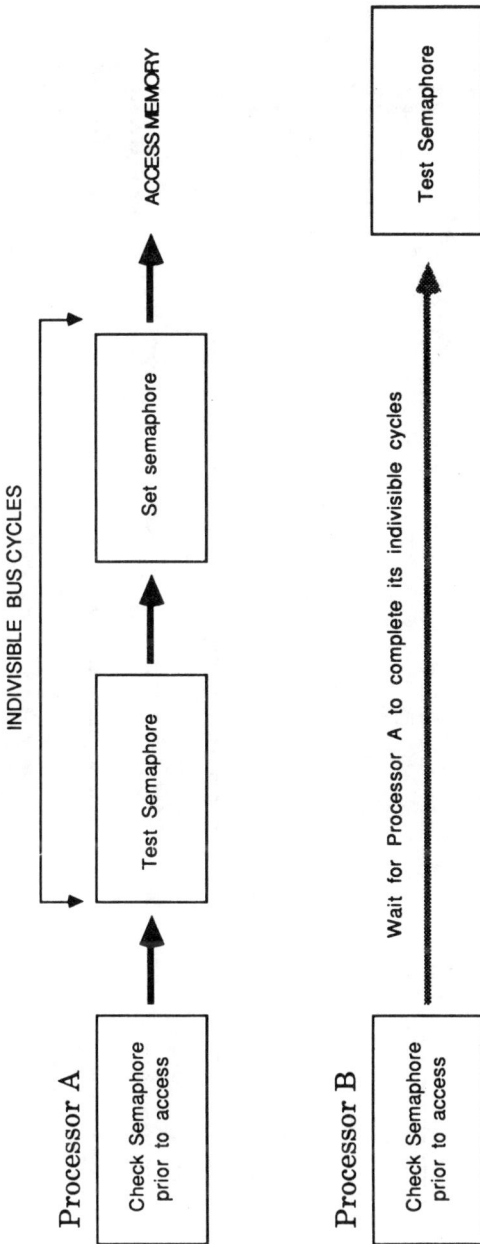

Figure 7.3 *Using a semaphore to control access to shared memory*

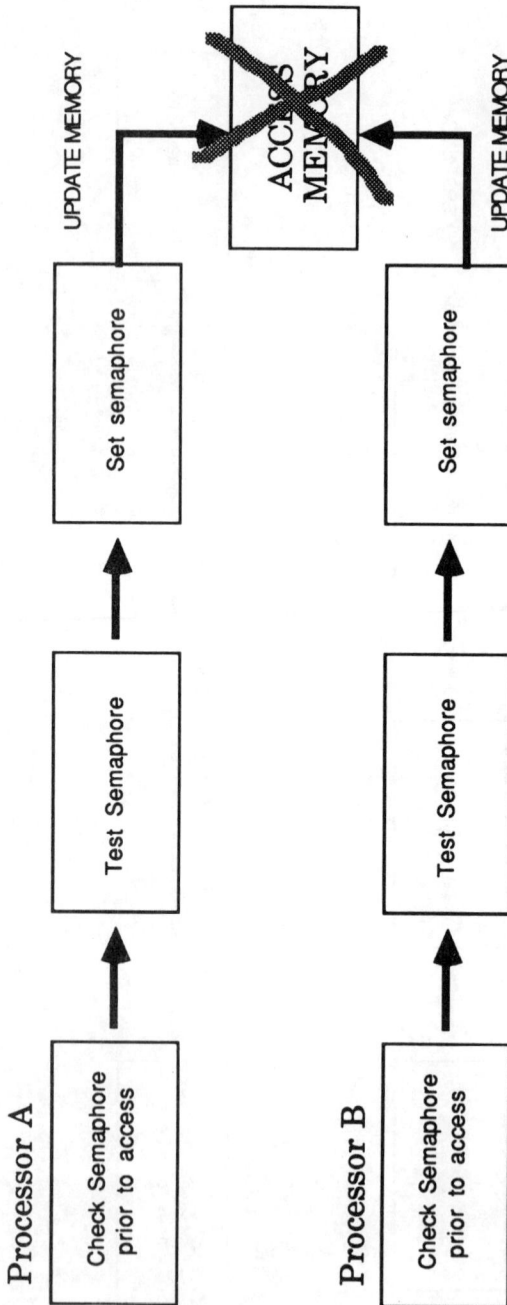

Figure 7.4 *Incorrect use of semaphores*

Two methods are generally used for the communications bridge: either serial or peripheral I/O devices can provide a communications link, or memory areas can be shared between multiple processors. The I/O communications link can provide low to medium speed data transfers but can cause tremendous system overheads for the connected processors unless sophisticated techniques using DMA are involved.

Using shared memory provides a medium which is capable of transferring data as fast as the processor can manage by using simple memory block moves, but requires careful system design to prevent bus contention and data corruption. Such circuitry may insert wait states into the access cycles and slow the process. The advantage of I/O links is their ability to be multipoint: they can send data to many processors simultaneously. Shared memory systems require each processor to access the bus in turn to inspect and receive the data. The aggregate time for this could be slower than a message via peripheral I/O. Given that these methods can provide the communication mechanisms required for controlling a multiprocessor system, there are choices in how the processors are allotted their work and controlled.

Multiprocessor architecture

There are two general types of multiprocessing architectures used. The first divides the required task into smaller components and executes them on the multiple processors in parallel. The second allows multiple tasks to be executed with one task allocated to each processor.

To illustrate this, consider a software task to consist of the operation of filling four small boxes and then putting them into a larger box. With a single processor system represented by a single worker, each small box would be filled and loaded in turn. After four boxes had been loaded, the box would be sealed to complete the tasks as shown in Figure 7.5. If another four workers were available then there are several possibilities open to improve the throughput of the system. One would be to simply have an additional four workers filling and loading boxes in parallel. Each worker would perform the five stages of each task sequentially, and would be wholly responsible for that complete operation. At any one time, five operations would be executed concurrently. Each worker would not need to know about the existence of the others, and any problems such as lack of filling would only affect one worker: the others would carry on regardless, albeit with less total system throughput. This is a 'multiple execution' type of system (Figure 7.6).

An alternative organization would be to split the task into small segments: four workers would be assigned to filling the small boxes and one worker would pack the four boxes into the larger box. By working in

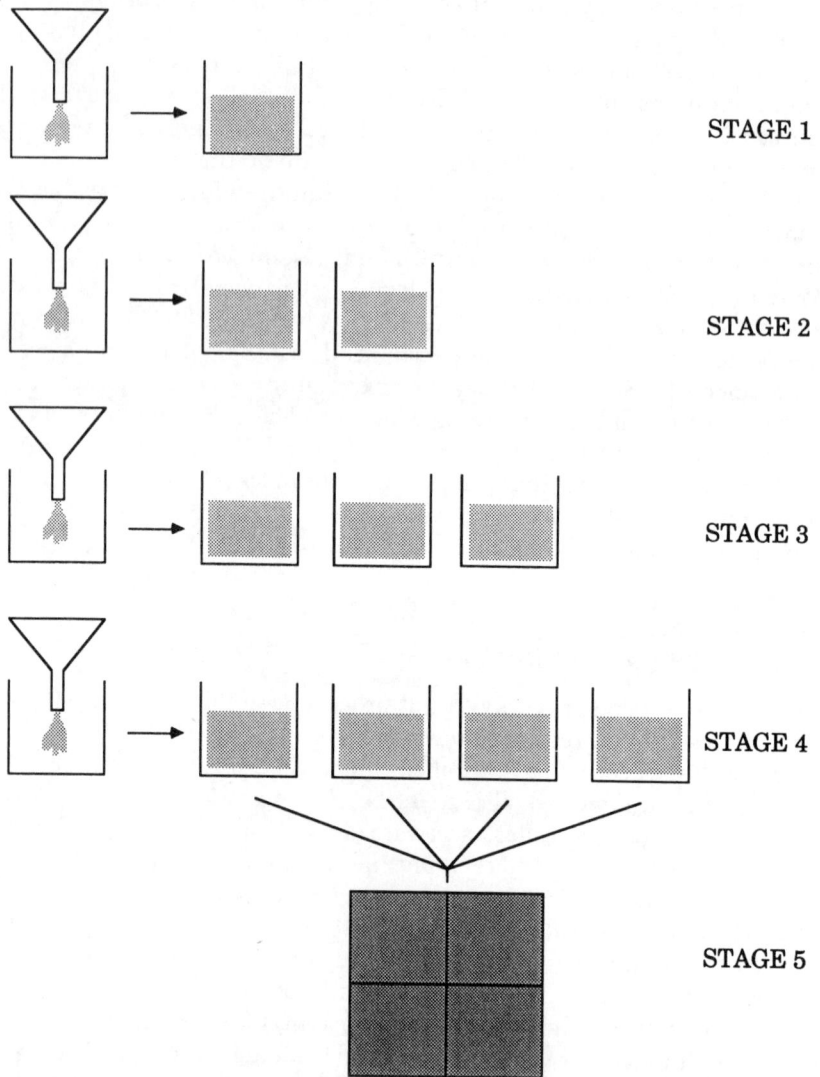

Figure 7.5   *Sequential task operation*

parallel, the four workers can provide four filled boxes simultaneously which the packer can then pack. While the packer is packing the big box, another four small boxes can be filled and loaded. If any of the four workers cannot provide a full box, then the whole system is liable to fail and will require major repairs before any system throughout can be obtained. This 'parallel execution' scheme as shown in Figure 7.7 relies on the operation being able to be split or dissolved into elements which

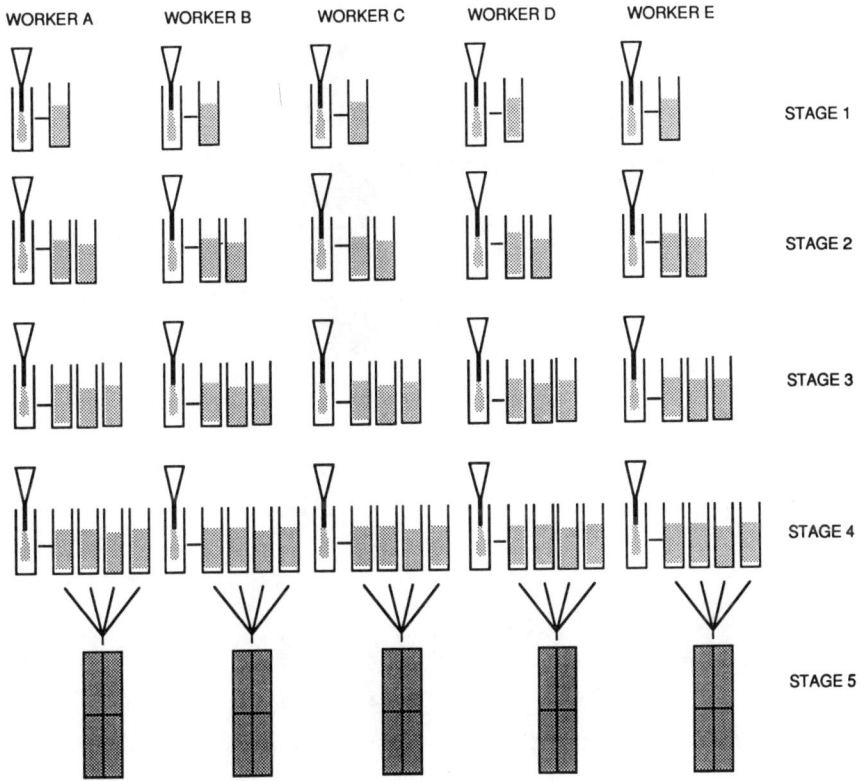

Figure 7.6   *Parallel processing through 'multiple execution'*

can be executed in parallel. If the operation is purely sequential, i.e. the four boxes are of different sizes and need to be packed inside each other like a Russian doll, the operation's elements cannot be executed in parallel. Each element's successful completion depends on the previous element and the order of execution, and therefore the only appropriate multiprocessing scheme is the first one.

These two schemes form the basis of the majority of multiprocessor hierarchies used in VMEbus systems. Both schemes require a controlling 'master' processor to direct the other 'slave' processors (the 'master' and 'slave' descriptions do not refer to the VMEbus definitions of MASTER and SLAVE).

The communications required for the two schemes are also different. In the 'multiple execution' scheme, the master processor normally performs supervisory functions and does not directly take part in any actual direct work. It simply provides a task for each slave processor and awaits the results. It only checks at the end of the task resulting in a system

FILLER A   FILLER B   FILLER C   FILLER D   PACKER E

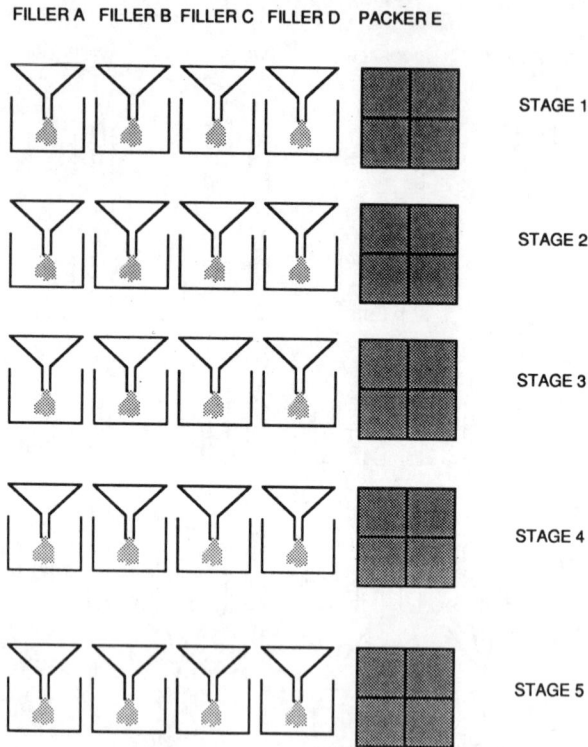

STAGE 1

STAGE 2

STAGE 3

STAGE 4

STAGE 5

Figure 7.7 *Multiprocessing with parallel processors*

granularity at the task level. Information is passed via a communications link between the master and each slave individually either through shared memory or I/O links. The number of slave processors that can be handled depends on the total communications bandwidth available and the portion of the bandwidth that each master-slave link needs. This is a function of the how the system is realized. This type of arrangement is typified by a point-to-point link for each slave. If the slaves require the use of the communication links for their own purposes, this will further limit the number of processors.

The 'parallel execution' scheme often uses the master processor to divide the task into its parallel elements and collate them after execution. Communication links are essential between the slaves so that they can synchronize and prevent unsynchronized execution from destroying the advantages gained by parallelism. Any skewing between the slaves adds processor overheads. These links also provide message pathways to allow the master to stop or control the system if something goes wrong. If these links are performed within shared memory, then the number of links is limited by available bandwidth, as described previously, and prevents simultaneous access. This adds to the skewing problem and decreases performance. This type of scheme is typical of applications using the inmos transputer and can easily be achieved using general purpose processors like the MC68020 with discrete communications links.

Sending messages

The communication techniques described provide the medium for message-passing and control. The method of detecting messages also requires consideration.

With any multiprocessor system, there are two ways of informing a processor that a message is waiting. It can either be interrupted or the processor can check at prearranged times. The interrupt technique uses interrupters activated by accessing certain memory locations so that processors can either interrupt individual processors or groups. This allows easy synchronization and control, irrespective of the architecture used. With the large number of elements in a 'parallel execution' model, the elements may need to daisy-chain the interrupt signals down through the model to complete global message-passing. The alternative is to poll.

Polling

Interrupt schemes place the responsibility on the peripheral or interrupter to inform the processor that it needs to perform some operation. If the processor does not receive an interrupt it carries on regardless.

Polling places this responsibility on the processor, which will periodically check peripherals, shared memory areas, etc. to see if there is a message waiting for it. This involves considerable overheads for the processor, especially if a fast response is only occasionally needed. The response time is dependent on the frequency of the polling routines, the number of sources that need to be checked and the order in which the sources are checked as shown in Figure 7.8. Checking sources at the end of the list may also be delayed due to the handling of received messages from earlier sources.

Some schemes use a combination of both techniques: groups of sources will generate a single interrupt and the interrupt handler will poll through the group to find the source that needs servicing. This is particularly useful when there are insufficient interrupt levels to assign uniquely or when generic interrupt handlers are used.

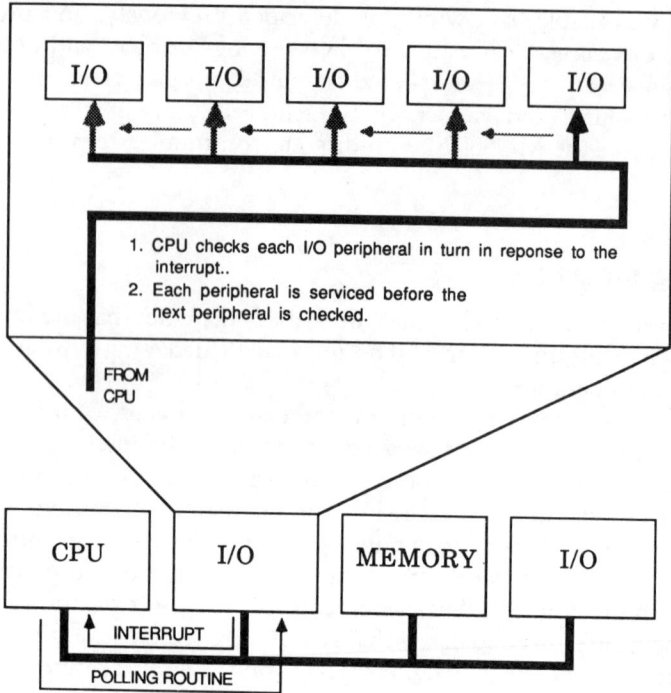

Figure 7.8   *Using a combination of interrupt and polling routines to service I/O peripherals*

Prioritized message-passing

Most systems require a selection of communication methods which can be used, depending on the service and volume of data that is required to be sent.

For low speed, low volume communications, a simple serial link can provide the ideal medium. For higher speed links (>38 000 baud), either a parallel bus, like the GPIB 488 standard, or a faster 10-Mbit serial link, based around Ethernet or the MAP protocol, would be sufficient.

As data speed increases, the processor load required to decode the data increases dramatically. For high speed MAP and Ethernet links, 32-bit MC68020 processors control special dedicated support silicon chips to provide the appropriate data. For communications between processors on a bus, the bus itself is used as the message-passing medium, using either polling or interrupt driven mechanisms to control the message priority. For low priority systems, a simple polling mechanism is used. For high priority messages, an interrupt scheme is used which can delay the processor's current activity until it has dealt with the priority message. By using various combinations, the right response can be achieved for the circumstances.

Software implications

Apart from the basic software implications of actually controlling and communicating within a multiprocessor system, there are three main concerns with message-passing and they are all concerned with the format of the message.

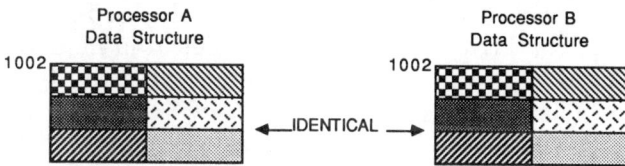

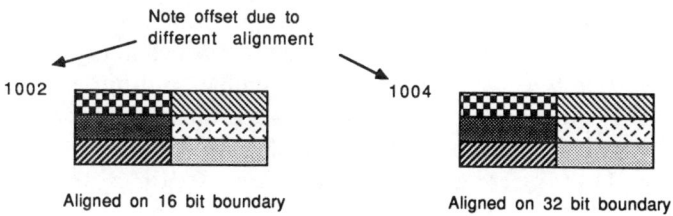

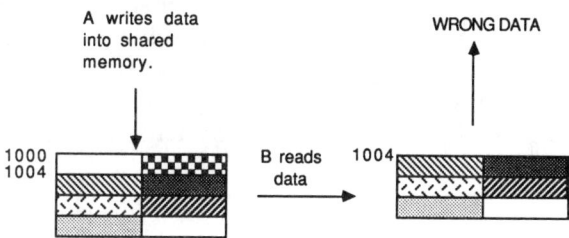

Figure 7.9 *Misaligned data structures and their problems*

The common method is to create a structure, if the programming language is 'C', or, if Pascal is being used, a record which takes a block of memory and defines a set of variables within it. With a multiprocessor system, where the processor architectures may be different and the software generated by different compilers or languages, it is essential that the sizes of the variables defined in the block are the same. 'C' compiler A may define a variable type *int* as 16 bits in length, while compiler B may use 24 bits or 32 bits. Such discrepancies mean that the data contained in the memory block are misinterpreted, causing a system crash.

The second concern is over how the compiler aligns its data blocks in memory. If compiler A aligns to a word boundary, while compiler B aligns to a long word, the data blocks may be misaligned again causing data corruption. Such alignment is often hidden from the user and is ultimately controlled when the software modules are linked with run-time libraries etc. Figure 7.9 depicts the problem in more detail: both processors start with identical data structures which should be at the same odd word address, but processor A's compiler aligns on a 16-bit boundary while processor B is 32-bit aligned. This means that processor B's data will be padded until it is completely aligned. This will cause no problem until data are passed between the two processors. When processor B reads processor A's data structure in memory, then it will read the wrong information and thus corrupt the data.

The third concern is over the byte ordering within the variables. There are currently two schools of thought about which bits are the most significant. The two organizations, little endian and big endian, mean that the same code to test a bit will actually produce different results from the two organizations. This is shown in Figure 7.10. If two processors which use these different organizations are used in a multiprocessor system, the software may be restricted in how it can bit test or manipulate data to prevent corruption. The bit testing of bit 15 in a little endian organization will access byte 1 within a 32-bit word. Performing the same bit test with a big endian scheme, byte 2 is accessed instead. Software that functioned perfectly with one memory organization now fails. This property can make many so-called 'machine independent' programs totally dependent on the memory scheme and hence choice of processor available for porting. Instead of direct bit manipulation, masking and quantity testing may need to be employed. Both these techniques can be slower and have an impact on performance. The next chapter will explore how multiprocessor systems are designed with the VMEbus.

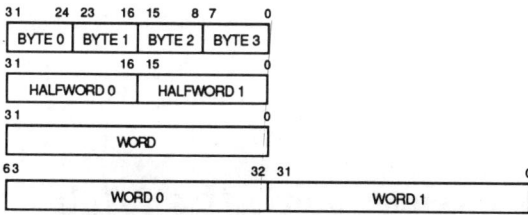

BIG ENDIAN BYTE ORDERING

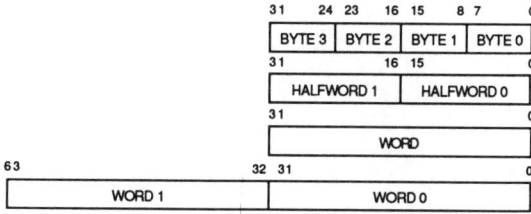

LITTLE ENDIAN BYTE ORDERING

Figure 7.10 *Little and big endian byte ordering*

8
Multiprocessing with the VMEbus

Basic concepts

The majority of multiprocessing designs using VMEbus boards use loosely coupled processors communicating through shared memory mailboxes accessed via the VMEbus. These mailboxes may be blocks of control registers, linked lists and tables, and can be accessed, for example, by processors, intelligent disc controllers and serial communications cards. They can contain whole files, new programs, or just a byte of data.

Response times can range from microseconds to seconds, depending on the mechanism used. A successful multiprocessor design takes these factors and trade-offs into account and allocates the most suitable communication configuration for each type required. Messages needing fast responses use interrupts, while simple system table updating uses a polling technique.

While I/O links such as RS232 serial lines can be used, they are very slow and need a lot of extra overheads to implement, compared with the ability to implement shared memory mailboxes supported by the VMEbus. I/O links, such as Ethernet and MAP, are used to provide communication between VME systems. These are discussed in chapter 15. Its bus arbitration schemes prevent a catastrophic simultaneous memory access by multiple masters. The bus lock provision supports indivisible semaphore testing and setting, allowing multiple accesses to the same address without interruption by another MASTER. This is performed by asserting the AS* signal throughout the multiple cycles. All that is required to set up such a multiprocessor system is to take a couple of processors and some VMEbus memory, install them in a rack, and declare the mailbox and associated semaphores address. This simplistic approach is easy to construct, but does not fully exploit the VMEbus potential.

A global message-passing bus

The VMEbus was originally designed as a global message-passing bus for multiprocessor applications. The most efficient multiprocessor designs aim to remove all local processor bus traffic, so that either large volumes of data can be passed between MASTERS or very fast transmission of small messages can be achieved.

In reality, most systems require a combination of both high volume low speed and high speed low volume message-passing. The time taken for a message to be sent is dependent on the software and hardware implementations and the VMEbus configuration itself. The total time required to pass a message on will depend on the message size, delays in accessing the mailbox and the method used to inform the receiver of the message's existence.

Accessing mailboxes

The first factor that determines the message-passing speed is the time taken to read and write the message into the mailbox. While the memory access time is constant and depends solely on the hardware design, the time taken to arbitrate and obtain the bus is not.

For a MASTER with a low priority within the arbitration hierarchy, the delay in obtaining the bus depends on the requirements of the higher priority MASTERS. If they are using the bus, the MASTER will have to wait until the bus is free. This highlights a recurring theme of VMEbus multiprocessor designs: a processor cannot be treated in isolation. Its performance ultimately depends on the rest of the system.

In a simple multiprocessor design which uses the VMEbus memory for local processor traffic, the bus utilization is extremely high and can

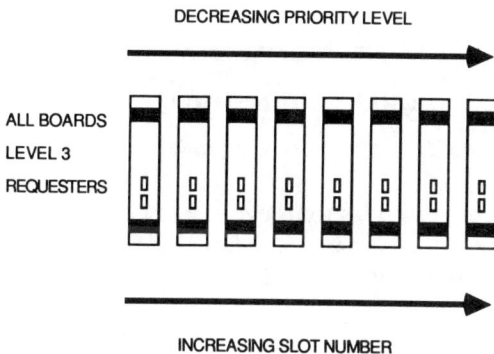

Figure 8.1 *Single level VMEbus arbitration hierarchy*

cause excessive arbitration delays. The obvious solution is to remove the local traffic from the bus. If this is unacceptable or impossible, the MASTER must be promoted within the arbitration hierarchy by changing the arbitration scheme or slot position.

The arbitration hierarchies that can be obtained are shown in Figures 8.1, 8.2 and 8.3. The single level scheme offers a linear hierarchy, where the board position in the rack determines the priority level. This is usually adequate for systems with only a few MASTERS.

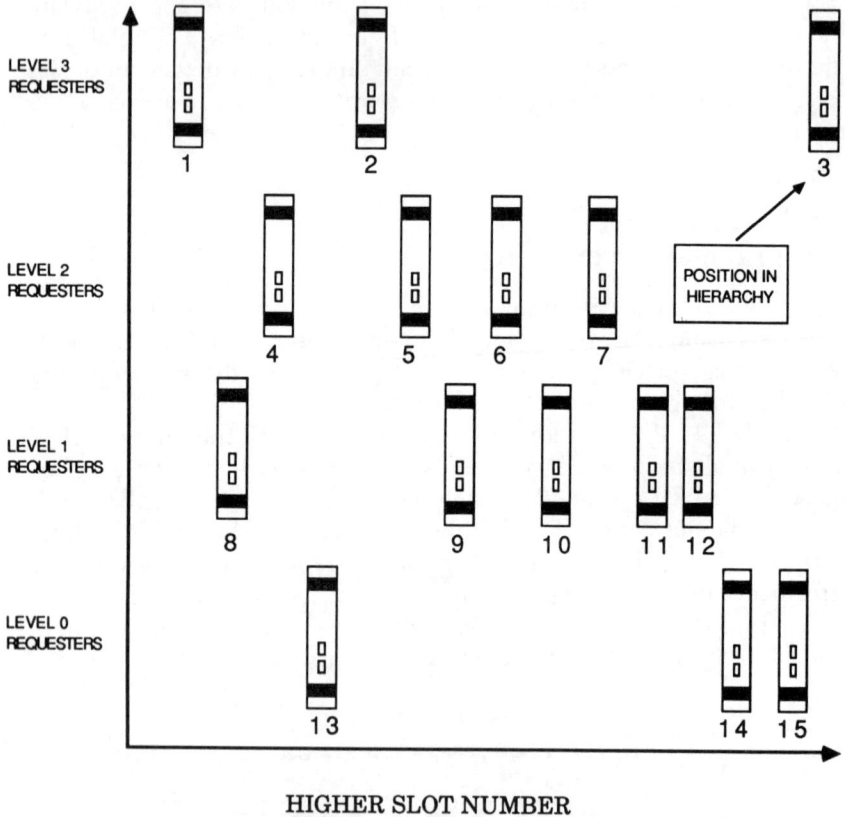

Figure 8.2   *Priority VMEbus arbitration hierarchy*

The priority scheme provides four levels of linear hierarchy, with each level being of higher priority than that below it. This scheme is normally used for large multiprocessing schemes, where certain MASTERS must have priority.

The third scheme is a 'round robin', where the highest priority is successively given to each level in turn, thus providing equal priority for each level. A linear hierarchy, based on board position, is applicable for

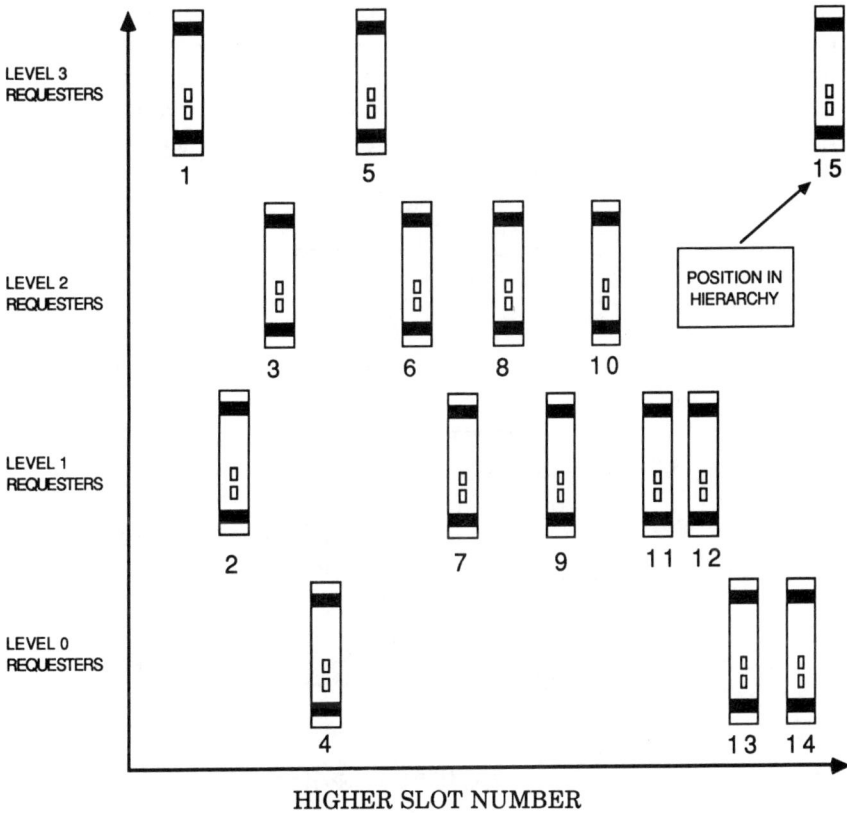

Figure 8.3 *Round robin VMEbus arbitration hierarchy*

each level. This provides an alternative scheme for large systems, where the bus access is more evenly distributed.

Mailbox locations

The location of the mailbox within the overall design can contribute to memory access delays. Figure 8.4 shows a system that comprises two processor boards with onboard memory. The memory is arranged to be accessible by both the local processor and VMEbus.

This most common implementation uses a shared memory design, which holds the local processor off the memory bus while it is being accessed via the VMEbus. The system does not have any other VMEbus memory and therefore parts of the memory block on processor A are defined as the mailbox. Whenever processor B accesses it, processor A is effectively stopped until the memory is free again. Processor A's performance therefore suffers. In addition, the extra logic required to form the 'sharing' interface causes the memory access time from the VMEbus to be several clocks longer than a typical VMEbus access. This further increases the delays, and affects the performance of both processors.

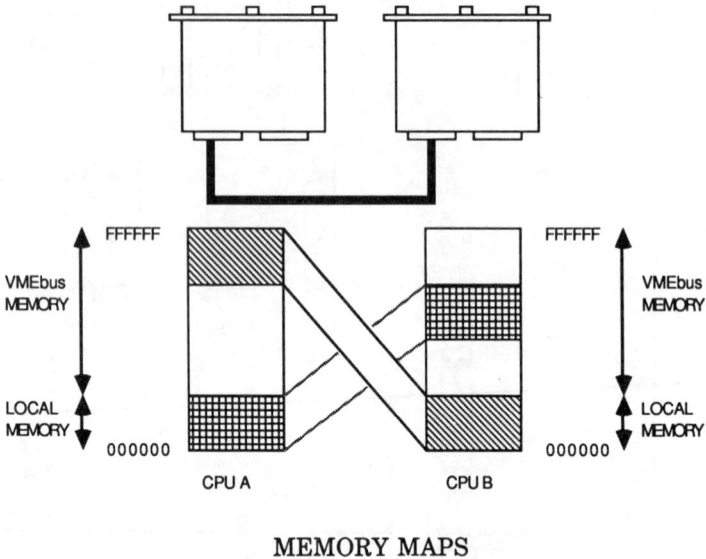

MEMORY MAPS

Figure 8.4   *A dual CPU shared memory configuration*

The solution is to use a separate VMEbus memory board for the mailbox as shown in Figure 8.5. This stops local shared memory design from consuming VMEbus bandwidth and prevents any local processor interruption. It provides a faster access to VMEbus memory for both processors which is beneficial to the whole system. Any increase in the time required to access the VMEbus consumes bus bandwidth and exaggerates any delays caused by arbitration schemes: the longer a MASTER takes when using the bus, the less time there is for others. While this may not be important where only small numbers of MASTERS are involved, the effect dramatically increases as extra processors are added.

The time taken to post a message into a mailbox depends on the access time, bus utilization and the arbitration position. All parts of this equation have to be considered.

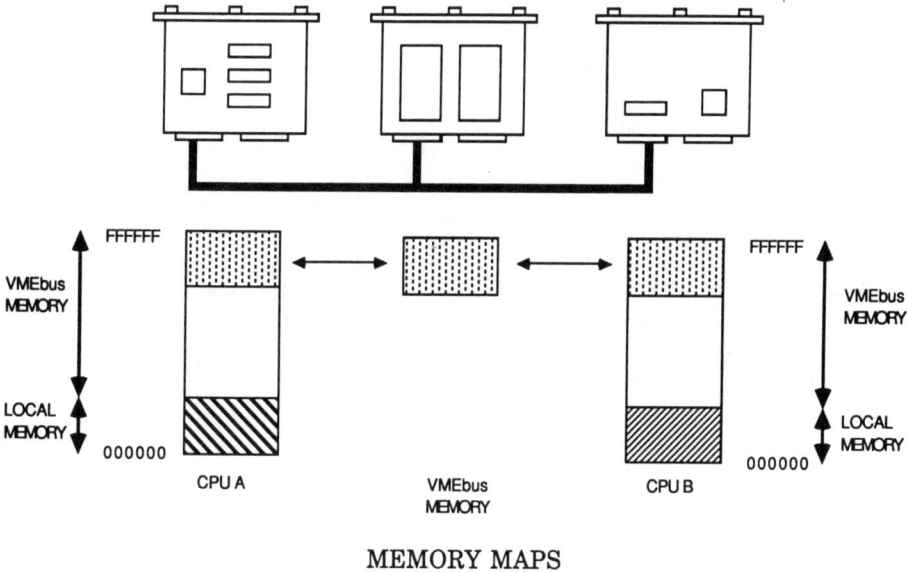

MEMORY MAPS

Figure 8.5 *Using VMEbus memory as a mailbox between two processors*

Notifying the addressee

Once the message has been posted into the mailbox, the addressee must be notified of its existence. For medium to slow transfers, polling is usually employed. Periodically the processors check the contents of each mailbox for new information. System response to such implementations is purely dependent on the polling periodicity. Decreasing the time between checks increases processor overheads and increases the amount of VMEbus traffic. The designer must therefore determine the best compromise.

Too many checks, poor message-passing times, and too much VMEbus bandwidth is consumed. In addition, the action of checking a mailbox may be more complex than it first appears. A message may contain information to identify the sender, when it was sent and what action is required. Mailboxes may require extensive examination which further adds to the overall VMEbus burden. This is even more significant if multiple messages are contained within the mailbox for more than one addressee. This situation is similar to the information received with a letter which has been delivered to a set of mailtrays. If a postal delivery has been made, individual trays will require checking. If a letter is present, further checking is needed to confirm that it is for you. Once that has been established, the additional information can be obtained. It is postmarked with the date it was sent, who wrote it, what reply is expected and who it is for. In comparison a telephone call is faster, will often not need any introduction and simply place a request and get an almost immediate response. The VMEbus equivalent is the interrupt.

Interrupt messages

If a MASTER wishes to inform another that a message is waiting or urgent action is required, an interrupt can be generated. The VMEbus supports seven interrupt priority levels to allow prioritization of resource.

Any board can generate an interrupt by asserting one of the levels. Interrupt handling can either be centralized, and handled by one MASTER, or can be distributed amongst many. For multiprocessor applications, distributed handling allows rapid direct communication to individual MASTERS by any board in the system capable of generating an interrupt: the MASTER that has been assigned to handle the interrupt requests the bus and starts the interrupt acknowledgement cycle. Here, careful consideration of the arbitration level chosen for the MASTER is required. The interrupt response time depends on the time taken by the handler to obtain the bus prior to the acknowledgement. If it has a low priority, the overall response time may be more than that obtained for a lower priority interrupt whose handler has a higher arbitration level. Figures 8.6 and 8.7 show the relationship for both priority and round robin arbitration schemes. A lower priority interrupt may be handled in preference to a higher priority one, simply because of the arbitration levels. To obtain the best response, high priority interrupts should only

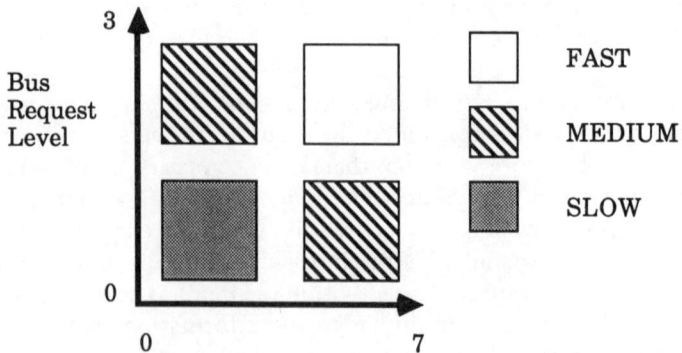

Figure 8.6 *VMEbus interrupt response times for a priority arbitration scheme*

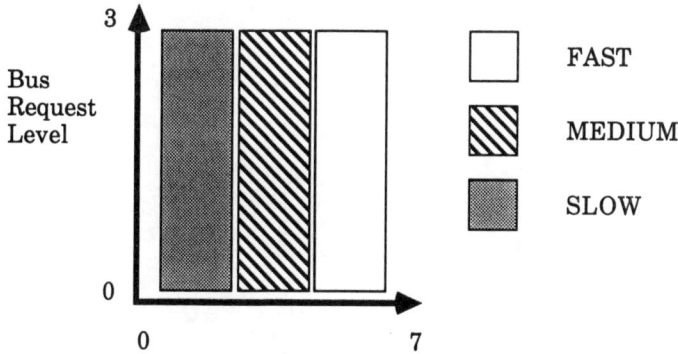

Figure 8.7 *VMEbus interrupt response times for a round robin arbitration scheme*

be assigned to high arbitration level MASTERS. The same factors, such as local traffic on the VMEbus and access time, increase the response time as the priority level decreases.

The VMEbus only allows a maximum of seven separate interrupt levels and this limits the maximum number of interrupt handlers to seven. For systems with a larger number of MASTERS, polling needs to be used for groups of MASTERS assigned to a single interrupt level. Both centralized and distributed interrupt handling schemes have their place within a multiprocessor system. Distributed schemes allow interrupts to be used to pass high priority messages to handlers, giving a fast response time which might be critical for a real-time application. For simpler designs, where there is a dominant controlling MASTER, one handler may be sufficient. Figures 8.8 and 8.9 show two examples of such configurations.

With all global mailbox systems, each MASTER needs to check the mailbox and read the message and this considerably increases the amount of VMEbus traffic. The most important goals with such designs are therefore:

1 removing all local bus traffic from the VMEbus,
2 minimizing VMEbus traffic associated with mailboxes and shared memory, and
3 the allocation of interrupt and arbitration levels.

Extending local resource

Many applications require more processor memory resource than can be placed on a single VMEbus board and the obvious solution is to place extra memory on the VMEbus and allow some local bus traffic. For

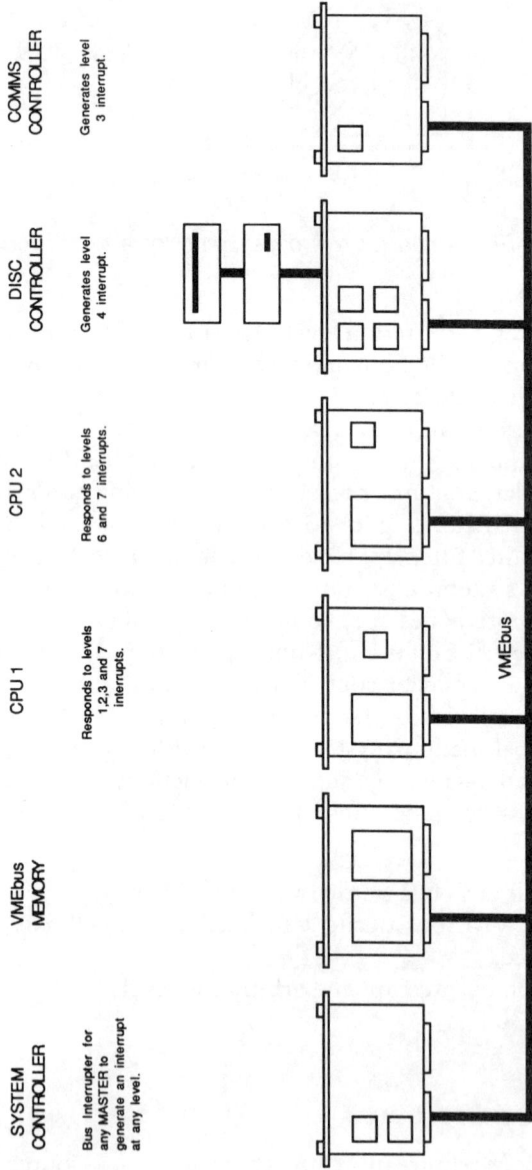

Figure 8.8   *Distributed interrupt handling VMEbus system*

SYSTEM CONTROLLER	VMEbus MEMORY	CPU 1	CPU 2
Bus Interrupter for any MASTER to generate an interrupt at any level.		Interrupt handler for all seven levels.	No Interrupt handler capability. Relies on semaphores for message passing.

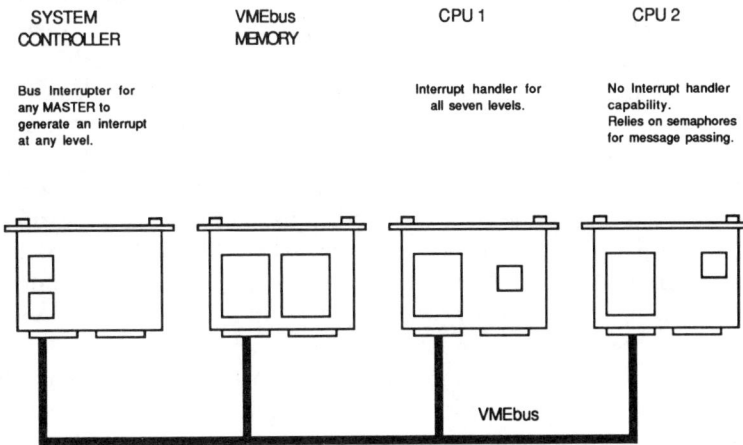

VMEbus

Figure 8.9 *Centralized interrupt handling VMEbus system*

simple systems, this is acceptable, although contrary to the idea of a global message-passing bus. In larger systems, however, there may not be enough bus bandwidth left to do this without causing performance degradation in the rest of the system, as described above.

There are two solutions normally used to solve this problem. The first is to add extra resource to the VMEbus and use cacheing techniques to reduce the bandwidth required to access it. This employs a cache memory to store the most recently used data locally. Memory cacheing works on the principle that software loops repeatedly fetch the same instructions and data from the same memory addresses each time the loop is executed. If this information is stored locally, the number of fetches to main memory can be reduced and the speed of access improved.

Cache memory system

This is a well established technique used in mini and mainframe computers, but only came to the notice of the micro world with the announcement of the MC68020 32-bit microprocessor which has an on-chip instruction cache to reduce the impact of memory delays and bus utilization. Shortly after this, the first VMEbus boards to use cache memory techniques appeared. One of the first available was the MVME121. It has a 4-Kbyte wait state free cache memory on board, in addition to its 512-Kbyte dual ported dynamic memory. The cache hardware is transparent to the user and provides wait state free access to either the data or instructions it contains. If the information is not available from the cache, the resulting miss starts a normal VMEbus cycle. The cache contents are automatically updated from such VMEbus accesses to preserve their coherence. Typically, a 4-Kbyte cache gives a 'hit' rate of about 80% although this figure is software dependent. Small routines will often achieve rates in excess of 99%. Such configurations are 'ideal' for benchmarking systems.

When a memory cycle starts, the cache tag RAM is checked to see if its contents match that of the address specified in the cycle. To perform this requires comparators for each of the address bits. These 32 comparators (one for each of the 32 address bits) require a large amount of logic and therefore most designs compromise and reduce their number. Figure 8.10 shows a typical implementation. The four middle order bits are decoded to form an index into the tag RAM array. The contents are then compared with the higher order address bits and, if there is a match, the remaining lower bits select the byte, word or long word needed from the cache line. If there is no match, the data are fetched from memory and an entry copied automatically into the tag and cache memory. If there is a cache line available, the existing entries are preserved; if not, one of the least used entries is replaced.

32 BIT MEMORY ADDRESS

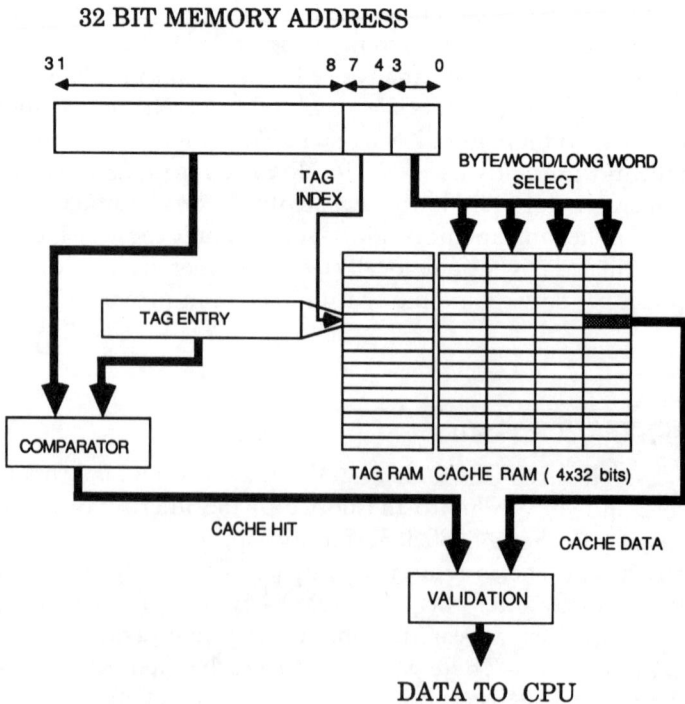

Figure 8.10 *Block diagram for a cache memory system*

Cache coherency is very important in multiprocessor applications. The first consideration is during a context switch. If the cache is on the logical side of the memory management unit, its contents must be cleared to prevent the data from the preceding task being supplied. With multiple tasks running at the same logical addresses, the cache would not know if the data it contained were for the currently running task. By clearing the cache every time a context switch is performed, no stale data can be supplied. However, the cache will need filling and its benefit will be

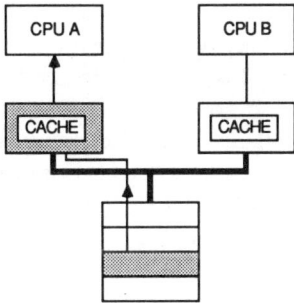

1. CPU A accesses main memory and caches the data in its cache.

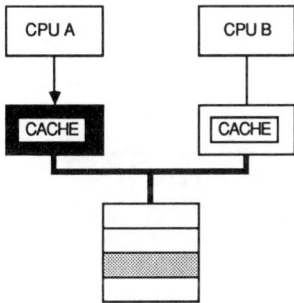

2. CPU A modifies the data in its cache, but main memory is not updated.

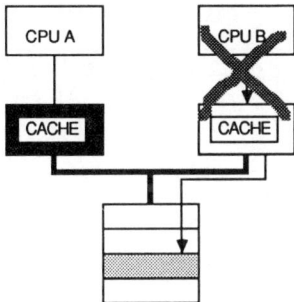

3, CPU B fetches data from main memory, but gets the unmodified stale data.

Figure 8.11 *A typical stale data cache coherency problem*

delayed. If the cache is on the physical side, this is not required because each physical address is unique.

For cached data, there is a potential problem associated with multiprocessor configurations where there could be multiple copies of the same data shared between two or more processors. Figure 8.11 shows a typical example of this dilemma. CPU A accesses shared memory and caches the data in its onboard cache. Subsequent processing alters the value, making the value stored in the shared memory stale. CPU B accesses the shared memory and reads the stale value that CPU A has cached.

The simplest solution to this is to make all write operations write through. Here, the modified data from CPU A is written through to the shared memory, so maintaining its validity. This does, however, increase the VMEbus utilization, especially if the data are modified many times before another CPU accesses them. A variation on this is to use a copyback scheme. This does not automatically update main memory when cached data is modified. To ensure cache coherency, some form of bus snooping is needed.

With bus snooping, the bus controller continually monitors the bus

System A: MVME121 in a VME-10 workstation running code in VME-10 RAM with MVME121 cache disabled.	136 seconds
System B; As for system A, but MVME121 cache enabled.	42 seconds
System C: MVME121 running code in on-board RAM, cache disabled.	55 seconds
System D: As for system C, but MVME121 cache enabled.	42 seconds

1. All code written in 68000 assembler and consisted of 1 million single precision floating point multiplications executed without a floating point co-processor.

2. The MVME121 has a code compatible MC68010 CPU with a MC68451 memory management unit, both running at 10 MHz.

Figure 8.12   *The performance of an MVME121 cache memory system*

and recognizes if another CPU is attempting to access a memory location where it has modified data. The controller can either act as a SLAVE, and provide the information itself, or abort the processor's cycle, update the memory and start a retry. Unfortunately, the VMEbus does not have direct support to implement such snooping schemes and therefore the write through mechanism is usually implemented for its simplicity, not performance.

An example of the improvements that can be achieved is given in Figure 8.12. The slow performance times for system A are caused by the VMEbus memory within the VME-10 workstation acting as local memory for the disc controller, graphics controller and processor, as well as being accessed by the MVME121 processor board. This is an example of using the VMEbus as a replacement microprocessor bus and the subsequent system degradation that can be experienced. Figure 8.13 shows an MVME121 processor and the cache RAM is located on the third row up on the left hand side.

Figure 8.13 *MVME121 processor board with cache memory*

A second method of achieving an improvement is to use a local extension memory bus like VSB.

VME subsystem bus

The VME subsystem bus (VSB) was developed from Motorola's VMX32 expansion bus used on its first generation MC68020 based VME processor cards, the MVME130 family. With its fast 32-bit data and address paths, dynamic bus sizing and cache control, it provided a local path over which processor, memory and peripheral modules could communicate. It evolved into VSB by the addition of a simple bus arbitration and interrupt scheme. A typical configuration is shown in Figure 8.14.

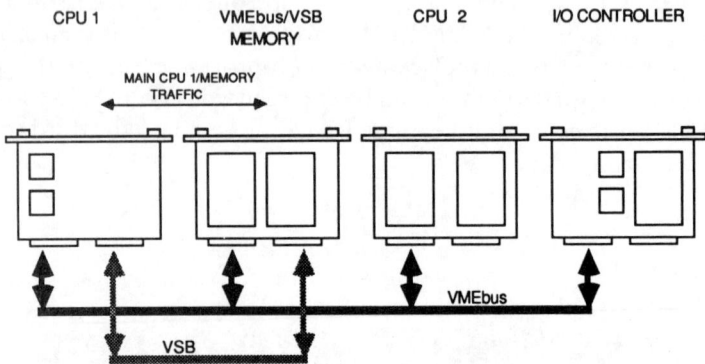

For CPU 1, all accesses to the memory are via VSB, and are not subject to VMEbus arbitration and delays.

All other traffic is via VMEbus.

Figure 8.14   *VSB as a local memory extension bus*

VSB is implemented using the user defined I/O pins on the P2 connector. It provides an elegant mechanism for removing local memory traffic from the VMEbus, and for increasing locally available resources, such as memory. This is an important feature because implementing a VSB interface, in particular bus drivers, consumes a large amount of board real estate. Local resource has to be reduced in order to provide space for the 15 or so discrete logic packs.

Because of these trade-offs, the decision to implement such a bus can be difficult to make. The effect that VSB has on overall system performance is often quite dramatic. If the VMX32/VSB bus is disabled on an MVME131 processor within a SYS1131 (Figure 8.15) running UNIX, an immediate performance reduction of about 20% occurs. From the system architecture, the reason is quite obvious. The MVME131 has very little local memory and uses its VMX32/VSB bus to extend that resource.

Disabling the extension bus puts the entire processor load on to the VMEbus, resulting in the observed system degradation. Fortunately this

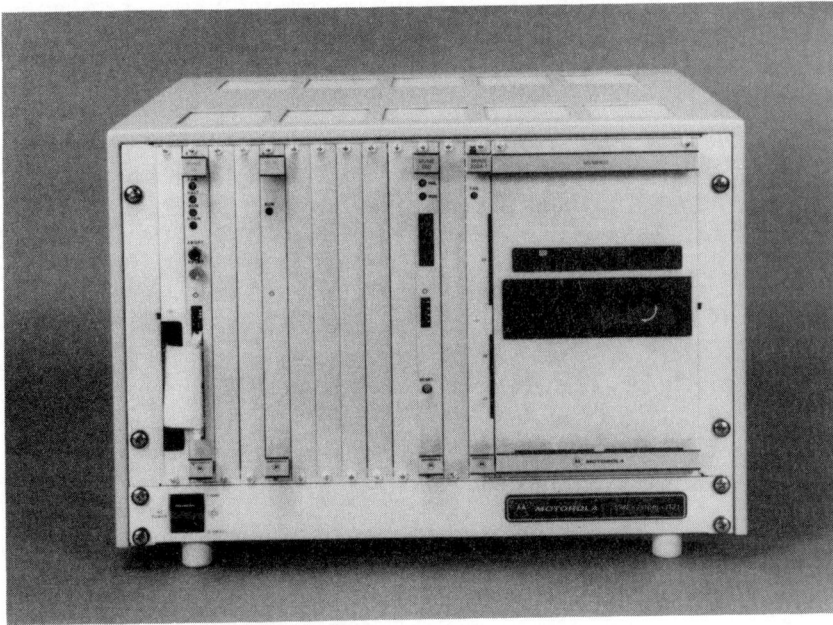

Figure 8.15 *SYS1131 VMEbus/VSB system*

degradation is reduced due to the action of the MC68020's on-chip instruction cache.

Synchronizing the system

The basic methods of communications described above allow a controlling supervisor processor to control and communicate with the subordinate boards in the system.

When the system starts up, the supervisor needs to allocate tasks to the subordinates and ensure that they are all synchronized. The supervisor processor is usually predetermined by a hardwired selection and cannot be changed.

A typical power-up sequence might involve each board going through a self check with the processor which explores the system to find out how many boards are functional and available. Global resources may need initializing and programs may be downloaded from disc. At this point, the supervisor can start each subordinate in turn.

If the system has less than seven processors, with each one assigned to handle at least one interrupt level, the supervisor can use a global bus interrupter to generate an interrupt for each one in turn. On receiving this interrupt, the processor can exit a waiting loop and start to perform its tasks. This is an extremely quick and efficient method of synchronizing the start-up of multiple processors. However, if there are more than seven processors, or no global bus interrupter to generate interrupts, or a MASTER that cannot handle interrupts, a polling technique must be used. Instead of the subordinate processors simply executing a waiting loop, a mailbox is checked regularly for its 'start' command.

On receiving its 'start' command, either through polling or by interrupt, the subordinate begins execution of its task. It may also move its code from global memory into local memory. This potential increase in bus traffic slows the other message-passing processes. As a result, the subordinate may require service from another subordinate before it is ready to supply it, and the system becomes potentially unsynchronized. Careful consideration must be given to the exact sequence used to start the subordinates; this may involve additional message-passing to provide confirmation that other boards are ready.

Handling errors

The most common error is the *bus error*. It is frequently used to size memory during a start-up phase. Memory addresses are incrementally accessed until a bus error is returned indicating that there is no memory present. This allows a system to determine exactly the hardware configuration present. Once this has been completed, it normally indicates a memory failure which may result in a system crash if it is unexpected, and not the result of a memory management operation, e.g. a page or write protect violation. The SYSFAIL* and ACFAIL* lines provide signals to detect both individual board failures and power failures.

SYSFAIL* is usually generated either by software writing to a register or by a sanity timer timing out. Most boards can choose to ignore it or route the signal through to generate a local processor interrupt. This is not a VMEbus interrupt. If a board has failed and asserted the SYSFAIL* signal, it is up to the handling processor to investigate the system and decide what to do. The signal simply indicates that there has been a failure somewhere in the system; it does not give any further information. If the failure has resulted in the VMEbus locking, the only possible action may be to shut the rest of the system down and attempt a system reset. When the fault is local to a board, less drastic alternatives are possible. In a multiprocessor business application, the faulty board may simply be removed from the ready list and not used any further. The system throughput is reduced but other processors are still functional. A simpler approach may be to simply reset the system and start again. If the failure is due to software, the system should reset and carry on, providing the circumstances which caused the software failure are not repeated.

The ACFAIL★ line is less vague in its interpretation. When asserted, it indicates that there has been an AC power failure and that the VMEbus DC supplies will fail within a very short time period. This period is dependent on the power supply used and its loading. Many power supplies can monitor the input supply and provide this type of signal. Again, this signal is routed through to generate a local interrupt. Once received, there may only be a few hundred microseconds available to store essential data and to bring the system down under control. Battery backup can extend this time.

In both these scenarios, a multiprocessor design has several possible handling mechanisms. The most obvious is if the signal is only monitored by the supervisor processor, and generates a non-maskable interrupt. The supervisor can then investigate the system to decide what action to take. This investigation requires the VMEbus, and the supervisor should have the highest bus priority, enabling it to grab the bus as quickly as possible. This is extremely important if the system needs to respond quickly.

Alternatively, all MASTERS can monitor the signals and respond to the local interrupt. The subordinate processors can stop their current processing, take preventative local action and then wait. The supervisor can then investigate the situation and decide what course to take. As all the other processors are waiting and not using the VMEbus, the supervisor's priority level is no longer critical to the speed of response. This system does, however, require that all MASTERS, including intelligent I/O controllers, respond in this manner and relinquish the bus. As many commercially available controllers are preprogrammed and often difficult to use in this way, the supervisor priority must be higher than any of these controllers to ensure a speedy response.

Protecting memory resources

A multiprocessor system has a great potential for data corruption caused by one MASTER overwriting another's memory structures. The obvious example is when two MASTERS are both running their own copy of an operating system. On power-up, both will size the external memory available and see some global VMEbus memory, which will be used as a mailbox area later. Unfortunately, the operating systems both attempt to use it for their own purposes prior to its allocation. They write their system tables there, causing corruption, and the system crashes.

The VMEbus protocols that allow multiprocessor systems to communicate can also allow multiprocessor systems to corrupt each other. It is essential to define exactly which MASTER can access each block of memory and what it will be used for. With operating systems, this involves modifying system table entries to restrict memory sizing; however, it is still possible for rogue software to access locations outside those allocated and cause corruption.

Hardware protection with memory management

Memory areas can be protected if a memory management unit (MMU) is used in conjunction with the processor. Normally, memory management is used to translate logical addresses to physical addresses and so allow code and data to be executed at any address without memory actually being there.

In multitasking systems, memory management allows multiple tasks to execute from the same start address without corrupting each other. This is achieved by partitioning the memory into blocks called either pages or segments and defining certain descriptors for them. Each block descriptor has the translation address and associated attributes, which describe the types of allowed access. Memory blocks may be read only, supervisor only and defined as shareable or unique. When a task is loaded, its code and memory requirements are stored in system tables, allowing the MMU to perform the correct translation and protection. If additional memory blocks are needed, they must be obtained via an operating system call prior to accessing them. Failure to do this causes the MMU to assert a bus error, so protecting the resource. Such methods can easily be used to protect mailboxes and other common areas within a multi-processor VMEbus system.

Most external MMUs insert at least one wait state into the memory access cycle and require a software driver to control the unit. Neither of these may be acceptable. In such cases, it is possible to use the VMEbus address modifiers to partition the VMEbus memory and provide protection, without using memory management. The address modifiers are six extra bits normally used to describe the addressing range being used and the type of VMEbus access, but can be used to act as memory block descriptors which have to be supplied by the MASTER as well as the address to obtain a successful access. Figures 8.16 and 8.17 show four typical examples. The most common use is to select the address widths that each VMEbus cycle will use. Another use is to use them as memory bank switches. Here two memory boards are physically addressed at the same location within the VMEbus memory, but respond to different address modifier codes. In this way the processor can bank-switch between them with ease. This switching can also be used to further partition the system where different SLAVE VMEbus boards require both correct addresses and modifier codes for a successful access. A variation of this involves the use of don't care bits within the address modifier decoding on SLAVE boards. This would allow hierarchical access: groups of MASTERS would be able to successfully access the SLAVE but others would be rejected by their address modifier code.

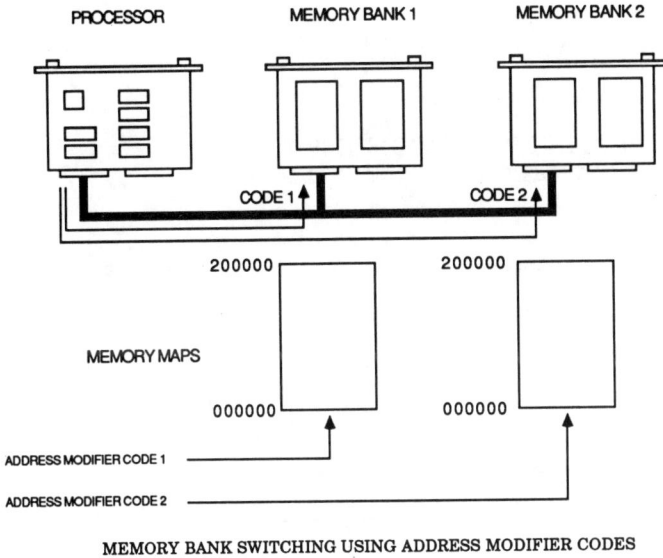

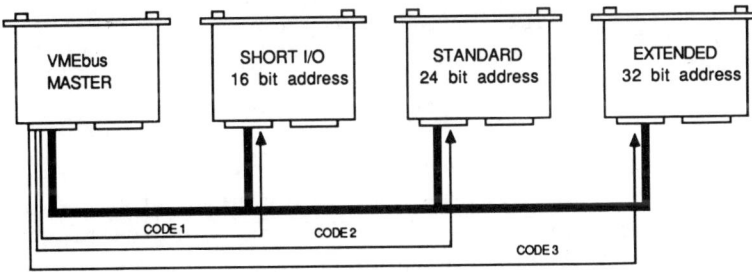

PROCESSOR   MEMORY BANK 1   MEMORY BANK 2

CODE 1   CODE 2

200000   200000

MEMORY MAPS

000000   000000

ADDRESS MODIFIER CODE 1

ADDRESS MODIFIER CODE 2

MEMORY BANK SWITCHING USING ADDRESS MODIFIER CODES

VMEbus   SHORT I/O   STANDARD   EXTENDED
MASTER   16 bit address   24 bit address   32 bit address

CODE 1   CODE 2

CODE 3

USING ADDRESS MODIFIERS TO SELECT THE ADDRESS WIDTHS

Figure 8.16 *Using address modifiers to partition the system (I)*

Multiprocessor organizations

With the bus arbitration schemes available within VMEbus, it is virtually

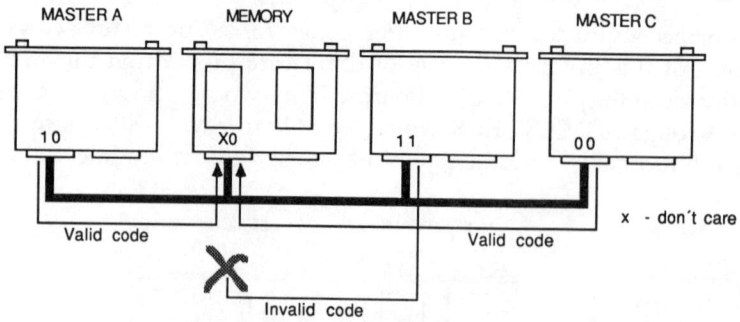

USING ADDRESS MODIFIERS TO GIVE
HIERARCHICAL ACCESS TO MEMORY

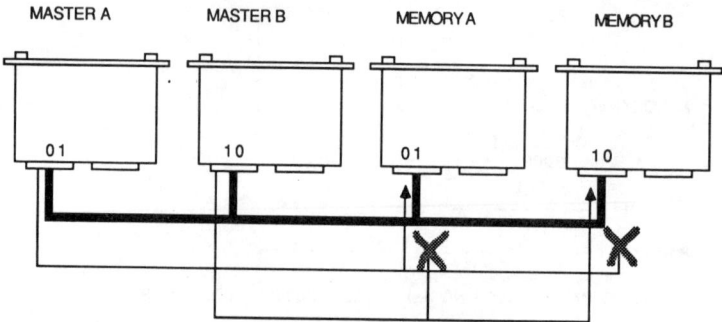

USING ADDRESS MODIFIER CODES TO
PARTITION THE SYSTEM

Figure 8.17   *Using address modifiers to partition the system (II)*

impossible to have a totally equal processor hierarchy. One processor
will always have a higher priority than the rest either through its slot
position or the arbitration request level. This processor must therefore
assume a more commanding role within the organization, and therefore
it is no surprise to find that the majority of designs adopt this approach
more formally.

The most common multiprocessor architecture is that of the master-
slave concept. One processor is declared the master and all other
processors act as slaves to it. Problems arise in determining which
processor is the master. Obviously, this can be hardwired but this is not
acceptable in systems which require dynamic configuration, such as fault
tolerant designs. Initializing such systems also presents problems. As
described previously, it cannot be assumed that on power-up all

processors running identical software will synchronize simultaneously. As soon as one processor accesses the VMEbus, the bus arbitration scheme excludes any other access and the rest of the processors lag behind. One solution to this is to organize processors into groups, allowing group message-passing and interrupts to be used by a master processor to maintain synchronicity within the system. This can be achieved in software, but places the design burden and overheads with the software designer and increases the software and bus overheads.

This type of facility is easier to implement in hardware, but does require board real estate which is often better used providing local resource and the VSB bus extension. The trend towards the heavier integration available from gate arrays and high density memories has released board space to provide such facilities.

The MVME135/6 processor board family from Motorola is typical of many boards that are available from manufacturers such as Radstone Technology, CompControl and Force that implement extensive hardware support for multiprocessor systems.

MVME135—VME, VSB and multiprocessing

The MVME135/6 is based around the MC68020 32-bit processor with its MC68881 floating point coprocessor and MC68851 paged memory management unit. It has 1 Mbyte wait state free (at 20 MHz) DRAM, with shared access between the VMEbus and the local processor. Two serial ports and both VMEbus and VSB interfaces are provided. The VSB interface uses the MVSB2400 gate array. VMEbus system controller functions are also provided.

What makes this processor board stand out is its multiprocessor support. It has hardware support to provide global access and control of several processor functions, virtual interrupts to selected processors, simultaneous interrupts to multiple processors and message broadcasting to within a group of processors. This is achieved by a set of registers accessible from the VMEbus called the Multi-Processor Control and Status Register (MPCSR).

The multiprocessing registers are shown in Figure 8.18. The first location at address offset 1 is the ID byte. This location is the image of the mapping switch S3. It provides two functions:

1 The first is to define, using bits D5 to D7, which group the processor belongs to and where the MPCSR is mapped in the VMEbus short I/O area.
2 Secondly, using bits D0 to D4, it defines the VMEbus mapping of the onboard DRAM and where the group location monitors are. This

Address Offset	D7	D6	D5	D4	D3	D2	D1	D0
1	ID BYTE							
3	BSY	SCON	FAIL	WDT				
5	KING	LM2	LM1	LM0	ISF	LKTR		
7	R & H				RONR			
9	H & H	UNDEFINED						
b	SIGLP	UNDEFINED						
d	SIGHP	UNDEFINED						
f		UNDEFINED						
11	MP0	UNDEFINED						
13	MP1	UNDEFINED						
15	MP2	UNDEFINED						
17	MP3	UNDEFINED						
19	MP COMM BYTE							
1b	UNDEFINED							
1d	UNDEFINED							
1f	UNDEFINED							

Figure 8.18 *Organization of multiprocessor registers of the MVME135*

provides one address for the location monitors and 31 unique VME DRAM addresses – more than enough for any system.

The second register, at offset 3, provides processor status information:

1 BSY indicates that the board is not ready to operate at system level and is executing confidence tests or initializing local resource.
2 SCON indicates that the board has been configured as a system controller.
3 FAIL indicates a local processor failure, and
4 WDT shows that a local watchdog timeout has occurred.

Checking of these bits throughout the system during initialization could identify a serious problem and allow a recovery plan to be executed.

Location monitoring

The third register has a bit ISF which can either be set locally or by other bus masters, preventing the processor from asserting SYSFAIL on the VMEbus as a result of a local failure and locking the bus. The LKTR bit can do the opposite and, when asserted, maintains VMEbus mastership for its processor until cleared. This allows whole software routines to be treated in a similar way to the TAS instruction and become indivisible bus operations. However, care must be exercised that other bus masters are not locked out to the extent that watchdog timers expire, causing bus errors—this bit must be used with caution.

The remaining bits KING, LM1, LM2 and LM0 are location monitors. The VMEbus is monitored, and when their address appears, the location monitors are set or cleared on all boards within the group simultaneously. This broadcast can cause various results: setting LM0 results in a local interrupt being generated on the board. LM1 and LM2 just record the current status and the KING bit is used during initialization to determine which processor is the master or system initializer.

The ability to use LM0 to generate a local interrupt also provides a mechanism to efficiently poll a semaphore: the processor using the resource clears LM0; the other processors, on finding LM0 clear, perform other tasks and wait until the first processor is finished and sets LM0. This immediately indicates to the others, via the generated interrupt, that the resource is available. One of the processors will then poll successfully and the cycle repeats. This means that waiting processors, rather than biding their time polling, can carry out useful work.

Software generated resets

The R&H and H&H bits allow other processors to directly control the local CPU. When R&H is set, the local CPU resets and holds until a system reset or the bit is cleared. The H&H halts the local CPU to aid code downloading into local DRAM. Fault tolerant designers therefore now have a simple mechanism to software reset a processor card without generating a SYSTEM RESET.

Other applications include synchronizing processors: a processor initializes itself, sets up its reset vector to point to its code, and then resets and holds using R&H. The system initializer (determined using the KING bit) can then start the processor at will by clearing R&H.

'Democratic' bus arbitration

RONR changes the processor's bus requesting algorithm to that of Request On No Request. The processor only requests the bus if no other requests are pending, thus allowing processors further down the daisy-chain access. This provides a more 'democratic' arbitration scheme, which can be activated under software control when required, and means that arbitration schemes are no longer totally dependent on slot position.

Processors can interrupt each other by writing to either SIGLP or SIGHP locations in the register model. SIGLP generates a level 1 interrupt to the local processor while SIGHP causes a level 6 interrupt. Both these interrupts and the broadcast interrupt LM0 can be masked by writing to a local processor control register.

Finally, there are four semaphore or handshake bits, MP0 to MP3, and a byte wide communications path MP COMM BYTE. These are provided for message-passing without using global memory.

Facilities similar to this are now appearing generally on the market and allow very powerful multiprocessing systems to be implemented with relative ease.

9
System integration

What is involved?

System integration is where the theoretical design starts to become a reality and it is often at this point that many of the potential pitfalls with designing and building a VMEbus based system are encountered.

The various layers of hardware and software are brought together for the first time. In practice it is usually unrealistic to expect that all boards, hard discs, tape drives, terminals, printers, operating systems and applications can be put together and work first time without a methodical, planned route for integrating the system. Integration can be likened to assembling a model construction kit without the instructions: the picture on the box shows what it should look like and all the parts are there, but how do they go together?

Work your way up

The best approach is to break the system into independent units. Each unit can be further split into hardware, onboard monitor or firmware, system level software and finally application software. The interaction between each unit should be checked as each of these layers is integrated. As this is performed, careful notes of exactly what has been done should be made so that an exact description of the configuration can be recorded. This often proves invaluable later, should faults need to be identified. Taking photographs of the VMEboards either using a camera or by laying them flat on a photocopier is a very easy way of recording jumper and switch settings. This information will ultimately form the basis of the instructions for building this kit of parts into a system and is essential if the system is to be reproduced.

Preliminary work

Before starting any integration work, the end result should be established in detail. The design definition should state which boards are in the system and how their user-definable options should be set. The most common hardware variables are memory addresses, sizes, and access times, bus request levels and interrupt handler settings.

It is extremely advantageous to have an already working system available which can be used for testing. It allows VMEbus boards to be tested in a known system, thus eliminating many of the variables associated with system integration.

A Obtain all the manuals for all the individual components
This includes the system specification, software, VMEbus boards, hard and floppy discs and any other peripherals.

With the majority of these items the relevant manuals are supplied. Exceptions appear to be anything to do with mass storage where manuals are often supplied as extras—however, without them it is almost impossible to set the drives up correctly. To save frustration, ensure that they are ordered at the same time. Any configuration documents or notes that are available may prove valuable. Much of the information they contain has been obtained from performing many system integrations and documenting such operations. It is advisable to document everything done during the exercise so that this information can become a configuration guide in its own right. An example is given in Appendix B.

B Test out racks and power supplies
Many racks are supplied ready built and tested. For those that require assembling, check that VMEbus boards will actually fit the backplanes, and runners are not misaligned or fouled. There is nothing more frustrating than reassembling rack systems.

It is highly recommended that power rails are checked under load. Six and 12 V light bulbs are a convenient load with a built-in visual indicator. It is extremely prudent to check that the 5 V rail is not 12 V before powering up an expensive VMEbus board. Many common power supplies can provide 250–300 W—more than enough to burn out cables, backplanes and boards if wrongly connected.

It may be possible to current-limit the supplies to minimize damage in cases of error. This can be difficult to set up, require constant resetting as each board is added, and cause voltage fluctuation.

It may also be worth considering monitoring the voltage rails and current during the integration to check that the power supply is capable of meeting the load placed on it.

An often neglected requirement is air flow. Many of today's highly integrated VMEbus boards require force air cooling. This is usually best provided by a fan tray either above or below the boards blowing air vertically between the boards as shown in Figure 9.1. The efficiency of such systems can be degraded by removing blanking panels, blocking air vents or by using extender boards—all activities extremely common during system integration when easier access is required. It may therefore be necessary to provide extra cooling during this phase.

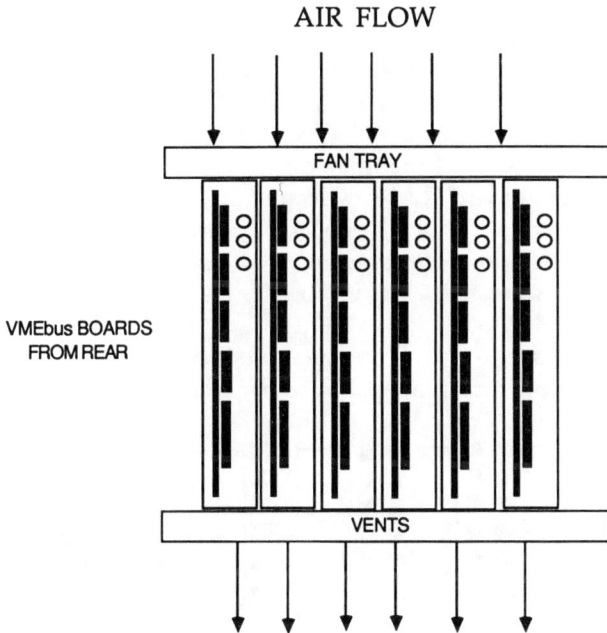

Figure 9.1 *Recommended method of force air cooling*

C Power up each board in turn

This simply checks each board. If a debugger is fitted, this can be used to act as test software. Set the board up as indicated by the debugger installation instructions, connect a suitable terminal, power up and wait for the prompt. If all is well, this should appear and the status lights should indicate a good system.

For peripheral boards or those that do not have debuggers, the status lights may be the only indication of a failure. If a fail light should come on, do not panic immediately. Many peripheral boards require software drivers to change the status from 'fail' to 'good'.

Do not assume that the shipped factory settings for jumpers and switches are the default for the debugger. They are usually the settings used for the test configuration prior to shipment. EPROM sizes and settings will invariably be different.

If a board appears to have failed, check the settings carefully. It is more likely that the failure is due the board setting than a board failure.

D   Modify boards to reflect the system specification

Change all the settings to those required by the system specification and check the boards individually again to see if they still function. If they fail, there could be a major design fault or some extra software/hardware needs may have been produced. This is not a good sign. If the debugger will not work in this configuration, it will be impossible to boot up operating systems or application software. Check what the new configuration actually means in terms of system usage. The processor board may now require external memory on the VMEbus for its stack area instead of using onboard RAM. Without that memory, the processor halts and fails. If the onboard system controller function has been disabled, bus arbitration requests may not be answered and again cause the processor board to fail.

E   Install a processor, system controller and memory boards

The system controller must be in slot 1 and it is advisable to jumper all the

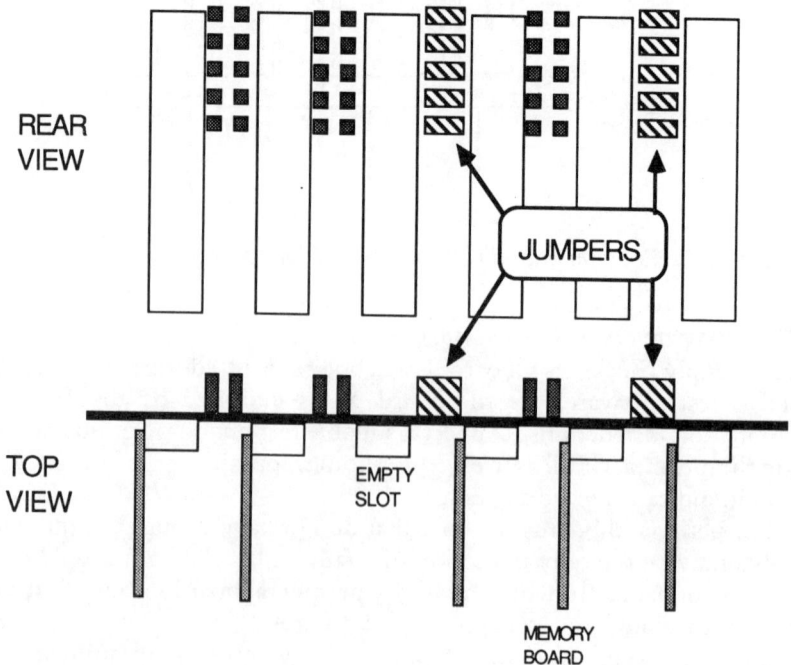

Figure 9.2 *VMEbus backplane jumpers*

bus grant and IACK★ signals on the backplane. Adding these functions may cure failures experienced previously. An example is shown in Figure 9.2.

If the processor board still fails, the system has been wrongly designed or it has failed because of some internal fault. Replacing the board and repeating the tests will identify which is the reason.

If it worked by itself, check bus request levels, arbitration schemes, etc. Anything that interacts between the system controller and processor is suspect. At this point, the integration process turns into a fault finding process. This is discussed in the next chapter. Appendix A details many of the common symptoms and failures.

F Run some memory checks

This confirms that the processor can access the memory in the system correctly.

Many debuggers have commands which will initialize, fill and test memory blocks and can be used to make sure the memory in the system can be accessed. However, these facilities can be restricted in their testing: they may not test all the data widths available and will only access the memory as a data area and not as a program area.

To provide more facilities, a simple assembler program can be entered using an on-line assembler. An example is shown in Figure 9.3. The

```
Version to read bytes:

START   MOVE.B  D5,(A0)+        moves data to data area pointed by A0
        NOP                     prevents MC68010 going into loop mode
        NOP                     and giving misleading results.
        DBEQ.L  D0,START        loop 1.
        MOVE.L  #$80000,A0       reset starting address for A0.
        ADDQ.W  #1,D7           D7 is a loop counter.
        DBEQ.L  D1,START        loop 2.
        NOP                     for breakpoint.

Version to read words:

START   MOVE.W  D5,(A0)+        moves data to data area pointed by A0
        NOP                     prevents MC68010 going into loop mode
        NOP                     and giving misleading results.
        DBEQ.L  D0,START        loop 1.
        MOVE.L  #$80000,A0       reset starting address for A0.
        ADDQ.W  #1,D7           D7 is a loop counter.
        DBEQ.L  D1,START        loop 2.
        NOP                     for breakpoint.

Version to read long words:

START   MOVE.L  D5,(A0)+        moves data to data area pointed by A0
        NOP                     prevents MC68010 going into loop mode
        NOP                     and giving misleading results.
        DBEQ.L  D0,START        loop 1.
        MOVE.L  #$80000,A0       reset starting address for A0.
        ADDQ.W  #1,D7           D7 is a loop counter.
        DBEQ.L  D1,START        loop 2.
        NOP                     for breakpoint.
```

Figure 9.3 *Simple memory test software*

program can be modified to write bytes, words or long words by changing the .L suffix to .W or .B.

If used with the MC68020 and MC68030, it is advisable to switch off the internal caches, forcing all accesses external and providing a better test by preventing the caches from masking any effects. This can easily be done from the debugger. The code can be run anywhere in memory simply moving the block to its different location. The branches are performed using a relative offset. Prior to use, the registers used in the program are initialized: A0 is loaded with the data starting address, D5 is loaded with the data that will be written out, D0 set to $FFFF and D1 set to $1F. Register D7 is cleared and a breakpoint set at the final NOP op code location. Various tests can be performed by executing the program from and by defining the different memory areas on and offboard. This program can also be used for testing with multiple processors.

If it accesses any non-existent memory, this will be detected by a bus watchdog timer and the program execution terminated with an error. The level of information provided is debugger dependent, but will usually provide the error address and the register contents. For further information the bus error stack frames can be examined.

G   Add peripherals and repeat stage 6

The peripherals required to form a minimum system for the operating system are now added.

When a peripheral board is added, the backplane jumpers may need to be removed in accordance with the hardware configuration. Failure to do so may cause problems with interrupt handling and bus arbitration. The debugger can be used to check that the processor can access the control registers and dual ported memory located on the peripheral boards. Some of the registers may be in the VMEbus short I/O addressing area, and may only occupy the odd or even bytes. Some debuggers may only allow 16-bit data access or automatically fetch the other byte, causing bus errors to be returned. Extra options may need to be specified on the command line to force the correct access.

The short I/O addressing block is located within the processor's memory map, usually at the top. Its location is determined by the processor board design and addressing capability and must not be assumed: a 24-bit addressing processor board may use address $FF1000 while a 32-bit addressing processor would use $FFFF1000.

Some debuggers provide higher level commands that will allow peripherals to be further tested. Serial and parallel ports can be configured and data sent to them to test the communications link. Disc controllers can be configured, and basic commands to format, read or write sectors to disc are provided. Again, if these commands are not present, simple software can often be written using the debugger to provide similar facilities. With disc controllers, the flashing of selected lights and whirring of discs provide good indications of correct functioning. Successful reading and writing to floppy discs can be verified by setting up memory buffers and examining them before and after an access. Do not use master discs or any that have irreplaceable contents. At this lower level, there are no second chances to undo a wrong command.

When accessing the disc, remember to test all the heads and several tracks. Track 0 can often be configured at a lower recording density than the rest of the disc. If the disc access is borderline, track 0 may often be accessed successfully and it is only when other tracks are specified that the problem is highlighted. Appendix A describes many of the common faults associated with peripheral boards, and their causes.

H   Add an operating system

Having confirmed that the processor board, memory and peripherals work together at a lower level, the operating system can be installed. The boot disc is placed in the drive and the boot command is entered. The drive should be accessed, some messages appear on the terminal and, finally, the operating system prompt should appear. If this is the case, initialize winchesters and copy the software as indicated by the operating system installation instructions.

Porting application software

Once the operating system is functional, then application software can be transferred and run. Providing the source system and the target system are functionally identical, then this should pose no difficulty. However, there are several potential pitfalls, all of which are associated with memory management. The first concerns the use of memory management and the choice of compiler libraries. If the source system uses memory management, then the libraries will often not be compatible with other systems that do not have hardware memory management. This results in applications that will run on one system but crash on another. Typical error messages indicate a load failure or memory not available. To ensure compatibility across such configurations, relocatable libraries for systems without memory management should be used.

Many systems without memory management have applications which will access physical memory without going through the operating system interface. Again this prevents such applications from functioning correctly.

What happens if the system is still faulty? At this point, the system integration turns into a fault finding procedure. Suitable techniques are described in the next chapter.

10
Fault finding

What to do if something goes wrong

Finding faults in any VMEbus system requires an understanding of the entire system. The interaction between application software, operating systems and hardware can easily hide problems and render their investigation difficult. An engineer therefore needs an understanding of the entire system and may often be required to become both a hardware and software expert.

Any VMEbus system consists of a series of layers with each layer primarily communicating with the layers above and below it but sometimes communicating directly with any layer in the system. An application program may make system calls to an operating system to access hardware such as a disc controller, or it may access the hardware directly. In these systems, the software and hardware are linked together and any change in one may have dramatic effects on the rest of the system. A good understanding of the system design and how it is partitioned is essential in diagnosing and identifying system faults. To show this interaction, consider the simple act of an application task writing to a memory location.

What is involved with a memory access?

The example system comprises an MC68020 based processor board with a disc controller and some global memory. Both the processor and disc controller are intelligent and a single level arbitration scheme is used, with the processor board providing the system controller function. The system is running a real-time operating system with memory management.

An application task needs to move 32 bits of data, currently stored in register D0, to an address pointed to by register A0. It executes the MOVE.L D0, (A0) instruction, which results in a total system crash and generates the fault 'BUS ERROR'. The instruction is valid and the address pointed to is correct. Obviously something has gone wrong but what? The address pointed to is valid, memory is present and can be accessed using the onboard monitor program, so where is the problem?

Addresses and address modifiers

To understand the possible causes, the interactions between the various levels have to be unravelled. The processor, on executing the instruction from the application task while running in USER mode, starts an external bus cycle with a valid 32-bit address. This address is translated by the memory management unit as directed by the operating system. If the operating system has not been informed that this address is physical, and should not be translated, either the MMU protects its memory by terminating the cycle with a BUS ERROR, or possibly another memory location is accessed. Either of these actions results in error.

Assuming the address is mapped as a physical address, the address decode logic determines that the location is not present on the processor card and that a VMEbus cycle must be started. At this point, a processor bus watchdog timer is started to allow 150 µs for the process to complete. The next decision to be made by the hardware is the address bus width to use. This is determined by hardware registers, under operating system software control, and forces a 32-bit address to be used. This information is then used, with the output of the processor function codes, to select the correct address modifier for a 32-bit address USER DATA access as shown in Figure 10.1. In addition, the logic also selects a 32-bit data bus and asserts the LWORD* signal. This, with the address

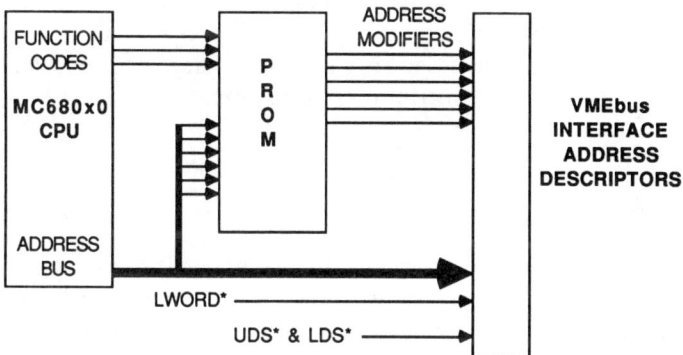

Figure 10.1 *VMEbus address and address descriptor bits*

modifier code, is issued with the address during a VMEbus cycle and requires a complete match for a VMEbus slave to respond successfully.

Instead of only one valid set of information resulting from the single instruction, multiple sets are possible. The one selected is dependent on system states and parameters, which may be invalid for the intended slave and thus cause the problem.

Bus arbitration

Prior to starting the bus cycle, the processor requires mastership of the VMEbus. Again, a watchdog timer is started with the bus request signal which will generate a BUS ERROR if the bus is not obtained within a set time period. If this time period is too short, conflicts may occur when the disc controller holds the bus while performing block data moves and the timer timing out, even though everything else is correct. These conflicts are often responsible for many transient BUS ERRORS. In this example, the bus is granted and the cycle starts. Unfortunately, the memory slave can only support 16-bit transfers and immediately asserts the BERR* signal and the resulting BUS ERROR crash.

Hardware or software to blame?

As this example shows, many of the faults found in VMEbus systems are due to the system environment which, if changed, may either cure or exaggerate the problem. Changing a control register bit, so that only 16-bit transfers are allowed, solves the problem and this may be the state of the register when the onboard monitor is used. In this environment, the instruction executes correctly. However, when control is passed to the operating system, the register is changed and the error returns. When faced with this apparent dichotomy, it is all too easy to blame either hardware or software in isolation when, in reality, it is a system error where both parties may contribute to the failure.

Further investigations

To discover the source of the error, the system needs partitioning so that the various components can be tested and eliminated from blame. This testing requires detailed information of the VMEbus boards in the system and how they are configured by both hardware and software settings. In addition, knowledge of the state of the system at the time of the crash is essential and may provide clues. However, it must be remembered that the system crash information may only describe the result of a fault and not the actual cause. If a memory management fault has occurred, resulting in a bus error which crashes the system, the stored information will reflect the bus error, not the original cause.

Faced with the previous problem, the first step in isolating the error is to interrogate the operating system to find out what has gone wrong and where. If the system is hung, assert the abort button on the processor card. If either the processor reset or VMEbus SYSTEM RESET is asserted, the system will reset, usually involving a memory initialization routine. This is not only destroys the processor's contents but also any information held in memory.

It is recommended that abort functions are not disabled during the debug stage so that there is an alternative available to stop a 'hung up' system. Once the system has been aborted, the processor contents can usually be examined, along with the processor user and system stack frames using the onboard monitor program. The stack frames will have sufficient information to describe exactly what went wrong with the processor. Again, remember that this may only be the symptom, not the cause.

Often, the operating system has a 'CRASHSAVE' area, where the system parameters at the time of the crash are stored. Reference to operating system manuals is required to interpret this information. If possible, find out what applications were running, the resources they required and their status prior to the crash.

Once this information has been gathered, it may be worth a simple test from the monitor program to provide an initial screen. For example, if the system detected a BUS ERROR at memory location $001A0000, reading and writing to that location may immediately identify the problem. In such cases, simple board replacement is required to confirm and cure the fault. This type of operation is logical and applicable to any system investigation. The real difficulty arises when simple tests do not highlight any fault. Then the system has to be partitioned, isolated and tested.

Partitioning the system

The example described shows how the simple act of executing an instruction to write data to an external memory location could result in many variations in the data presented to the VMEbus. To partition the system, the causes of these variations have to be understood so that, if necessary, each one can be isolated and tested. The simplest way is to remove all the boards from the VMEbus and replace them, one at a time, while running a series of tests. As each successive test is completed, another system layer can be added. By building on the layers, only one variable is added at a time, allowing easier investigation. The best way to explain this is by means of a case study.

In this example the basic system (Figure 10.2) comprised:

1   MVME131 MC68020 based CPU board acting as system controller and as the highest priority processor.
2   MVME204 2-Mbyte DRAM board supporting both VMEbus and VSB accesses.
3   MVME320 disc controller with a 5.25″ floppy disc and winchester attached.

The system ran the VERSAdos operating system version 4.51 and worked well until the addition of a MVME350 QIC II tape controller and its associated tape streamer. The operating system simply refused to recognize its existence, despite being configured for it.

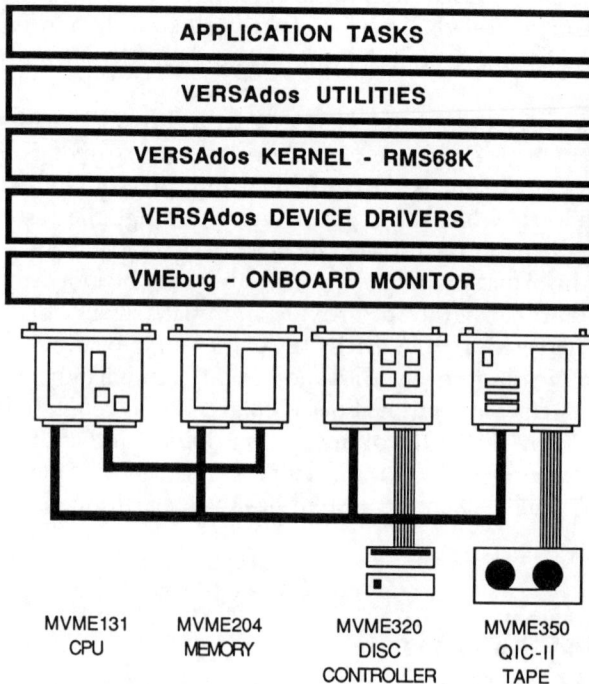

Figure 10.2 *Case study of VMEbus system*

The initial investigation had failed to find anything obviously wrong and, as a result, it was decided to partition and test the system to see if there were any clues to the failure.

Master processor and VMEbus memory

The first partition comprised the MVME131 CPU and MVME204 DRAM board as shown in Figure 10.3. The CPU ran 130BUG (an onboard debugger/monitor program) successfully on power-up. This proved that the basic CPU was functional. The debugger was then used to access the DRAM. A succession of memory block fills were executed and the contents examined. However, debuggers often achieve a 32-bit read by generating four 8-bit reads, and this does not test the system's reactions to 16- and 32-bit data accesses. To give greater confidence, a small memory access program was written using the 130BUG single line assembler/disassembler. This program was executed from both onboard RAM and MVME204 DRAM.

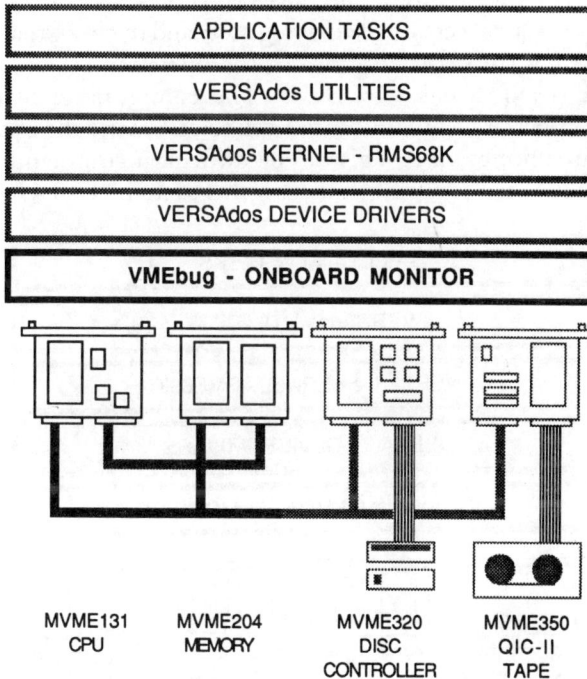

Figure 10.3 *System partitioning—processor and memory*

Subordinate processors and VMEbus memory

The MVME320 disc controller appears to the VMEbus system as a master and, in that respect, is no different from a processor board. During DMA transfers from its own buffers to VMEbus memory, it arbitrates for the bus and can cause problems for the MVME131 if it requires access at the same time.

To simulate and test this reaction, a second processor was added, an MVME101 MC68000 based CPU complete with its debugger, VMEbug. The board had its interrupt handler and system controller functions disabled, and requested the bus on level 3. Similar tests were performed using blockfills and the memory access routine. As a final test, both processors ran the tests simultaneously, proving that the system was capable of coping with two masters.

Processors and peripheral boards

The MVME101 was removed and the MVME320 disc controller added. The first test was to access its control registers and to check that the board was addressed at the right location for the operating system to find it. This can be performed by 130BUG. The configuration is shown in Figure 10.4. A better test would have been to command the board to read a sector from a floppy disc. This can be difficult if command structures have to be initialized by hand, but with this system, 130BUG provides

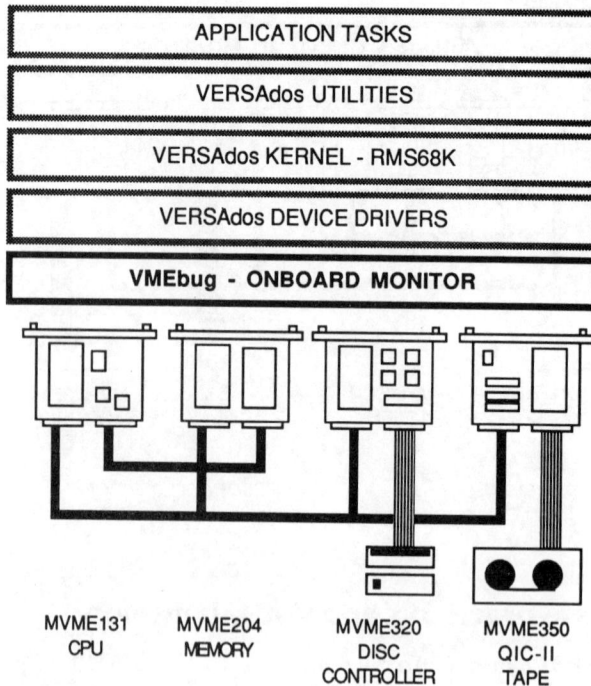

| APPLICATION TASKS |
| VERSAdos UTILITIES |
| VERSAdos KERNEL - RMS68K |
| VERSAdos DEVICE DRIVERS |
| VMEbug - ONBOARD MONITOR |

| MVME131
CPU | MVME204
MEMORY | MVME320
DISC
CONTROLLER | MVME350
QIC-II
TAPE |

Figure 10.4 *System partitioning—processor and peripherals*

low level commands for disc access. The system accessed discs successfully.

The procedure was repeated for the MVME350: its registers could be accessed, but no low level commands were available and the structures were complex. It was decided to assume that the board was functional. If nothing could be found, then some hand-coding would be required to create the control structures needed to further test the board.

Adding the software layers

Satisfied that the basic hardware appeared functional, the basic version of VERSAdos without the MVME350 driver was booted. This came up correctly and functioned perfectly when asked to perform a disc coherency check, using the REPAIR command, on the winchester drive. This configuration is shown in Figure 10.5. Next, the version including the MVME350 driver was booted and tested. It also functioned correctly but did not recognize the MVME350 board. This indicated that the problem lay with this customized version and not with the configuration as shown in Figure 10.6.

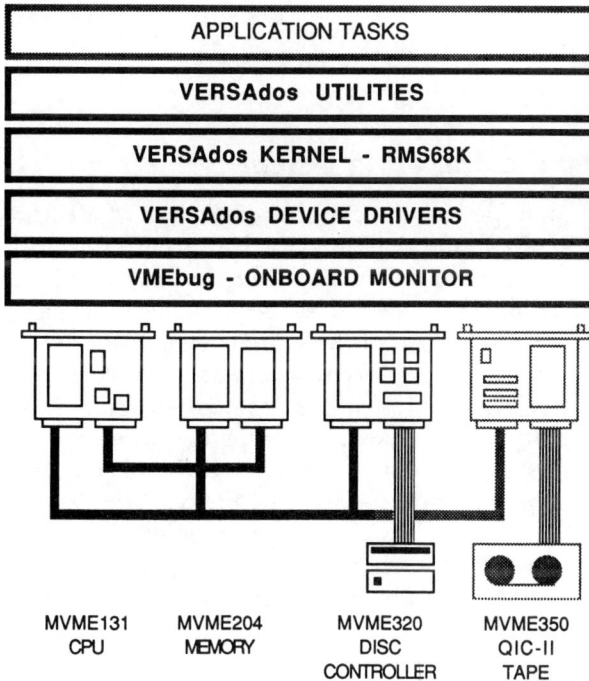

Figure 10.5 *System partitioning—basic VERSAdos system*

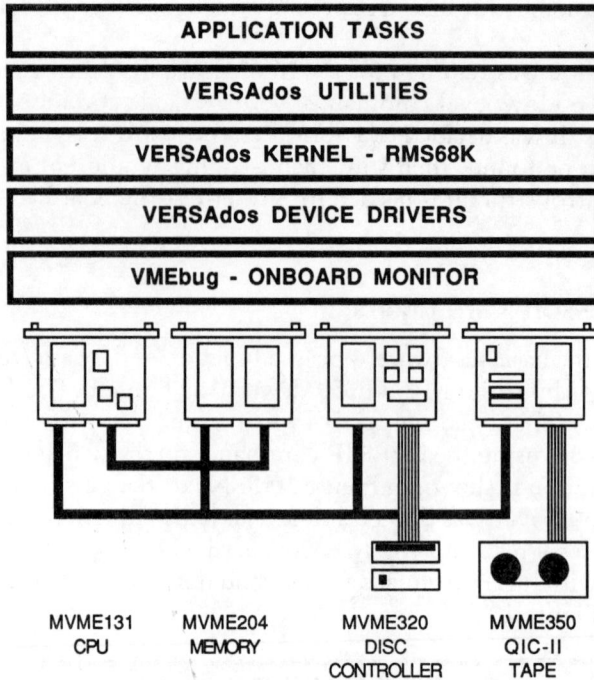

Figure 10.6   *System partitioning—basic system with MVME350*

Customizing the operating system

The configuration files for the customized version of VERSAdos were checked and it was found that an error had occurred in including the driver. The system–build information revealed that the driver had not been included, although the switch had been changed. Further inspection highlighted the error: instead of the switch being set from 0 to 1, it had been set to ! (shift 1). The mistake was corrected and the system rebuilt.

When this new version was run, the system recognized the MVME-350: it now appeared in the system device tables but the card immediately went into a halt state. The initial hardware tests indicated no problems and, at last, the board was recognized by the operating system. At this point, it was decided to use a VMEbus monitor (made by Concise Technology) to see exactly what was happening on the VMEbus.

The CTVMEBM1 VMEbus monitor plugs into a VMEbus rack, monitors the VMEbus signals and presents the data on the front panel. Address and data buses are displayed as hexadecimal data and the signal states by light emitting diodes. The analyser can trigger on various events, such as bus errors and interrupt acknowledgement cycles, or can free run. The ability to trigger on an external event is supplied by an oscilloscope or logic analyser connected elsewhere in the system. This monitor allows the actual transactions on the VMEbus to be viewed without using a processor board to process and present the data, and therefore allows investigation of the system without imposing any other criteria which may confuse the issues.

Using a monitor

The monitor showed that the MVME131 only accessed the VMEbus to communicate with the MVME320 disc controller or the MVME350 tape controller. All accesses to the MVME204 DRAM were over the VSB and did not appear on the main bus. VMEbus traffic was at a minimum and therefore it was unlikely that bus arbitration problems were the cause.

The monitor was set up to free run and it soon became apparent that bus errors were occurring. The start of the MVME350 driver routine was found from the VERSAdos build files and the operating system booted and halted using the BH 130BUG command. A break point was then put at the driver start and the operating system started. At the break point, the bus monitor was set to trigger on a bus error and the operating system restarted. The next bus error was decoded and found to be a non–existent address. The operating system continued, but would not respond to any attempts to access the MVME350 board. Any attempt resulted in an 'unrecoverable channel' error. Further inspection of the bus monitor revealed that the attempted transfer was 32 bits wide using a 32-bit address, but that the decoded address appeared to be missing the top 8 bits. The only bus master that needed to perform a 32-bit data and address transfer was the MVME350. It was almost as if the bus was only a 24–bit address 16-bit data. Was this a clue?

The VMEbus rack was investigated (Figure 10.7) and it was found that the P2 backplane, used for the I/O and VMEbus extension pins, only supported the I/O pins which were connected by a ribbon cable to form the VSB interface. The MVME320 only had a 24–bit address 8-bit bus capability and therefore did not see any problem. The MVME350 required a full 32-bit bus and was therefore receiving corrupt data because of the missing bits. The board would eventually crash while trying to access non-existent memory. The driver automatically assumed a full 32-bit implementation and several driver switches had been set accordingly. On installation of the boards in a full 32-bit rack (Figure 10.8), the system worked first time.

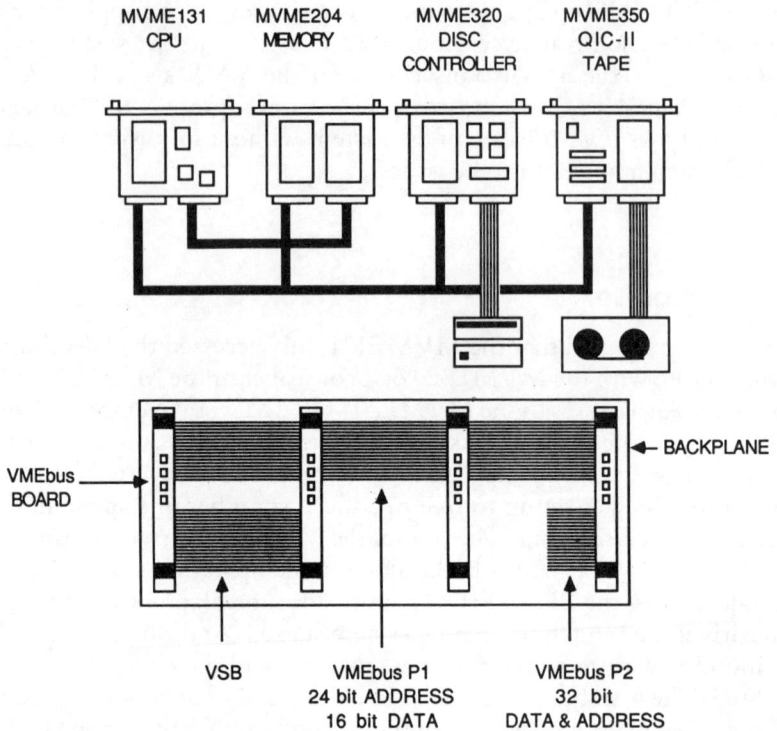

Figure 10.7 *The problem*

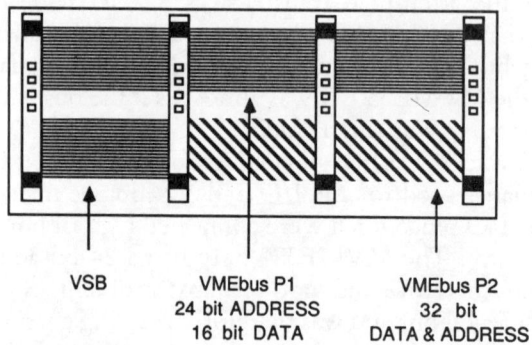

Figure 10.8 *The solution*

Using instrumentation

Without using a piece of dedicated VMEbus test equipment, the problem described above would have taken many more hours to solve than it did.

In addition to the CVMEBM1 VMEbus monitor, Concise Technology produce a bus ownership module, CVME0M1 (which identifies which slots are responsible for bus requests, ownership, interrupt handling and generation), a VMEbus stimulator CVMEBS1, to generate interrupts and bus requests for testing system responses, and a VMEbus power supervisor to provide continual monitoring of the power supplies. Figure

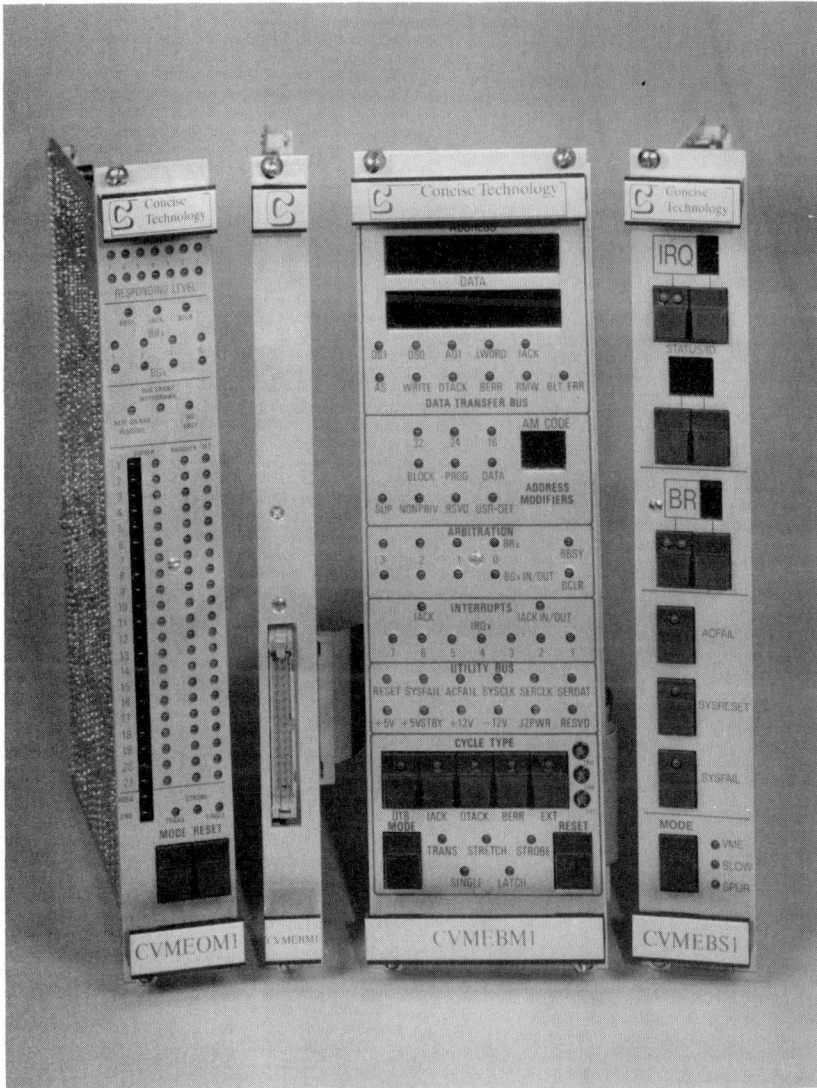

Figure 10.9 *VMEbus instrumentation from Concise Technology*

10.9 shows the CVMEBM1, CVMEOM1 and CVMEBS1. Other available instrumentation includes a VMEbus combatibility tester from VMETRO, a Norwegian company. This tests for the majority of specification violations to ensure compatibility. They also manufacture a logic analyser for the VMEbus which stores the backplane signals and displays them on a terminal or personal computer. The common types of errors and causes are described in appendix A. Typical specification violations are described in appendix C.

11
A design methodology

Designing VMEbus systems requires experience of not only micro-processor systems, but also of system architectures previously only found in mini- and super-minicomputers. The previous chapters have described the various techniques and design considerations that have to be evaluated during any design process. Unfortunately, every decision has advantages and disadvantages, and these influence other decisions.

The key to a successful design is making the right trade-off decisions for the required implementation. The modularity and flexibility of VMEbus systems does not impact a 'hit or miss' approach as much as a discrete microprocessor design would. If a VMEbus processor does not have sufficient performance, it can often be replaced with a faster version, whereas a custom built microprocessor design might require a complete redesign. However, in VMEbus systems, the final overall complexity is far greater than is often attempted with discrete implementations. A poor design often does not show up its failures until late in the design cycle, where it is more expensive and difficult to cure. There is nothing more frustrating than having to fundamentally modify a system to cure a design fault with only a few days to go before a demonstration.

Many of these inbuilt design faults come from a lack of understanding of the pros and cons associated with each design decision. There is no simple right or wrong way of building a VMEbus system. The criteria for assessing the pros and cons form part of the design process and therefore may change from application to application. This chapter describes a design methodology to guide designers.

Design methodology

The methodology described below is an iterative process, using detail only determined later in the chain to further define the original specification.

A Define the functional blocks required to fulfil the basic system requirements

The functional blocks are the basic system requirements in terms of processor, memory, mass storage, I/O, etc. These functions should be defined to provide the initial specification of the system. At this point, avoid the temptation of getting involved in too much detail too soon; specifying in detail at this stage often freezes that part of the design on the basis of initial criteria which will often change as the design proceeds. Be prepared to reiterate the process as problems are highlighted and/or a better understanding of the system is obtained. Do not forget to include operating systems and application software. These often require a certain minimum hardware configuration to run and this may further modify the specification.

B Define the time critical functions/mechanisms within the system and their importance to the system

Analyse each block in turn and determine where possible time critical functions or system bottlenecks may occur. Define, if possible the minimum and maximum times, repetition rates, transfer rates and the priority and impact on the system. As the system progresses, it may not be possible to fully satisfy all the requirements, and the impact priority analysis will help identify where design relaxations can be achieved.

C Define the hardware/software required for each functional block and check it meets the performance requirements defined in B

This is where the theoretical requirements are matched against data-sheets. From this, details such as minimum processor speed required, disc access, memory access and software techniques will come out. If a new point arises, repeat step A and use the information to improve the initial definition. Unless unlimited budgets are available, approximate financial limits should be defined in addition to the technical specification.

The question of building or customizing all or part of the system may arise. This is often an extremely difficult decision to make and may rely on many external factors. The cost of building complex VMEbus boards, especially when low numbers are involved, should not be under-estimated. The visible costs of components are often small compared to the design, testing and maintenance costs, all of which need to be considered as part of the equation. Ten days of an engineer's time spent debugging a custom built board might buy a very sophisticated VMEbus board that, at first glance, appeared to be too expensive.

D *'What resource, i.e. memory, interrupts, etc., does each function require?'*

This is the most difficult aspect of a multiprocessor system. The full system definitions are now required and these must cover, in detail, the requirements for both the hardware and software.

It is often useful to divide these requirements into three categories: mandatory, desirable and optional. Mandatory requirements must be met by the system; desirable facilities should be included if possible. Optional needs are the lowest priority and should disappear first in any trade-off decisions.

At this point, the hardware and software interactions of the system start becoming apparent. If they are neglected, or not considered correctly, any initial design flaws will not surface until late in the design cycle, when it is either too late or extremely expensive to cure. For inexperienced designers, many problems stem from common misconceptions about implementing VMEbus systems; these have been described as a set of observations:

'In terms of the hardware interface and requirements, any VMEbus board capable of acting as a VMEbus MASTER and initiating data transfers across the bus, should be treated as a processor board and its bus, interrupt and memory needs taken into consideration. In addition the system should be designed as a multiprocessor system.'

This means that the majority of disc controllers, graphics boards and serial communications boards are all VMEbus MASTERS. They are similar to processor boards but have been dedicated to a particular function. The result is that even a simple VME system is often a multiprocessor system.

It is important that bus arbitration and interrupt requirements are adequately supported. A design may require a four level VMEbus arbitration scheme, while the VMEbus MASTER acting as a system controller may only support a single level option. Within a distributed interrupt handler scheme, where different VMEbus MASTERS handle different interrupt levels, care must be taken to ensure that all levels are handled by a unique handler. Designing and debugging a system where interrupts can either be left hanging or answered at random by different handlers is not to be recommended.

'To achieve maximum performance, the VMEbus should be used as a medium for passing messages between VMEbus MASTERS and SLAVES and not as a replacement for the native microprocessor bus.'

The modularity of VMEbus boards allows their use as building blocks by using the bus as a microprocessor bus replacement. The problem is that an MC68000, through its pre-fetch and pipeline mechanism, uses about 80% of the external bus bandwidth. So, where the majority of bus use is processor traffic, the scope for multiprocessing is reduced due to the small bus bandwidth available. This processor need can be reduced by the use of 32-bit processors (such as the MC68020 and MC68030), which use on–chip caches to reduce bandwidth requirements to about 50–65%, and by the use of extension memory buses or increasing local resource.

It follows that the use of intelligent boards is recommended to reduce the bus bandwidth burden of dealing with I/O functions. The use of 'dumb' boards should be restricted to low performance designs.

'Every VMEbus MASTER on the VMEbus has its own memory map which may overlap or be localised: i.e. memory may appear at different locations in different VMEbus MASTERS memory maps and may be local or globally available.'

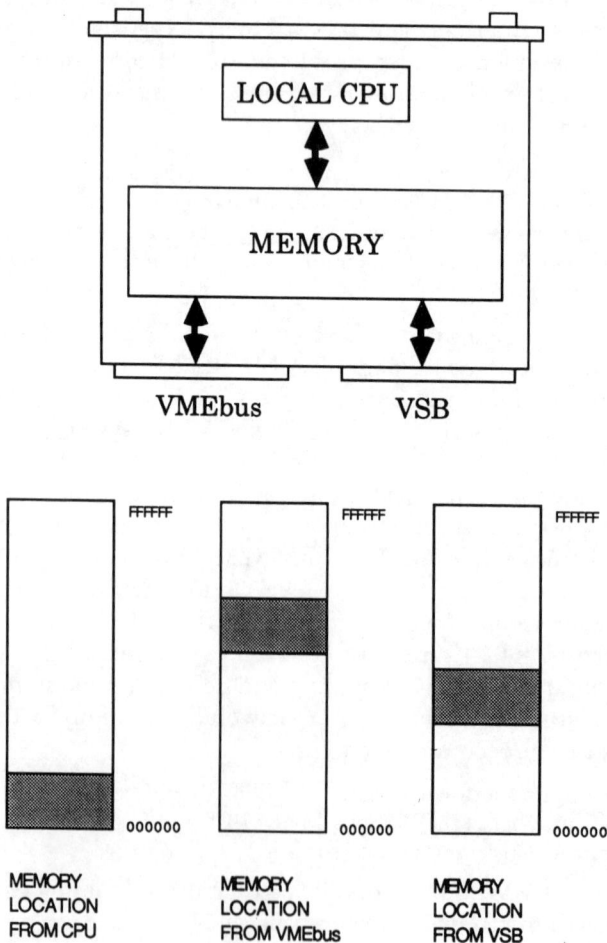

Figure 11.1   *An example of triported memory*

It is important that memory maps are determined. Within a VMEbus system, memory and I/O devices may either be local to a processor on a VMEbus board or be globally available via a bus. In addition, memory may be multiple mapped within a system or may be addressed differently depending on which path is used to access it. Figure 11.1 shows such an example. The processor board has a memory block which is accessible by the onboard processor as local memory, and via both VMEbus and VSB interfaces. The memory responds to different addresses depending on which interface is used. This has to be taken into account when software is written. For instance, if a pointer is used to reference a memory buffer for a disc controller, then the value used by the disc controller will be different from that used by the local processor. If the local processor is instructing the disc controller where it will find memory for the data buffer, then the pointer it passes will need translating.

Add to this the address modifier codes, which indicate a 16-, 24- or 32-bit address, and there is a potential for much confusion. Defining individual memory maps gives the view that each VMEbus MASTER has of its memory. This allows checking, to prevent duplicate memory addressing, and all required accesses can be achieved using the appropriate data path.

Again, software has a large influence over the hardware implementation: address modifiers may change depending on which state, user or supervisor the program is running in. Onboard registers may need initialization to allow certain memory pathways and enable hardware facilities. However, these registers settings should not be arbitrarily set to suit a hardware configuration without first confirming that this does not conflict with an operating system requirement.

'Interrupt response is the result of not just the interrupt level but also the bus arbitration request level and the local processor interrupt level and mask.'

The interrupt mechanism within the VMEbus involves the interrupt handler successfully arbitrating for the bus prior to acknowledging an interrupt. The handler processor may further delay the process due to an internal or external interrupt mask or because of some higher priority exception processing. Therefore, for the fastest response, a combination of high bus arbitration request, at both VMEbus interrupt level and local interrupt level, is required to reduce the response time throughout the whole interrupt chain. Time-critical functions which are not allocated these resources will be impacted. Again, by creating a table showing the bus request, interrupt levels for all the VMEbus MASTERS will show where a possible conflict might occur.

Figure 11.2 shows a typical chart and highlights some potential errors. The most common error often concerns allocation of interrupt handlers. The diagram highlights that there is no handler allocated for level 4 and that there are two sources of level 4 interrupt. This immediately raises two issues: firstly, which processor is assigned to be the level 4 handler and does the interrupt handler know that it will possibly have to poll to establish the source of the interrupt. The third concern questions the bus request level assigned to CPU 1 when it has five levels of interrupt to service which appear not to be used. There is obviously an omission or error in the design.

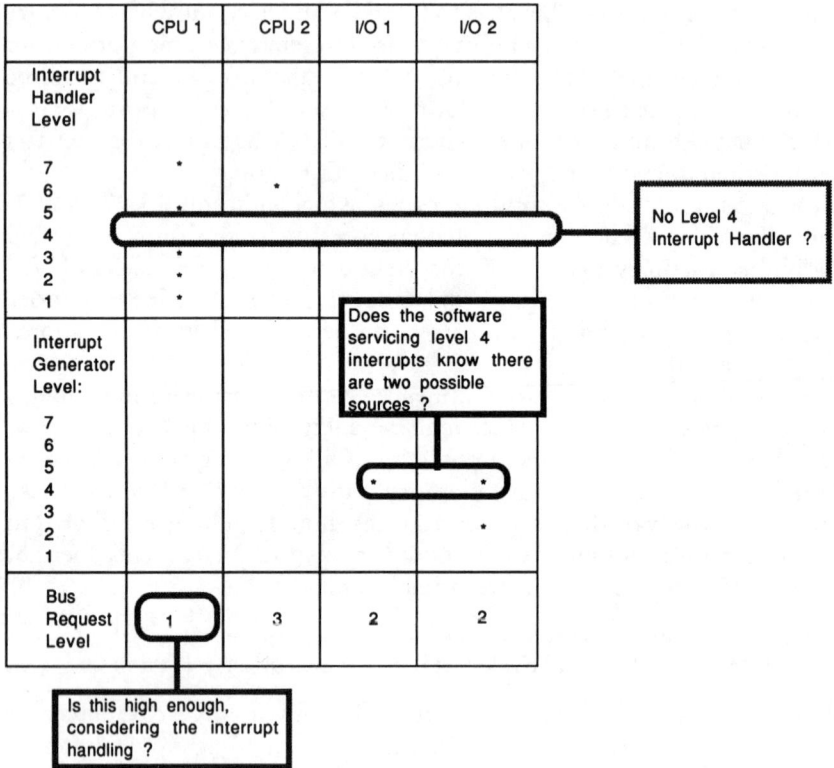

Figure 11.2   *An example of a configuration table and some typical problems*

'Every VMEbus MASTER has equal potential for enhancing the system or degrading it.'

Every time a VMEbus MASTER board is added to the system, it has the capability to hog or lock the VMEbus, rendering useless a system that functioned correctly prior to its addition. To prevent this, careful consideration has to be given to the bus bandwidth requirements, bus request and interrupt handling and the processor's memory usage. A board that executes software stored in global memory will either impact the other system MASTER's performance, by absorbing all the band-width, or will be impacted itself, due to its use of the bus.

Full consideration should therefore be given to speed upgrading or system redesign before the decision to add another processor is made.

E 'How does the system handle errors or system failures?'
It is all too easy to overlook how a system will respond if it encounters a failure either externally or internally. VMEbus provides basic support for detecting failures through the use of watchdog timers which assert special failure signals or high priority interrupts. It is important that the system software knows about these circumstances and reacts accordingly. Many software packages treat these conditions as standard faults and may just simply halt the system. This is generally not acceptable and means that modifications maybe required.

The most common cause of a 'system failure' is the incorrect setting of a bus watchdog timer, which causes the generation of a bus error signal if a data transfer is not completed within a certain time period. This facility ɜ necessary to prevent system hangs due to the truly asynchronous nature of the VMEbus and MC68000 family interface; however, if the timer value is too short or a VMEbus MASTER hogs the bus, a bus error is generated which is interpreted as a system failure. Thorough checking of timers and their values is therefore recommended.

F 'How much performance capacity is not being used? Is this sufficient to give confidence that the hardware/software can meet requirements?'
This is extremely difficult to evaluate without some practical information typical of the end system. Some microprocessors in circuit emulators and logic analysers will provide timing and bus utilization information while executing software. This software could be part of the actual end application or a test suite designed to emulate characteristics of the end application. The use of boards, which allow microprocessor speed and/or memory upgrades, provide a simple insurance policy if the system is unable to meet specification—the hardware can always be upgraded to obtain the extra performance.

G 'Actual information is worth a thousand guesses.'
Try to base all decisions on real information rather than guesses or hunches about the sytem characteristics. This may not be feasible or possible in all cases, and therefore extrapolation and interpretation should be used, providing the criteria used are both reasonable and conservative. Extrapolating from known data using unrealistic assumptions can often be less accurate than guessing! If a system is not providing the performance required, an immediate 'guess' may be to increase the processor speed to provide more performance. If the system bottleneck is

due to disc performance, increasing processor performance will not solve the system problem. Indeed, it may even make it worse.

This methodology should prevent or highlight many of the simple and more common mistakes that are made with VMEbus designs, i.e. while the design is still on paper where such errors are easy and cheap to correct.

12
Design case studies

The case studies described in this chapter demonstrate the flexibility of the VMEbus for system applications and the type of engineering trade-offs that can be made.

Simple production machine simulator

The application here was a machine simulator to train operators of a customized plastic moulding machine. The machine in question controlled plastic injection equipment working 24 hours a day, producing various mouldings. Due to high production commitments, the machine was only available for a limited time for training new operators—the commercial cost of losing only two hours' production was extremely high. The simulator allowed operators to learn the machine basics before any access to the machine, reducing the amount of training time needed on the actual machine. They learnt where the controls were and what function they performed, the relationships between them and what to do in case of error.

A simple mock-up of the machine, with all the controls reproduced, required a computer control system to provide the simulation. It would need to take inputs from the controls, calculate the machine's response and then display it. A terminal would allow an instructor to monitor results and to create error conditions to test the trainee's progress. The basic concept is shown in Figure 12.1.

The basic I/O requirements were for 12 channels of A/D (analogue to digital), eight channels of D/A (digital to analogue), four DC inputs and 16 DC outputs, with updating or sampling every 50 ms. This provided the interface to the controls and display units. An instructor terminal would be provided to allow monitoring and the production of

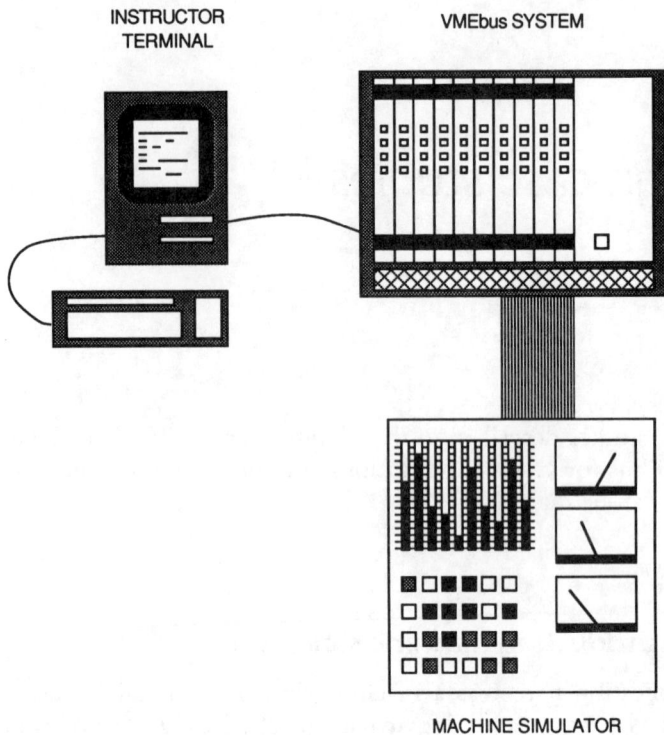

INSTRUCTOR
TERMINAL

VMEbus SYSTEM

MACHINE SIMULATOR

Figure 12.1 *Case study 1—the overall concept*

error conditions. The terminal would have a simple text display of the
I/O status.

The first stage was to decide how the system would be partitioned. To
meet the A/D requirements required 240 conversions a second which,
with a typical conversion time of 30 µs, would take only 7.2 ms. The
D/A would need 160 updates at 30 µs, i.e. only 4.8 ms. This left plenty
of time to perform the preprocessing and digital I/O across the VMEbus.
Although the I/O requirements are not difficult, it was decided that some
form of intelligence would be used to preprocess the information and
control the simulation locally. Although placing the I/O directly on the
VMEbus was initially considered, it was dismissed due to restrictions it
would place on further expansion—the addition of extra simulators
would require a multiprocessor solution which would be restricted by the
extra bus loading in accessing the I/O. The simulator module would
comprise a processor using a local bus to access the I/O functions.

The next decision concerned the instructor terminal. This function
could be part of the I/O intelligence, making the whole system a single

processor solution. This had obvious advantages concerning cost, but did impose some restrictions—the addition of extra machine simulators, under the control of one instructor, would require the instructor function to be independent to prevent the additional work from overloading the simulator module. If the results were to be stored, the instructor would need an operating system and this would not be easy to provide if the function was still integrated. It was therefore decided that the instructor function would have a dedicated processor unit and that it would access the simulator modules via the VMEbus to obtain a system status update.

With the hardware basically blocked out, as shown in Figure 12.2, consideration was given to the software structuring. Communication between the two processors would be via shared VMEbus memory. The system memory maps are shown in Figure 12.3. The simulation could be divided into two types of data: Boolean and analogue. The Boolean data came, for example, from switches and detectors that were either on or off. The analogue data came from control settings and temperature and pressure readings, for instance. The Boolean data and status could easily be simulated by straight Boolean equations.

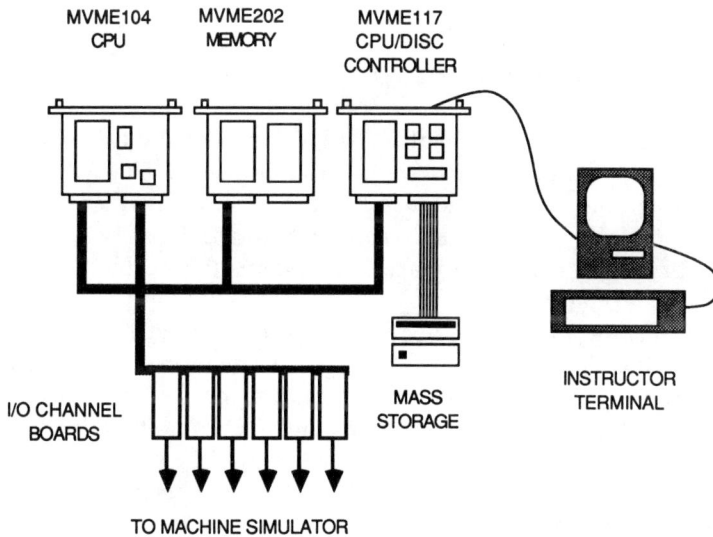

MVME104 CPU MVME202 MEMORY MVME117 CPU/DISC CONTROLLER

I/O CHANNEL BOARDS

MASS STORAGE

INSTRUCTOR TERMINAL

TO MACHINE SIMULATOR

Figure 12.2 *Case study 1—the basic system*

The analogue data could be simulated by look-up tables, which contained the results for various conditions. A major advantage of look-up tables, is that data can be modified on the fly to change the simulation dynamically to provide error conditions.

The choice of either a high level language or assembler had to be made.

c

```
FFFFFF          I/O
              CHANNEL
FF0000

200000
              VMEbus    VMEbus    VMEbus
              RAM       RAM       RAM
180000


 80000

              LOCAL               LOCAL
              MEMORY              MEMORY
0000000


              SIMULATOR           INSTRUCTOR
                CPU                  CPU
```

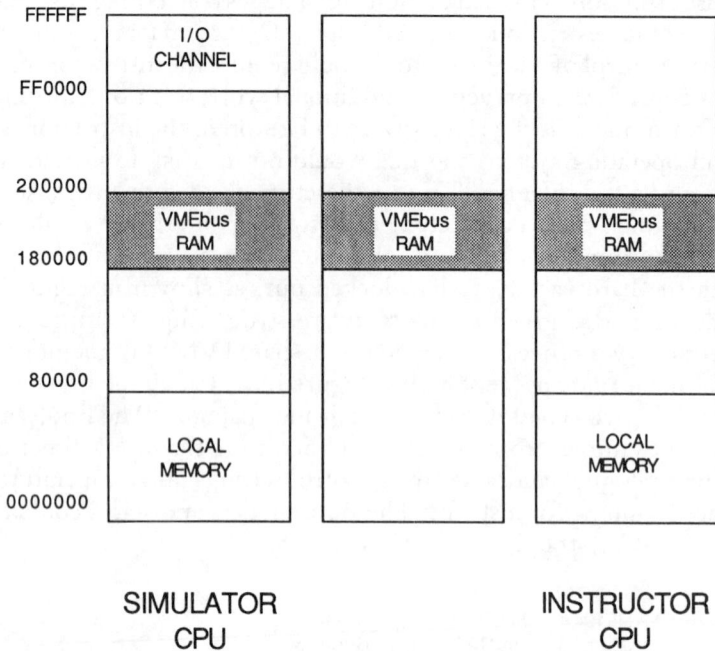

Figure 12.3 *Case study 1—the system memory map*

It was decided to use 'C' for software development and to download the simulation tables by the instructor into the simulator. This would require both an operating system and mass storage, confirming that the decision to separate the simulator and instructor functions was correct. The instructor would periodically access a system status table to obtain the latest simulator status.

Changing the look–up tables would be performed by the simulator accessing the new tables stored in global memory. Every time the simulator performed its sampling, it would check a semaphore to see if it should update the tables. If so, it would fetch a pointer, perform the transfer, reset the semaphore and carry on with the simulation process-ing. The basic structure is shown in Figure 12.4. This method forced the simulation processing to be performed in discrete packages and pre-vented the processing from using half-modified data—a situation which could have occurred if the instructor processor wrote directly into the simulator memory.

The simulator processor is made from an MVME104 MC68010 based processor board with 512 Kbytes of dual ported RAM. It uses the I/O channel to control an MVME600 A/D controller with an MVME601 extender to provide up to 16 channels of A/D. Two MVME605 D/A controllers, two MVME625 DC output modules and an MVME620 DC

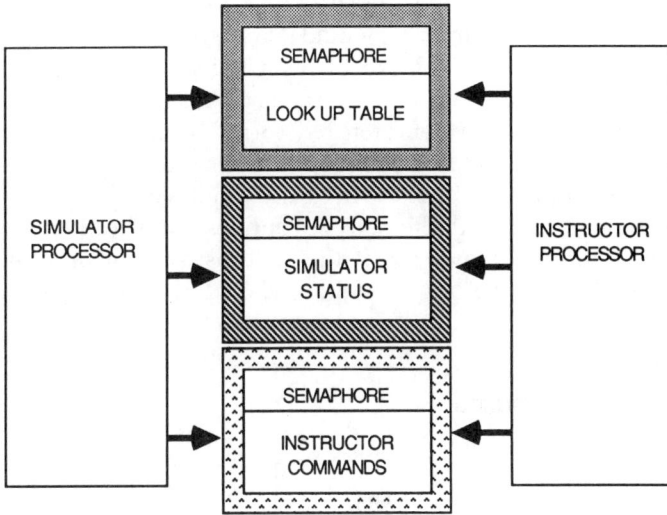

Figure 12.4 *Case study 1—using shared memory for processor to processor communication*

input module provide the remaining I/O facilities. The instructor processor is an MVME117 single board computer running VERSAdos as its operating system. While both memory boards have onboard local memory, additional memory for semaphores and table downloading was added. This was an MVME202 512-Kbyte RAM board.

As this system was only designed to be used for tutorial purposes, all error handling has been ignored. Neither of the processor boards will respond to power fail etc.

A data processor

In this requirement, the initial design brief was for a data processor which could take data from 16 analogue channels at a 2 kHz sample rate and provide a statistical analysis on the incoming data in real time. The resolution of the analogue channels was to be 12 bit or greater and no data was to be lost throughout the measurement period. This example appears to be very similar to the first, except that the I/O requirement was more stringent and required more careful design.

Figure 12.5 shows the basic functions. After blocking out the basic functions of a processor to fetch the data and analyse it—16 channels of analogue to digital I/O and some memory—the critical functions were determined. Obviously, the capture of data was the most important and would result in a heavy processor load. To capture 16 channels at a 2kHz sampling rate requires 32 000 separate data transfers which, if polled for 30 μs (a typical conversion time), would take 960 000 μs or 96% of the bus bandwidth. The use of a 32-bit processor, with its wider data path, would not have been advantageous because the data was less than 16 bits wide and was not available in concatenated form. If an interrupt software scheme was adopted, and each interrupt routine took an average of 15 μs (again a typical figure), 48% of the bus bandwidth would be used. If some data loss could be tolerated, the analysis routines could be interleaved into the polling routines. However, if the analysis overran or some other exception took place, polling would be delayed, resulting in subsequent

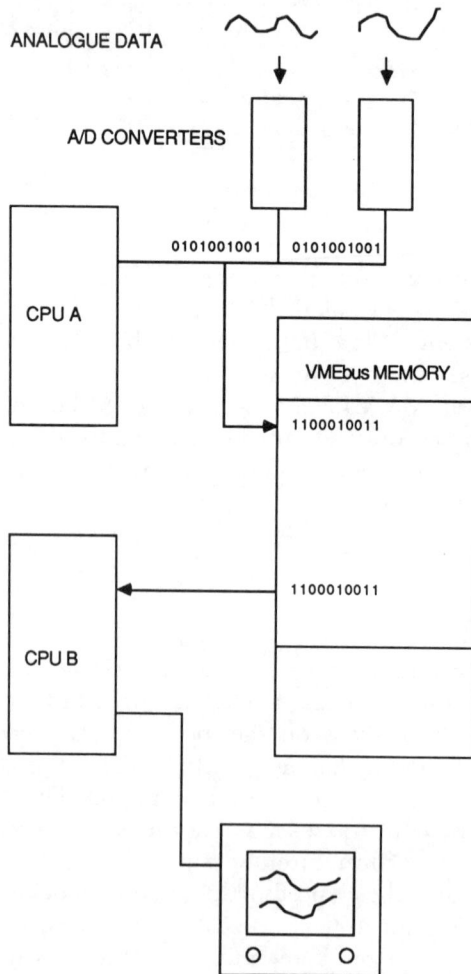

Figure 12.5   *Case study 2—basic block configuration*

data loss. Simply placing a dumb A/D board on the bus would dissent from the design methodology by using the VMEbus as a replacement microprocessor bus.

The most obvious solution was to put some intelligence with the A/D board to remove this overhead. The chosen solution was to use an MVME110 SBC which, like the MVME104, has its own local I/O channel interface. On the I/O channel is an MVME600 with an MVME601 extender providing 16 channels of A to D conversion. The combination of these units gives a single, intelligent, A/D unit.

The adopted solution is shown in Figure 12.6. The delegation of system functions is straightforward: the MVME110, with the MVME600/601 A/D boards, collates the information from the A to D converters, preprocesses it and then writes it into global VMEbus memory. A second processor board, an MVME101, takes the information, analyses it and displays it on a terminal. Both these boards have 8 MHz MC68000 processors with onboard RAM/ROM.

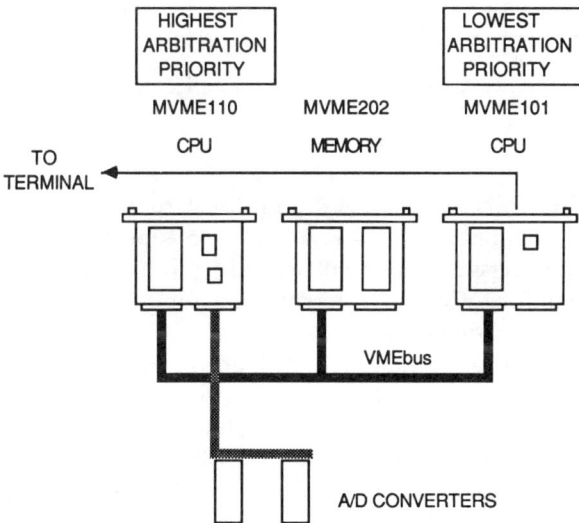

Figure 12.6 *Case study 2—the VMEbus solution*

The addition of the MVME110 enhances the system, providing consideration is given to its requirements. In this example, the two processor boards are tightly coupled and the interboard communication is critical to the design. From the memory maps shown in Figure 12.7, the only area of commonly accessible memory is provided by the MVME202 RAM board. Therefore, data must be stored in this global memory using circular buffers of sufficient depth as depicted in Figure 12.8. Access is required by both processors but priority is given to the MVME110 to ensure data is stored without loss. The MVME110 thus has the higher bus arbitration request level. If the MVME101 had the higher level, access to the global buffers would only be given to the MVME110 when the MVME101 had finished using the bus. No guarantee of access would certainly result in data loss and system degradation.

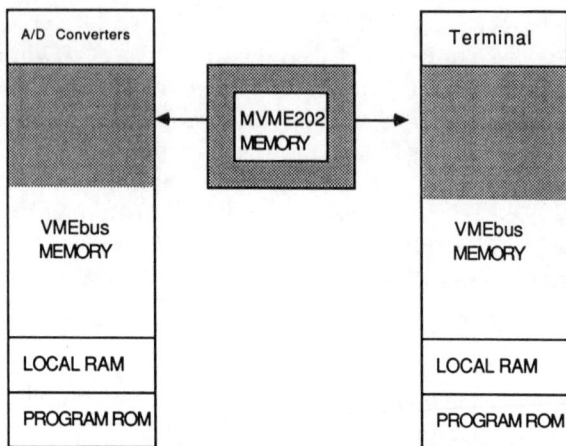

Figure 12.7   *Case study 2—memory map*

The rest of the system design is straightforward: both processors have their code stored in onboard ROM and use some local scratchpad RAM. Synchronization between the two processors is achieved by polling a memory semaphore. VMEbus interrupts are not used because of the lack of a bus interrupter function on either SBC. Only local interrupts are processed. The code is written in assembler for speed and compactness.

Error handling is simplified by disabling the SYSFAIL VMEbus line such that neither processor recognizes it. A bus error signal is treated as an indication of a global error: the MVME101 sends a message to the terminal indicating possible data loss, and the MVME110 holds as much data locally as it can. Both boards will retry the access periodically to see if the system will recover.

A cable harness tester

This appeared to be a simpler application to the previous one but required careful design. The specification was for a cable harness tester that would accept a range of harnesses and check for the correct connections, open and short circuits. The system should require no setting up and be able to

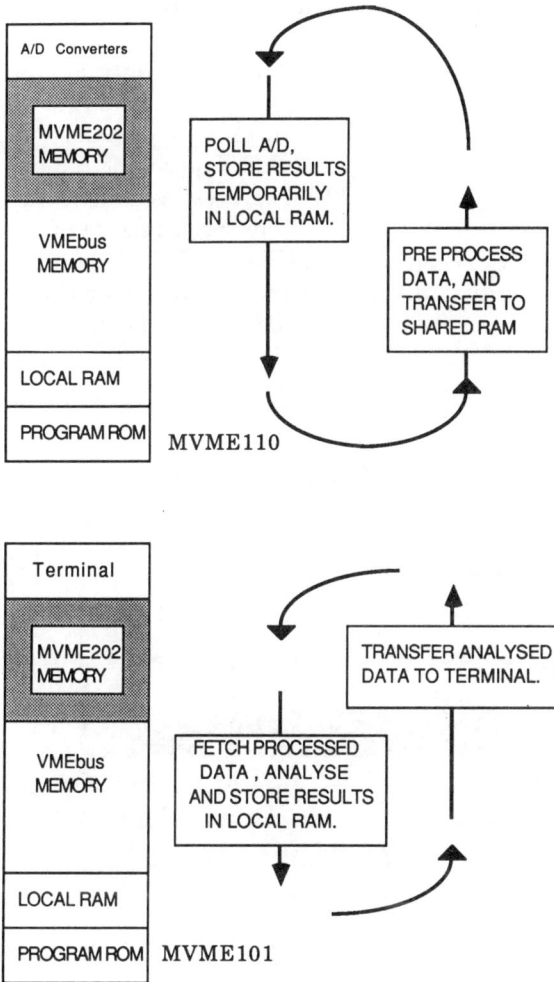

Figure 12.8 *Case study 2—memory map and data movements*

recognize cables by comparing the connection map it obtains with a reference library in memory. The harnesses have only two or three connectors, connecting up to 220 individual wires. The method of operation is simple: a harness is plugged in and the test run. If the harness pattern matches one of the recognized configurations, a conformance test document is printed for it. If it fails, a test pattern indicating the failures is printed to allow easy reworking. A learning procedure is inbuilt, allowing new patterns to be learnt and stored by the machine.

The initial block diagram, Figure 12.9, has a processor communicating with several parallel I/O boards over the VMEbus. The largest number of connections required many boards to be used. The larger VMEbus formfactor permitted larger numbers of I/O lines per board and was therefore an obvious candidate. There was only a single MASTER present and so the VMEbus loading by the I/O boards was not significant. The processor board controlled the printer and performed the testing and pattern matching routines. To provide the fastest performance, an MC68020 based 32-bit processor board was chosen. Its additional addressing modes and faster performance provided very fast pattern recognition—an area which analysis had shown would be the bottleneck. The patterns were held in 1 Mbyte of battery backed up memory. The general operation is depicted in Figure 12.10.

CABLE HARNESS UNDER TEST

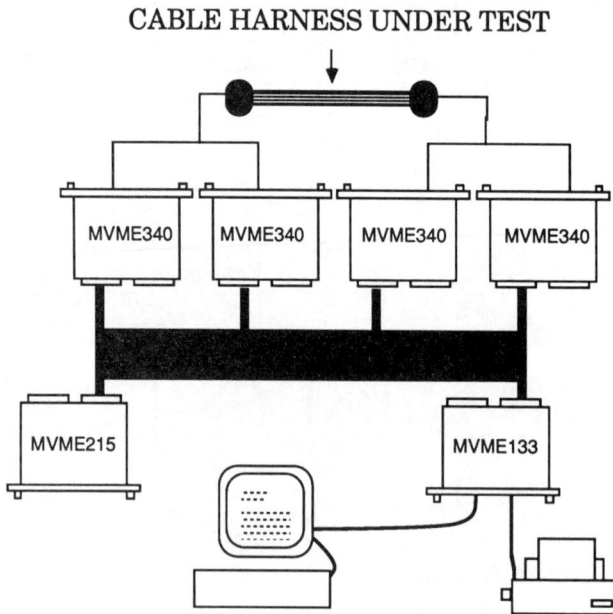

Figure 12.9 *Case study 3—system block diagram*

For performance reasons, it was decided to write the program in MC68020 assembler. However, the I/O calls to processor peripherals were used to minimize the code generation. These calls were provided by the onboard monitor and offered simple data input and output to serial ports etc. They were invoked by the creation of parameter blocks and the execution of a processor TRAP instruction. The processor would poll the parallel I/O lines and not use interrupts. The final configuration was based around an MVME133 processor board with a 12.5 MHz MC68020 processor and 1 Mbyte of shared DRAM. The parallel I/O was provided by 4 × MVME340 64 line I/O boards communicating on the VMEbus. An

1. Test the harness to derive pattern.

2. Compare patterns.

3. If incorrect, compare with library stored in memory.

4. If there is a match, cable is identified and certificate printed.

Cable 2.3 Type 456
Tested O.K.

5. If there is no match, print out the pattern data.

Cable 2.3 UNKNOWN TYPE

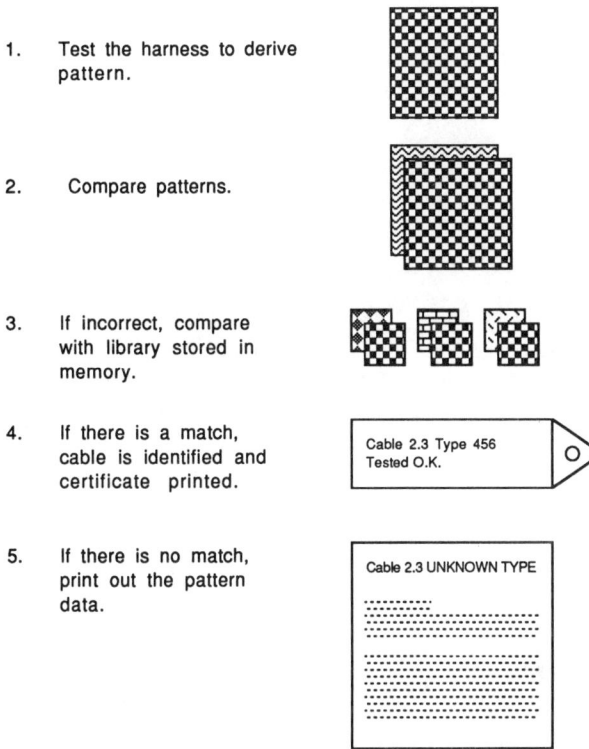

Figure 12.10   *Case study 3—general operation*

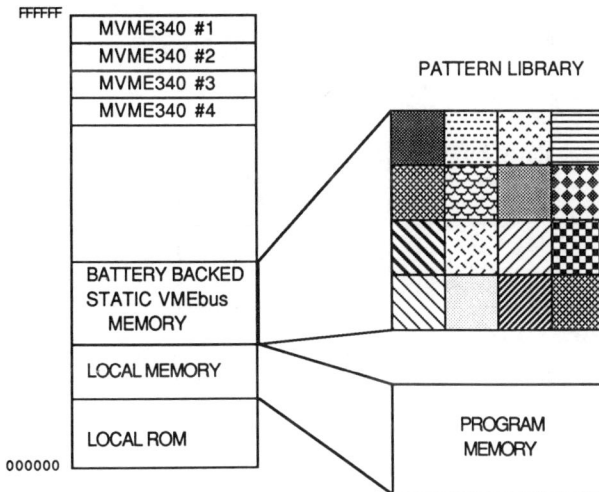

FFFFF

| MVME340 #1 |
| MVME340 #2 |
| MVME340 #3 |
| MVME340 #4 |

PATTERN LIBRARY

BATTERY BACKED
STATIC VMEbus
MEMORY

LOCAL MEMORY

LOCAL ROM

000000

PROGRAM
MEMORY

Figure 12.11   *Case study 3—system memory map*

MVME215–3 provides 1 Mbyte of battery backed up static RAM. The system memory map is shown in Figure 12.11.

With only a single processor, the choice of arbitration scheme is not important. A single level three is the obvious implementation; with a polling technique being used, interrupts were disabled. This example is using the VMEbus as a simple connection bus.

A UNIX based cable harness tester

This example is based on an upgrade to the previous system. The original tester now needed to be linked into a UNIX environment where test patterns could be downloaded and results sent back to the UNIX system for archiving and use within a database. The UNIX and the tester systems would communicate over the VMEbus using shared memory to act as the communication media. The UNIX system would require a disc system, a processor with memory management and at least 1 Mbyte of system memory.

The initial draught, shown in Figure 12.12, appeared to be quite sound and, from the hardware considerations, eminently practical. However, the interaction between software and hardware had not been considered. The initial design replaced the task performed by the MVME133 in the original design by the UNIX system. Effectively, the four I/O boards

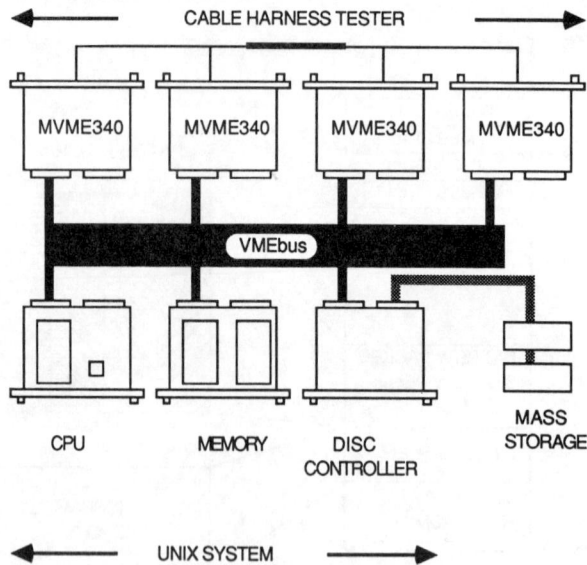

Figure 12.12   *Case study 4—initial UNIX configuration*

were placed into the UNIX VMEbus rack and the testing software run as a UNIX task.

The critical routine of receiving and analysing the data required a guaranteed response and access to physical resources, such as global memory and possibly interrupts. The UNIX environment used its hardware memory management to prevent processes running under it from accessing these resources. Simply writing some code which accessed location $100 compiled and ran, but the physical memory location accessed was translated and not $100. In addition, the UNIX operating system required large amounts of disc access, even when it appeared to be dormant, which would conflict with accessing the MVME340 I/O boards. Changing to an interrupt scheme would not help, as the UNIX characteristics did not guarantee when an interrupt would be serviced.

If a database application was running under UNIX, it would increase the total test time taken due to the increased time-sharing needed to run both tasks simultaneously. A worst case condition may occur if the database had a higher priority, when the testing may not actually commence until the database had finished. Neither of these scenarios was acceptable.

The solution was to include the original MVME133 board to perform the original task and communicate with the UNIX environment via a shared memory segment. (This is supported in SYSTEM V/68. A dummy device driver is built into the kernel and a system call is used to attach to the shared segment.) This provided a shared memory com-

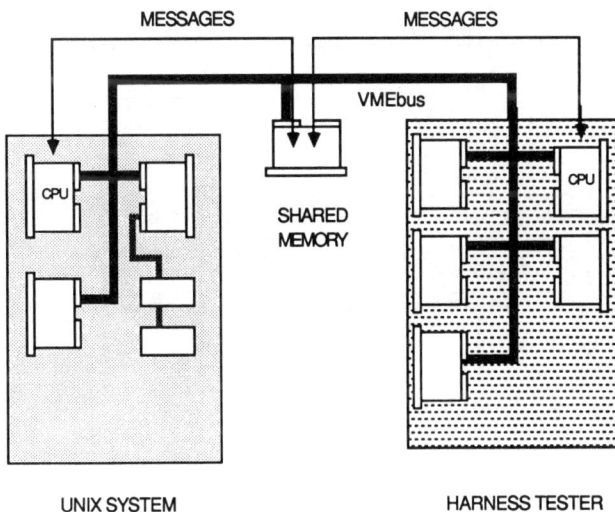

Figure 12.13 *Case study 4—a multiprocessor solution*

munication path between the processors and allowed the tester to operate in real time.

Unfortunately, this second arrangement was not ideal. A close inspection of the configuration in Figure 12.13 shows that there are three VMEbus MASTERS present on the bus: the UNIX processor, the tester processor and the intelligent disc controller. In addition, the high bus traffic between the tester processor and the I/O boards caused further complications. If the tester was declared the highest priority processor, the UNIX processor and disc controller were locked out for large periods of time thereby degrading performance. If the priority was reversed, the tester suffered.

A partial solution was to use the VSB for the UNIX processor, removing its loading from the VMEbus. This still left the disc controller and the trade-off decision over which has priority: UNIX or the tester processor. Both processors use the VMEbus for the majority of their accesses, and any choice would affect one of the processors.

A possible solution was to implement a round robin arbitration scheme, where the bus ownership is evenly distributed between VMEbus MASTERS. This was not practical for this solution unless a separate system controller was added to provide this function. The even distribution would simply share the degradation between the MASTERS, not remove it.

The obvious decision was to give each unit its own separate bus, which was then bridged to form a link. This is what the final configuration in Figure 12.14 does. Two VMEbuses are used: one for the UNIX environment and the other for the tester. The link is formed by a memory

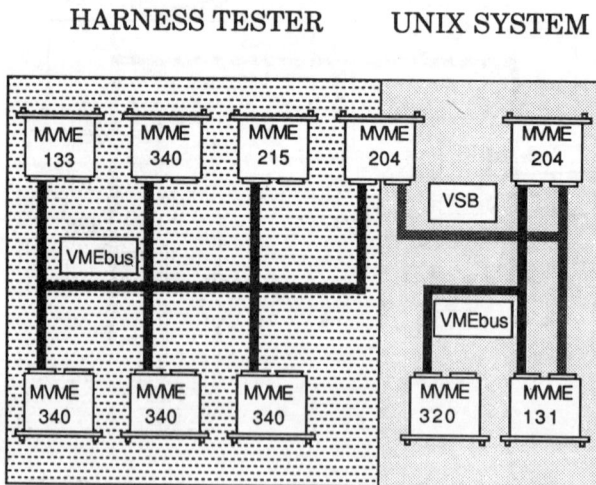

Figure 12.14   *Case study 4—dual VMEbus solution*

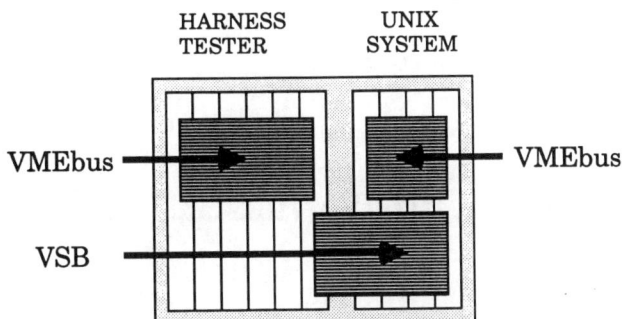

Figure 12.15   *Case study 4—backplane configuration*

board which is dual ported between the VSB and VMEbus using a backplane configuration similar to that in Figure 12.15. The UNIX processor accesses the memory via VSB, and the tester via VMEbus. For both normal accesses, each MASTER uses its own bus. This removes the bus traffic conflict, allowing each unit to operate at maximum performance. The tester uses the same MVME133/MVME215–1/MVME340 configuration with the addition of an MVME204–2F 2-Mbyte VSB/VMEbus RAM board.

Whilst it is straightforward to configure the hardware to provide the correct accesses, the SYSTEM V/68 kernel will search and size memory within certain boundaries and will use any memory it thus finds. Therefore, these boundaries must be modified to prevent the use of the second MVME204–2F memory for general use, keeping it dedicated purely to shared memory communication.

There are no 16-bit processor boards within the system which could cause problems when address pointers are passed: a 16-bit board may only pass a 24-bit pointer which may cause a 32-bit board, expecting a 32-bit address, confusion and conflict. With both systems acting virtually independently, bus arbitration and interrupt handling is not critical and the standard configuration for the UNIX and tester system can be used. The tester software is then modified to use the shared area via semaphore control, and the UNIX applications generated using a high level language such as 'C'.

13
Interfacing to the VMEbus

It cannot be stressed enough that the only reference documents that should be used for a design are the bus specifications themselves, which define the protocols and their required timings. The VMEbus specification is unlike many specifications, in that it makes many observations and recommendations for practical design. These have come from many inputs and have been coordinated by the many VMEbus User's groups worldwide. As a result, it is an extremely usable document.

This chapter describes the general techniques used to implement VMEbus interfaces and highlights some of the areas requiring careful implementation. As stated before, the only design document that should be used is the VMEbus specification itself.

Buffering

The VMEbus uses a terminated transmission line design backplane for its signal transfers. This is necessary to prevent corruption of the signal levels such as ringing, over- and undershoot. The termination networks normally used for termination effectively prevent the direct connection of devices, such as microprocessor buses, to the VMEbus. To meet this bus driving capability, drivers are normally used to provide the 48 mA drive current required by the VMEbus specification.

This buffering consumes board space but also provides a cheap protection between the bus and the more expensive microprocessors and peripherals. Because of the high transients that these bus drivers can generate, extreme care must be taken with PCB design. Track lengths must be kept short and the copious use of ground and power planes is recommended. It is not uncommon for very high performance VMEbus boards to use a 12 layer PCB.

SLAVE interface

The SLAVE interface is the simplest to implement. For a 16–bit wide memory board, the VMEbus data bus is simply connected to two banks of byte wide memory. The VMEbus address lines and data strobes are decoded to generate the appropriate chip selects and address lines for the memory.

If dynamic RAM is being used, an additional DRAM controller is required. The read/write line is connected to the memory banks.

Address decoding can be achieved in several ways. Usually it needs to be user selectable, so the memory can be mapped anywhere within the VMEbus memory space. An easy way to implement address decoding is to use a comparator, which compares the upper address bits with a pattern selected by a jumper field. If the addresses match, a valid address signal is generated. This signal can then be qualified by AS* to indicate the start of a valid bus cycle.

Decoding address modifiers

The address modifiers can either be decoded in a similar way or by using hardwired logic, but this does not allow user modifications or the easy support of multiple address modifiers. The memory board is normally expected to respond to a valid address with either of the user/supervisor/program/data standard address modifiers. This is often implemented using the address modifier bits with some of the higher order memory bank address bits to access a bipolar Programmable Read Only Memory (PROM). Figure 13.1 shows a typical design. The high order bits allow the memory to be divided into separate banks for which a valid/not valid code can be stored in the PROM for each possible address modifier code. This enables the user to easily customize which address and modifier codes the board responds to; memory banks can then be partitioned and protected. The data strobes and LWORD* signals are used to enable

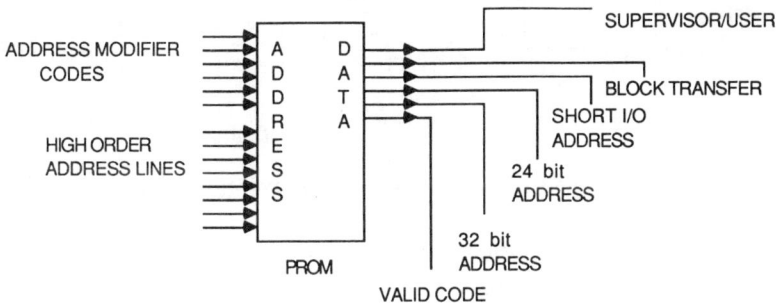

Figure 13.1   *Using a PROM to decode address modifiers*

the bus drivers so that the correct information is read or placed on the bus at the right time.

Using a PROM to decode the address modifiers allows the recognition of block transfers. An additional bit can be programmed so that it is used to preload and enable the address counter needed to increment the memory address during a block transfer. The counter is incremented using the data strobe signals.

Generating DTACK*

The SLAVE must generate a DTACK* to signal the successful completion of a memory transfer. This can either be a fixed value, suitable for a populated memory board, or variable, depending on the address or a user-defined setting. This allows different speed peripherals and memory chips to be used on a single board. Fixed values can be generated by a monostable initiated by chip select and AS* signals, or a system clock could be divided down to provide a suitable delay.

To generate variable times, another counter can be used which divides a reference clock down. Figure 13.2 shows a suggested circuit. The AS* signal is used to start the counter and the outputs are gated with a valid address signal to generate the DTACK* signal at the correct time. The gating can be combined with a jumper field to allow easy selection. In the example either four or eight clocks delay can be selected.

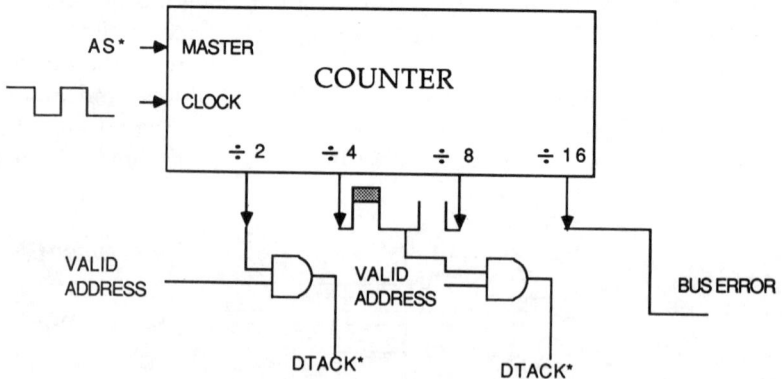

Figure 13.2   *Generating DTACK* for different memory blocks*

The bus error signal should only be generated if a long word access is attempted that the SLAVE cannot support. Bus error watchdog timers are best implemented on MASTERS or as a SYSTEM CONTROLLER function.

Interfacing 8-bit peripherals

The VMEbus DTB interface assumes a 16–bit wide data bus and uses the lower and upper data strobes to select either the odd or even byte within the 16-bit word. The address generated is on a word boundary and this can cause complications with many 8-bit peripherals. These peripherals will accept a few address lines which are then used to select the internal registers.

In an 8-bit system, both odd and even addressed bytes use the same bus. This is not the case with the VMEbus. Although address line A0 is

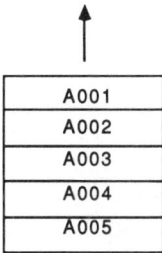

A001
A002
A003
A004
A005

8 bit peripheral to 8 bit data path

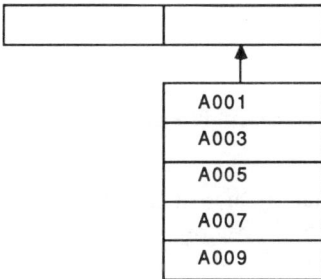

8 bit peripheral to 16 bit data path using A1

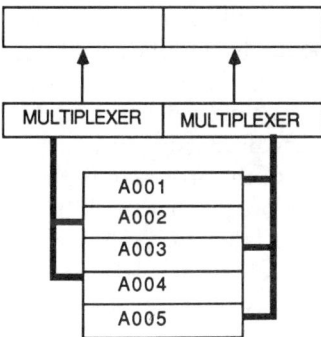

A001
A003
A005
A007
A009

8 bit peripheral to 16 bit data path using multiplexers

MULTIPLEXER   MULTIPLEXER

A001
A002
A003
A004
A005

Figure 13.3   *Connecting 8-bit peripherals to the VMEbus*

missing, it can be reconstituted from the lower and upper data strobes to select the registers correctly. However, the 8-bit data bus is usually connected to either the lower or higher 8 bits of the VMEbus. For every other access, the data are presented on the wrong half of the VMEbus databus.

There are two solutions to this. The first simply offsets the VMEbus and peripheral address lines so that the VMEbus A1 address bit is used as the A0 peripheral bit. This changes the register addressing so that each register is accessed every other byte; for example, register A is at $A000, register B is at $A002, etc. This may cause problems when porting software from an 8-bit arena to the VMEbus environment. The MC68000 family has a special MOVEP instruction to support this arrangement which writes a 16- or 32-bit value out on consecutive odd or even memory locations. It is therefore recommended that, in such a solution, word and the unused byte accesses should generate a bus error signal.

The second solution uses a multiplexer to switch the peripheral data bus from one half to the other. This increases the interface hardware required but does provide a software transparent solution. The various configurations are shown in Figure 13.3.

Interfacing the MC68000 as a VMEbus MASTER

The MC68000 bus signals are so similar to that of the VMEbus that all that is required is to buffer the signals and possibly synchronize them to generate the correct timing specifications. The AS★ signal is such a signal, and may need synchronizing as shown in Figure 13.4. The signals can then go straight across to the VMEbus interface. This simply relies on the sequential appearance of the signals and will assume that there is no barrier preventing the VMEbus from being driven. If the VMEbus is not available, then the bus cycle must be prevented from starting, so that the correct signal sequence and timings can be preserved. Once the MC68000 has asserted its strobes, the signals will remain steady until the peripheral replies. This can be easily achieved by use of the processor bus arbitration pins. If the VMEbus is not available, the processor bus is arbitrated away. It will then delay any external bus cycle until the bus is released back to it. This appears to be a simple solution. However, the cycle that is delayed may not need to access the VMEbus and may reference local memory. If ownership of the VMEbus is a prerequisite for any processor bus cycle, then all local accesses will effectively need VMEbus bandwidth although the bus will only be held and not used for the actual data transfer. This is not a satisfactory design; it loses all the advantages that local memory offers.

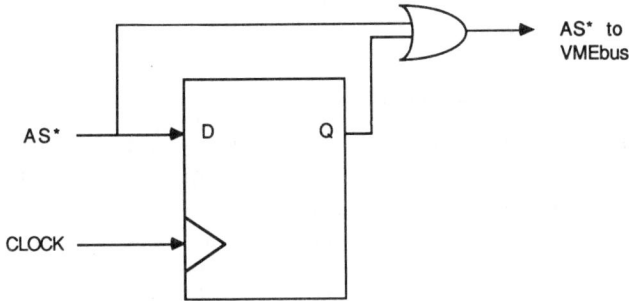

Figure 13.4 *AS* delay logic*

The main consideration is in differentiating between local bus cycles and cycles destined for the VMEbus. When the processor is accessing its local resource, there should be no holding of the VMEbus which prevents other MASTERS from using it or consuming bus bandwidth with local accesses. Usually, the decision to use the VMEbus for an access is taken after the address has been decoded. To try and give as much warning, many designs decode the address prior to the processor address strobe being asserted and then use that signal to validate the decoding. This saves time and allows more time to be allotted to the rest of the memory cycle and determining which data path it will use. Once the processor has started the cycle, the cycle will finish depending on where the memory is located. The interface needs to take into account three types of access.

Local accesses

Here, the decoding inhibits accessing the VMEbus and the processor memory interface uses standard techniques. The decoded address is validated by the processor address strobe, and is used with the data strobes to produce a memory chip select and address information. An onboard DTACK generator similar to that used for a SLAVE interface generates the DTACK★ signal to complete the cycle. There should be no interaction with the VMEbus.

VMEbus accesses: bus already held

In this case, VMEbus access is allowed and effectively should be treated in the same way as a local access. The address and strobe information is driven on to the bus and the processor waits for a reply. The designer can use the processor bus sequence within the interface logic instead of waiting until processor signals are stable before generating the VMEbus timings. It is usual to start a watchdog timer so that BERR⋆ can be asserted to abort unsuccessful accesses. The SLAVE supplies data and signals a successful transaction using DTACK⋆. Again this is simple design.

VMEbus accesses: bus not held

In this case, the address information cannot be driven on to the bus until the bus is requested and granted. The processor generates its strobes etc., and waits until it receives a response.

There are two ways of handling this situation. The first is to insert wait states into the processor bus cycle while the interface logic requests and gains the bus. However, the processor will have asserted its strobes, and its bus signals will be stable. The interface logic generates the correct VMEbus timings once the bus has been granted.

Another method is to use the hardware retry mechanism provided by the MC68000 family. Here, the BERR and HALT pins are asserted together to abort the current cycle. Once the cycle has been aborted and the HALT signal removed, the processor retries the bus cycle. If this is only performed when the VMEbus has been granted, the cycle restarts and the interface logic can use the signal sequence from the processor to generate the appropriate interface logic for the VMEbus.

Generating address modifiers

To allow customization, the modifiers are usually generated by a PROM, which inputs function codes and higher address bits to fetch a 6-bit value from its memory, as shown in Figure 13.5. This allows the designer to

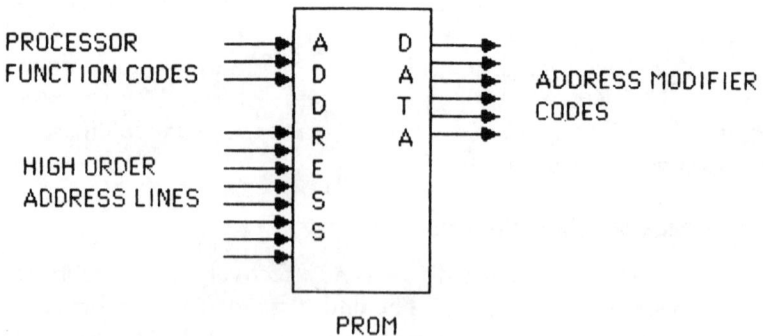

Figure 13.5 *Generating address modifiers for different memory accesses*

program both the address modifiers for each block of memory and the function code outputs to suit the application. Some implementations allow specified address modifier bits to be preset by writing into a special software register. This allows customization via software control.

For a 16 bit MC68000 processor, only the standard and short I/O address modifiers are generated. The short I/O is generated by decoding a 64-Kbyte memory space as the area, so that the processor will specify a full 24-bit address, while only the lower 16 bits are used on the VMEbus itself. The full 24-bit address is required to generate the correct address modifier codes which specify a short addressing range. The top 8 bits are decoded to generate the short I/O modifier which is then driven on to the VMEbus with the lower 16 address bits. Normally, this area is defined as the top block in the address range (i.e. $FF000–$FFFFF). Similar mechanisms are used for 32-bit processors.

Interfacing the MC68020 and MC68030 processors

Both the MC68020 and the MC68030 have additional facilities with their asynchronous bus interfaces. The first obvious difference concerns the replacement of the MC68000 type signals with new ones: the upper and lower data strobes are replaced with a single data strobe. The individual byte strobes are decoded from the A0 and A1 address lines and the two size signals SIZE0 and SIZE1. In addition, there are two DSACK signals, which not only perform the same function as the previous DTACK signal, but also indicate the data width of the transfer. This allows the processor to use 8-, 16- or 32-bit data ports for data transfer, with the size selected by the peripheral or memory.

This dynamic bus sizing is normally performed on a cycle by cycle basis on the native processor bus. The processor automatically assumes that the port is 32 bits in size. If the memory width is only 8 bits, the processor recognizes this on receipt of the 8-bit width DSACK signals, automatically reorganizes the data and starts another bus cycle. The size pins indicate that there are now 24 bits of data left to transfer. This process is repeated until the full 32 bits of data are transferred.

The MC68020 allows any combination of transfer, for example, 8, 16 and finally 32 bits. The MC68030 uses the same port size throughout the operation. If the returning DSACKs indicate an 8-bit port, the remaining transfers are all 8-bit. While dynamic bus sizing has many advantages and is supported in the VSB specification, there is no direct support within the VMEbus, and dynamic bus sizing support has to be synthesized.

Supporting dynamic bus sizing

While the data present on the size pins and lower address A0 bit can be decoded to generate the upper and lower data strobes needed for the VMEbus using logic shown in Figure 13.6, there is only a single DTACK★ signal available and therefore dynamic bus sizing cannot be directly supported.

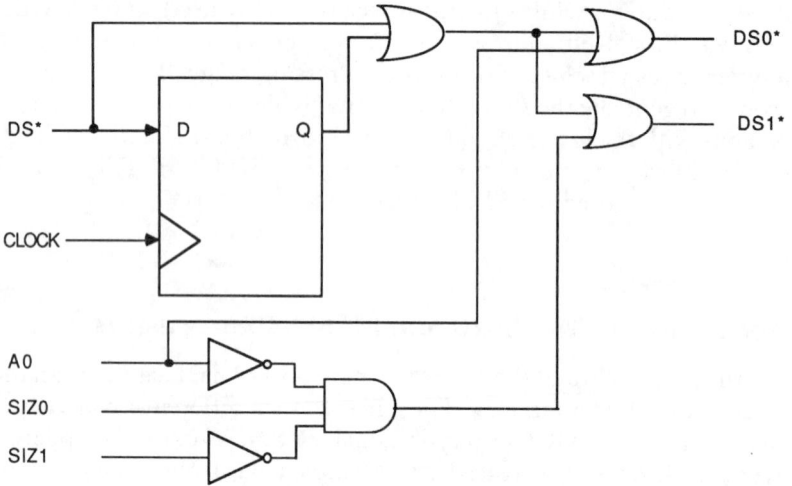

Figure 13.6   *Generating DS0* and DS1* for an MC68020/68030 processor*

There are several solutions to this dilemma. They all generate the DSACK signals from a combination of the VMEbus DTACK★ signal and some onboard memory mapping information, either provided by the processor or by a local resource. The first uses a mapping PROM (the same one that generates address modifiers, perhaps) to define the data width for each block of memory. This information provides the LWORD★ signal, which can be used with the VMEbus DTACK★ signal to generate the correct DSACK response for the processor. The logic for this is very simple and consists of an OR gate as shown in Figure 13.7. The LWORD★ signal is ORed with the DTACK★ signal to generate the 32–bit DSACK response.

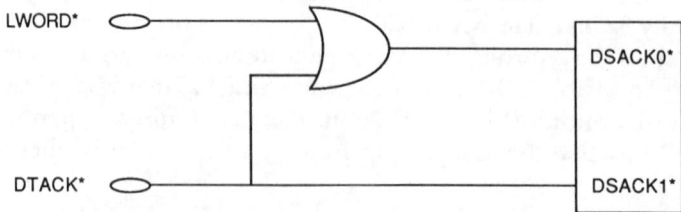

Figure 13.7   *DSACKx* logic*

For all other cases, a 16-bit response is generated. If there are sufficient bits available within the PROM, both DSACK0* and DSACK1* can be supplied and are gated by the VMEbus DTACK*. This is fine for all aligned transfers, but is further complicated for misaligned transfers where transfers of differing sizes may need to take place. The system does require the system to be predefined and can therefore be limiting.

An alternative is to use an aborted VMEbus cycle to indicate that the data width is too great. At the start of each cycle, the maximum data width is always assumed. If the cycle is aborted by a BERR*, the cycle is restarted with the next smaller data width. This is repeated until either the data are transferred successfully or a bus error occurs on a byte transfer.

The advantage with this method is that dynamic bus sizing does take place without having prior knowledge of the system. The disadvantage is that several cycles may be attempted before a 'real' bus error is recognized. This slows down system response and additional software is needed to investigate bus error conditions and recover partially corrupted data.

Consider a VMEbus MASTER attempting to perform a 16-bit write to an 8-bit peripheral port which only accepts even byte access. Such an attempt would normally indicate a failure by producing a bus error. With this scheme, the processor attempts the cycle again but with an 8-bit bus. The SLAVE responds correctly with the first even access but a bus error occurs on the second odd access. The processor recognizes this last access as a real bus error and calls the software bus error handler to investigate the situation. Unfortunately, the SLAVE location has been erroneously modified—a situation which the handler has to identify and correct.

	A1	A0	SIZ1	SIZ0	DS0*	DS1*	MUX*	LWORD*
LONG WORD ALIGNED BOUNDARY	0	0	0	0	0	0	1	0
	0	0	0	1	0	1	0	1
	0	0	1	0	0	0	0	1
	0	0	1	1	0	0	0	1
WORD MISALIGNMENT	0	1	0	0	1	0	0	1
	0	1	0	1	1	0	0	1
	0	1	1	0	1	0	0	1
	0	1	1	1	1	0	0	1
ODD WORD ALIGNED	1	0	0	0	0	0	1	1
	1	0	0	1	0	1	1	1
	1	0	1	0	0	0	1	1
	1	0	1	1	0	0	1	1
BYTE ALIGNED	1	1	0	0	1	0	1	1
	1	1	0	1	1	0	1	1
	1	1	1	0	1	0	1	1
	1	1	1	1	1	0	1	1

Figure 13.8 *Multiplexing logic truth table*

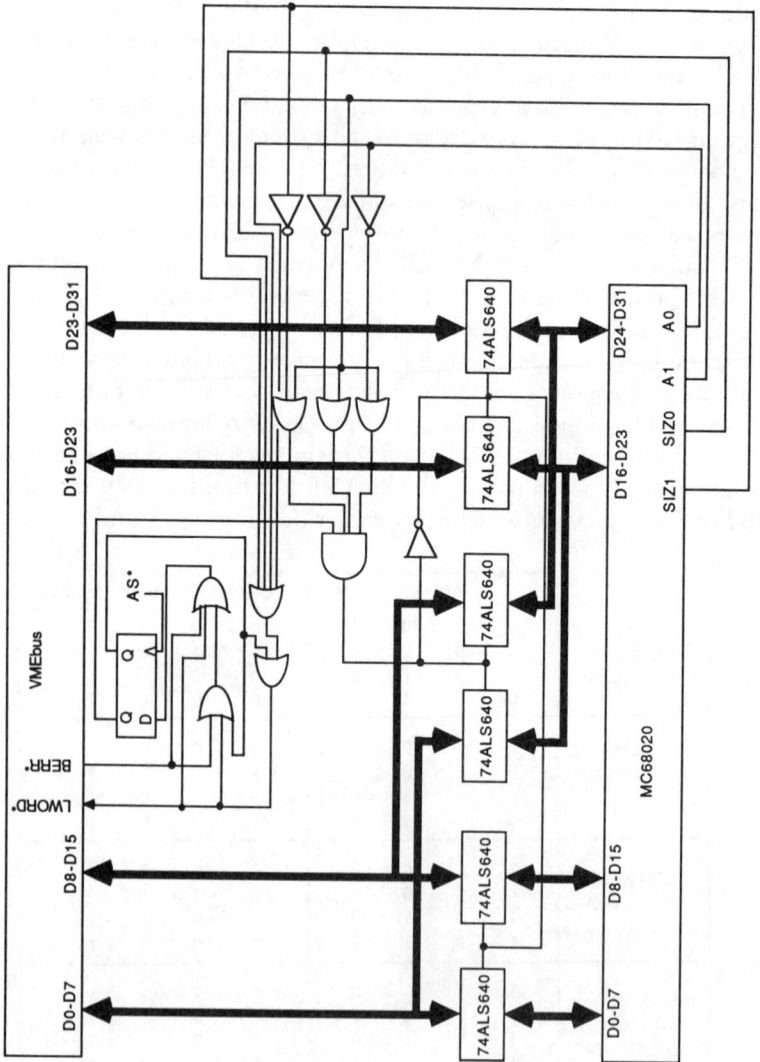

Figure 13.9   *Multiplexing and retry logic for an MC68020 to VMEbus interface*

Location of words on 32-bit buses

In addition to the complexities of dynamic bus sizing, both the MC68020 and the MC68030 differ from the VMEbus specification over which parts of a 32-bit bus are used for a word transfer. The VMEbus specification uses bits D0–D15 (right justified) while the processors are left justified using D16–D31. To solve this discrepancy, multiplexing logic using octal transceivers, such as SN74ALS640–1, can be used. The logic needed to implement a multiplexing design, with the automatic bus error retry mechanism as previously described, needs to comply to the truth table shown in Figure 13.8. The block diagram of the interface is shown in Figure 13.9.

A simpler solution is to have a switch or jumper which predefines the access to either A24/D16 or A32/D32. This assumes that either all slaves support this type of access or responsiblity is placed on the system software to ensure they only access 8-bit ports via bytes, 16-bit ports with words or bytes and only specify long words at addresses with 32-bit ports. For single systems, where complete control can be maintained over compilers, operating systems and applications, this is acceptable. Where software is transferred from one system to another, this restriction may not be adhered to, causing great difficulties in porting and debugging.

Whichever method is used to generate the DSACK signals, the different word locations will require multiplexing. This is often incorporated into the signal buffering.

Read–Modify–Write cycles

Read–Modify–Write (RMW) cycles on both the VMEbus and the MC68000 processor are indicated by the holding of the address strobe and the second strobing of the upper and lower data strobes. Such cycles assume that the addresses of the read and write cycles are identical and do not change during the process.

The MC68020 and the MC68030 perform the RMW cycles differently and, by virtue of their CAS and CAS2 instructions, perform RMW cycles where the addresses are different. Both the MC68020 and the MC68030 indicate an RMW cycle by the assertion of an RMC★ pin. During such a cycle, the address strobe is released and reasserted and must therefore be gated with RMC★ to maintain a stable AS★ for the VMEbus. Before the second half of the cycle is started, the second address must not have changed. If it has, the VMEbus address strobe must be released and reasserted with the new address. This destroys the indivisible cycle and can cause problems within a multiprocessor application—another MASTER could be granted the VMEbus and start accessing the same location with disastrous results. If the address is the same, the VMEbus can cope.

The only way around this is to hog the bus so that it is not released and thereby maintains the indivisible cycle. This is done by feeding a bus lock signal into the requester logic that is derived from the processor RMC signal. When asserted, the requester refuses to release the bus.

Multiple arbitration schemes, and system lock-ups

There is a further potential problem with indivisible bus cycles and dual ported memory as shown in Figure 13.10. Consider two processors with

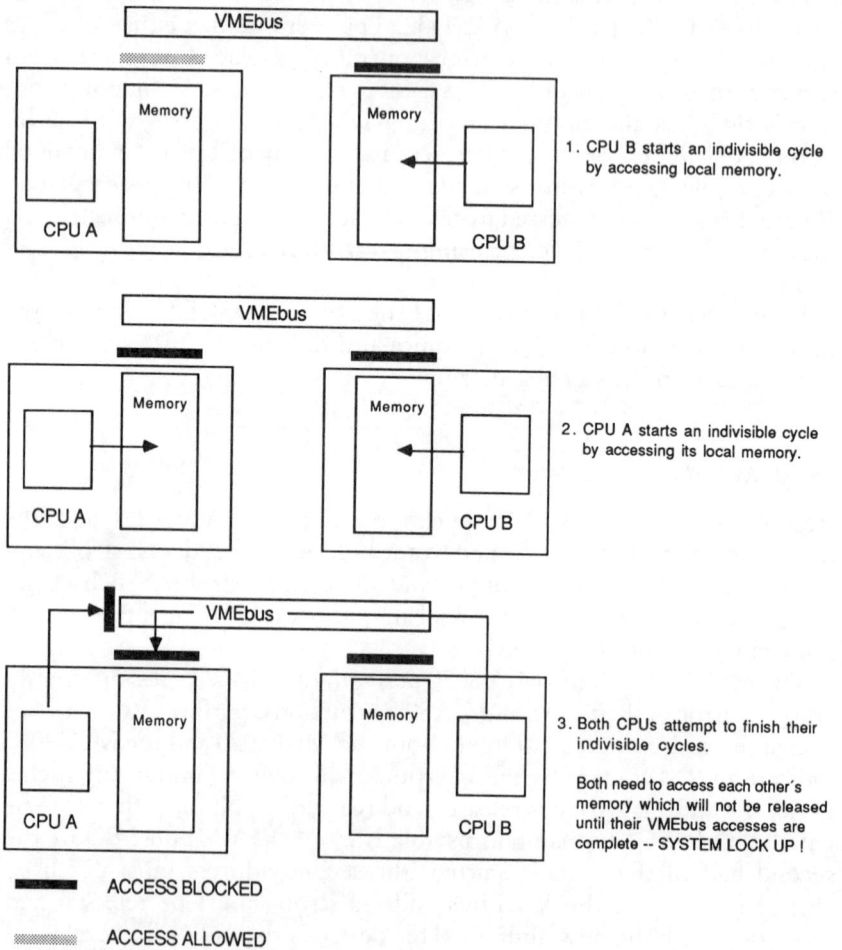

1. CPU B starts an indivisible cycle by accessing local memory.

2. CPU A starts an indivisible cycle by accessing its local memory.

3. Both CPUs attempt to finish their indivisible cycles.

Both need to access each other's memory which will not be released until their VMEbus accesses are complete -- SYSTEM LOCK UP !

ACCESS BLOCKED

ACCESS ALLOWED

Figure 13.10 *Potential system lock-up with dual ported memory and read–modify–write cycles*

onboard memory dual ported between the VMEbus and the local processor. CPU A's memory is located at address $100000 and CPU B's memory at $200000. Both start an indivisible bus cycle, which accesses their own local memory first and then each other's memory, via the VMEbus. Both processors successfully access their own locations and then arbitrate for the VMEbus. CPU A wins the contest and attempts to access the location in B's memory. CPU B will not relinquish the local memory until it has completed its indivisible cycle, which it requires the VMEbus to do. CPU A will not release the VMEbus until it has completed its own indivisible cycle. The system is in deadlock. In practice, but timers would abort the cycles, removing the deadlock but causing an awful mess for the two CPUs' software to handle. This problem arises because two arbitration mechanisms are involved.

There are several solutions to this: the most obvious is to restrict the use of RMW cycles to indivisible operations using only a single address. Software could locate all its parameters and semaphores to VMEbus global memory where the single arbitration scheme would prevent such deadlock. This increases VMEbus traffic, especially for locations that have heavy local access and light access via the VMEbus.

A hardware solution is to declare the VMEbus as arbiter so that mastership of the bus must be obtained before any RMW cycles are started. In such a scheme, CPU A would get the bus prior to accessing its local memory. CPU B would thus be prevented from starting its RMW cycle until CPU A had completed. Such a scheme must not require VMEbus ownership prior to all accesses; such an implementation destroys any system advantages that local access offers.

Using silicon support chips

The majority of today's VMEbus interfaces are constructed using programmable array logic (PAL) devices. PALs are cheap, fast and allow hardware modifications to be easily implemented if a design problem appears in the product during its lifetime. Full support chips which provide a complete interface (often including drivers) are only just becoming available and the decision to use them should be carefully considered—they are often expensive due to the advanced technology required to drive many pins at 48 mA per pin. Their high pin counts need expensive multilayer printed circuit boards. Typical costs are about $US200 a chip. As a result, they are not economic to use for the average designer. Their appeal should improve once prices start to come down.

Currently, there are many companies and organizations, including VITA (VMEbus International Trade Association), using gate array technology to implement such designs. At the present time (1989), the only single chip implementations have come from Motorola Computer Division and Performance Semiconductors. Other VME manufacturers, such as Force, have developed their own interfaces for their own use but these have not yet appeared on the open market. An alternative to using a support chip is to buy a VMEbus board with the appropriate interface logic already present, leaving a large wire-wrap area for prototyping. Xycom produce a series of such boards, which allow cheap and quick prototyping. Their range covers prototyping boards with simple interfaces through to boards with MC68000 processors and associated glue logic. All have wire-wrap prototyping areas.

The MVME6000 VMEbus interface chip

This chip, available from Motorola's Computer Division, provides the VMEbus functional modules for MASTER, SLAVE, requester, arbiter, interrupter and handler, global and local watchdog timers, and both global and local control/status registers. It is typical of the designs that are either planned or in development. It has been designed to interface to an MC68020/030 processor and has external signals to control the necessary data swapping buffers. With the exception of the ACFAIL* line, all VMEbus signals from the chip meet the current drive and can be connected directly. Address modifiers are either calculated by the chip from the processor function codes, or can be programmed by software control of an address modifier register. It has 132 pins, of which 120 are active, and the remainder are used for power or ground connections.

The interface chip supports both cache filling, where a full 32-bit access is performed irrespective of the required data size to allow the prefilling of cache lines. This provides a more efficient interface to memory systems allowing the use of faster nibble and page mode accesses. Write posting, where an early acknowledgement is provided to the processor, releases it to carry on local processing while the latched address and data are written out across the VMEbus. This further improves the performance of the system and makes the local processor less prone to VMEbus delays.

If the chip's slave interface is enabled, the local processor's VMEbus bound write cycle is not acknowledged until the processor is granted VMEbus ownership. This prevents system deadlocks in cases where the current MASTER is attempting to access the local onboard resource at the same time. The SLAVE interface can support this write posting facility. A block diagram is shown in Figure 13.11.

VSB bus interfaces

The main design problem with using VSB is that the hardware support

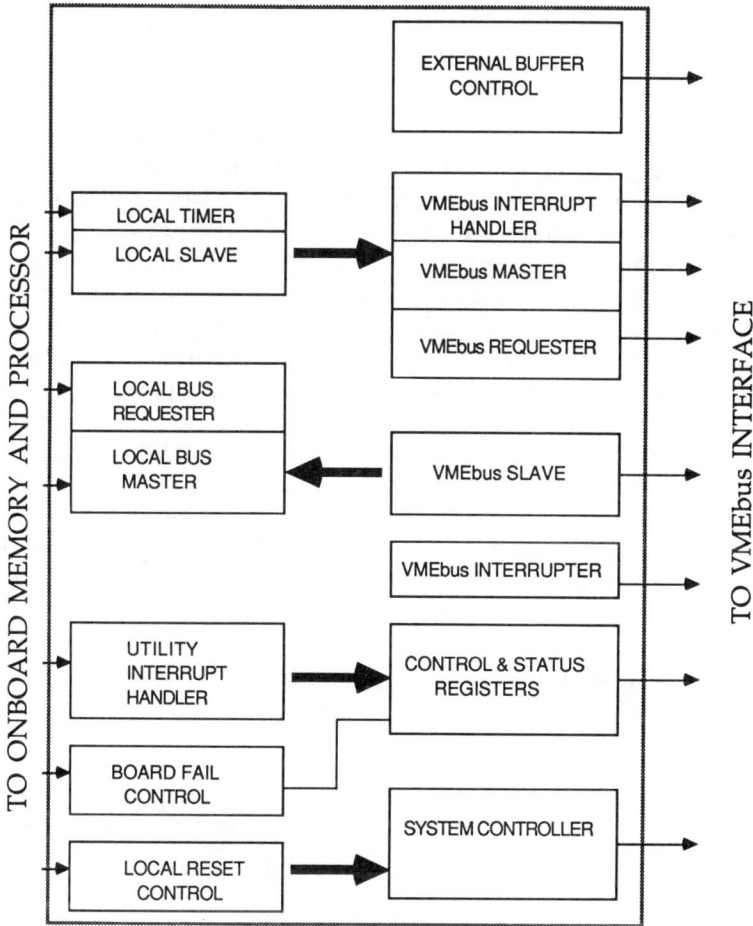

Figure 13.11   *VME6000 VMEbus interface chip block diagram*

(bus drivers, in particular) consumes a large amount of board real estate. A typical VSB implementation requires about 15 logic packs to implement. However, this drawback can be overcome by replacing the standard circuitry by using another standard interface chip: the MVSB2400 interface chip from Motorola Computer Division.

The MVSB2400 is a low power bipolar LSI gate array which contains all the VSB address/data multiplexing circuitry, a VSB requester and arbiter with associated timeout module, status and control registers and the capability to provide 48 mA drive to the VSB lines directly. It will interface to a local 16- or 32-bit microprocessor, such as an MC68010 or MC68020.

The device is packaged in a 14 × 14 pin grid array, where 120 of the pins are active. It supports data transfers either on a single or multiple cycle (block) basis, where only the initial address is generated. The chip provides software control of the bus interface via two addressing registers and a control/status register.

The block transfer register has a dual function: it provides a byte count during a block transfer of data and, when in MC68010 mode, provides an upper eight address bits to extend the MC68010's 24-bit addressing a full 32 bits. The second addressing register contains the address decoded to access the control/status register. This is set to $FFFA0000 on reset. The control and status registers allow the control of bus timeout values, block transfers, write access to the bus, slave or master modes and provides diagnostic information on the cause of bus errors during a data transfer.

With the increasing availability of programmable logic and even 'soft' semicustom integrated circuits, the tools are becoming available to allow designers to define their own interface support chips. With the increasing competition amongst VME manufacturers and the importance of a good VMEbus interface to offer the maximum performance within the market-place, other factors may influence the silicon used to implement such interfaces. Custom or programmed logic makes proprietary designs easier to implement and allows other facilities to be offered which will differentiate it from other similar products in the market-place.

Appendix G lists interface chips suitable for the VMEbus.

14
High integrity VMEbus systems

The use of VMEbus systems, in applications ranging from simple data loggers to automated steel rolling mills and operating in environments found from laboratory to battlefield conditions, has placed a tremendous responsibility on the VMEbus manufacturer and designer to ensure that such systems have at least a high integrity if not complete fault tolerance. The VMEbus specification has given designers the capability to build complex systems by integrating many microprocessor based functions into system building blocks. This level of integration forces system reliability to be designed into the system at the outset. It is not something that can be added at a later stage.

Basic system integrity

To demonstrate how system integrity can be designed into a system using standard VMEbus hardware, a design for a standalone data recorder, used for collating information from remote locations, is considered.

The basic requirements are to record eight channels of digital data every 15 s and to store these data in battery backed up static RAM.

This information is retrieved by replacing the RAM pack every 14 days and analysing the data at a base station. The system is powered by the combination of a rechargeable battery and a solar cell. Each set of entries is date stamped with data from a real-time clock.

This is a straightforward VME bus design. However, as the system is to remain unattended for at least 14 days and could be susceptible to possible power failure, careful consideration has to be given to its design.

The basic hardware design

The system, blocked out in Figure 14.1, comprises an MC68000 based processor, running at 8 MHz clock rate, with 1-Mbyte battery backed up CMOS static RAM. The CMOS parts were chosen because of their reduced power consumption. The controlling program and vector table are stored in 64 kbytes of EPROM. Both of these areas are address modifier code protected.

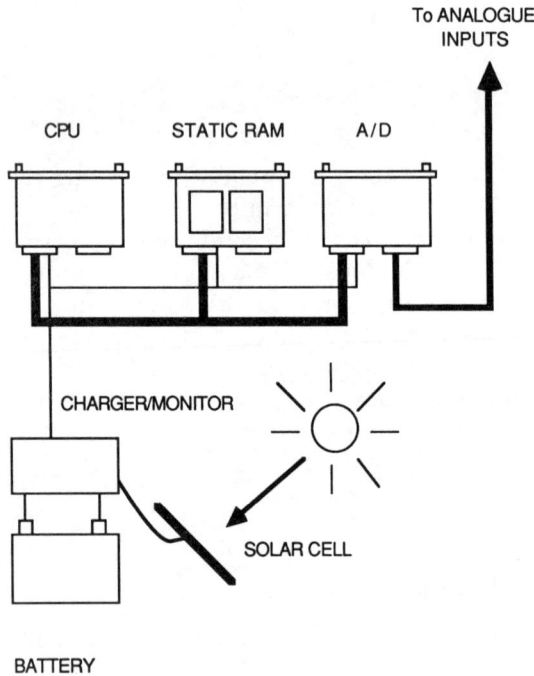

Figure 14.1 *The basic system*

A battery backed up real-time clock provides the date stamping information for the digital data received from an 8-channel analogue to digital converter located on the VMEbus.

Throughput is not critical to the system design. The static RAM board is separate, so it may be easily removed and replaced. Power is provided by a rechargeable battery, kept charged by an external solar cell. This effectively provides an uninterruptable power supply; however, the charging circuit monitors power levels and will assert ACFAIL* when the supply is likely to fail.

The static RAM is parity protected. Parity is a simple way of detecting simple single bit faults by storing an extra bit with every byte. The bit is set depending on the number of bits set or clear within the memory byte. If a bit were to fail, then the parity bit would become invalid, indicating a memory fault. It would not detect a double bit fault which would cancel itself. To detect multiple failures and restore such lost data usually requires error detection and correction circuitry which stores a special code allowing data corruption to be detected and corrected. Such systems can easily be identified by their required memory organizations as shown in Figure 14.2. The trade-off is the increased chip count and the delays needed before the detection and correction procedures.

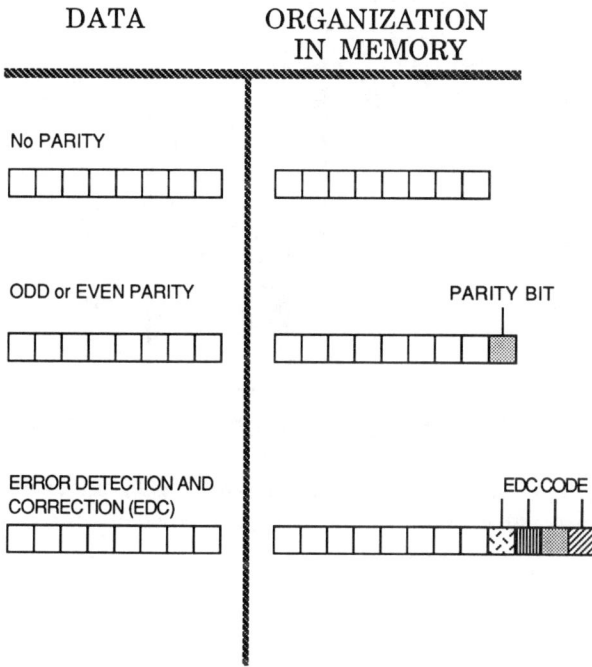

DATA   ORGANIZATION
IN MEMORY

No PARITY

ODD or EVEN PARITY   PARITY BIT

ERROR DETECTION AND   EDC CODE
CORRECTION (EDC)

Figure 14.2 *Memory protection and organization*

In this example it was decided that the risk of losing small amounts of data can be tolerated. The decision to trade off reliability against implementation cost is a recurring theme in high integrity designs. It was decided, however, to use the address modifiers to partition the memory system into various areas (e.g. mailbox, supervisor program and data, etc.) as shown in Figure 14.3. Each area has its own unique address modifier, which means that if one of the address generating components fails, the address modifier would still be invalid, and thus prevents an incorrect access.

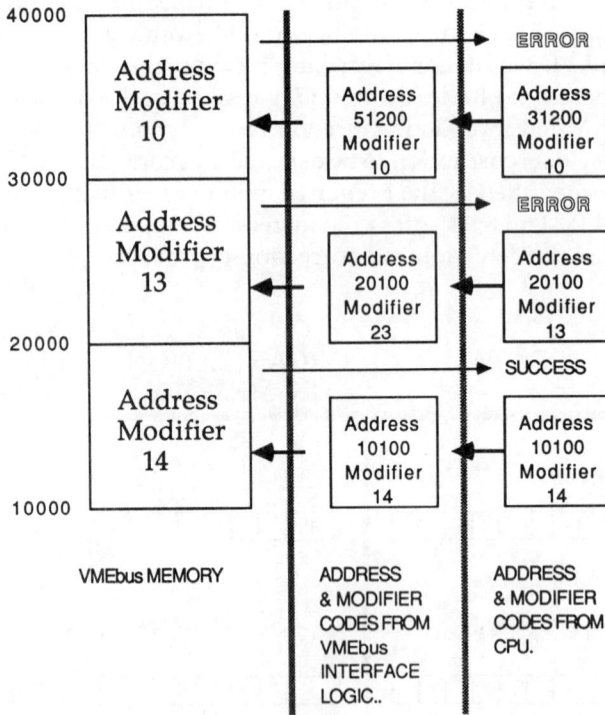

Figure 14.3   *Using address modifiers to protect VMEbus memory*

The normal bus watchdog timers are implemented, with one timer dedicated to a sanity timer function. This timer generates a system reset unless periodically reset by software.

The software philosophy

The hardware design described uses a minimum of boards and provides detection of nearly all hardware faults. It also independently monitors software execution, to ensure that the system operates correctly.

The philosophy behind such a high integrity system is to recognize a system error, preserve the data and restart the system at a known point. To help recognize faults, an area of the memory map is used to hold system parameters, provide a mailbox facility and to act as a reset log so that on system reset, software can determine past history and if necessary modify its behaviour accordingly. This could, for example, remove an area of faulty memory from use.

The software tasks needed for this system are straightforward: after routines have sized and checked memory across the VMEbus, using BERR* to signal non-existent memory, and checked the system parameter area, the system is initialized. During initialization, the memory system and mailbox are checked to identify if this reset is the first or the result of a system failure. If there are valid data which were obtained prior to the system reset, the appropriate memory area is excluded.

After initializing, the processor uses the STOP instruction to effect-ively stop the processor and tristate the external bus until a periodic interrupt is generated. When the periodic interrupt is received, the processor is woken up. It checks the time, compares it with the last access to make sure that no entry has been missed through failure, and proceeds to read the ADC channels and store the information in the main RAM. Before powering down with the STOP instruction, it updates the system status area ready for the next awakening and resets the sanity timer.

A great deal of consideration is required for the exception handlers, which need to perform a lot of detective work to find out what has gone wrong and then decide what to do. During initialization, only the bus error and interrupt handlers are used during normal operation: these are used to size and check the system. Once the system is operational, only the interrupt handler associated with the periodic interrupt is valid. All other exceptions are indicative of a system error and must be handled appropriately.

Bus error handling

The most likely cause of an unexpected exception is the bus error. The initial problem is to determine where the error occurred and then to decide if it is a transitory or permanent fault by investigating the stack frame built by the processor, the access address, function codes and the status of the read/write line. The instruction and status registers at the time of the error are also present.

By comparing this information with a system resource map compiled during initialization, the fault can either be diagnosed as an external hardware fault (i.e. an access to a valid address), or the result of corrupt program or data. If it is hardware, the instruction can be restarted, in case it was a transient problem. With a software fault, all that can really be done is to reset stack areas, note the failure and restart at a known point (i.e. execute the STOP instruction and wait for the next interrupt).

If everything is bad, a software reset may be called for. This is achieved by noting the time and nature of the fault in the system parameter's memory area, masking out all interrupts and placing the processor in a halted state by executing the HALT instruction. With the processor halted, the external sanity timer will expire and reset the system.

Other exceptions

The ACFAIL* signal is routed through to the processor to generate a level 7 non-maskable interrupt. The software handler brings the system down after updating the system mailbox. The MC68000 processor traps other exception conditions and allows their separate handling.

Some errors, e.g. divide by zero, misaligned addressing and check bounds violation, are primarily due to hardware faults. All 256 vectors are handled, albeit with a general handler that simply notes the exception and returns. This is essential because any vector could be selected if there was an external hardware fault during a vectored interrupt acknowledgement cycle. For this reason, an autovectored interrupt hardware scheme is used. This limits the choice to the vector for that particular interrupt level and does not use an externally supplied vector to find the exception handler. However all the vectors are covered in case of a hardware fault.

Improving fault tolerance

This example shows how careful software design can use simple hardware facilities provided by the VMEbus to design a system capable of detecting failures and indicating where data have been lost or are unreliable. Its software philosophy, of designing reliability in at the beginning, differentiates it from other implementations based around a similar hardware configuration. However, such integrity cannot be 100% guaranteed. The system still has many single point failures, such as the processor, static memory or even the VMEbus backplane itself. A failure in any one of these units causes the system to, at best, miss data or simply lock up the complete system. To improve fault tolerance, the single point failures must be eliminated by providing redundant systems to automatically replace failed units. This can be performed at many levels within the design, depending on the required reliability and system importance.

EDC and battery backed up memory

As previously mentioned, error detecting and correcting (EDC) memory uses extra memory bits to mathematically encode checking data which allow the data to be reconstituted if a failure has occurred. This, coupled with battery backed up RAM, allows a processor to shut itself down by dumping its internal registers into memory and then halting. On restart, the contents are reloaded and the processor carries on as before.

This technique can be used to allow a second redundant processor to replace a faulty processor. It requires that both processors have access to the same memory and that this memory is used for program execution. The VMEbus is an obvious choice for this bus but it does have the performance impact associated with program execution across the bus. An alternative may be to use the VSB to provide an alternative route.

It is interesting to note that the reliability of modern memory technology has improved so much that many systems disable any parity checking in favour of reduced access times and greater system performance.

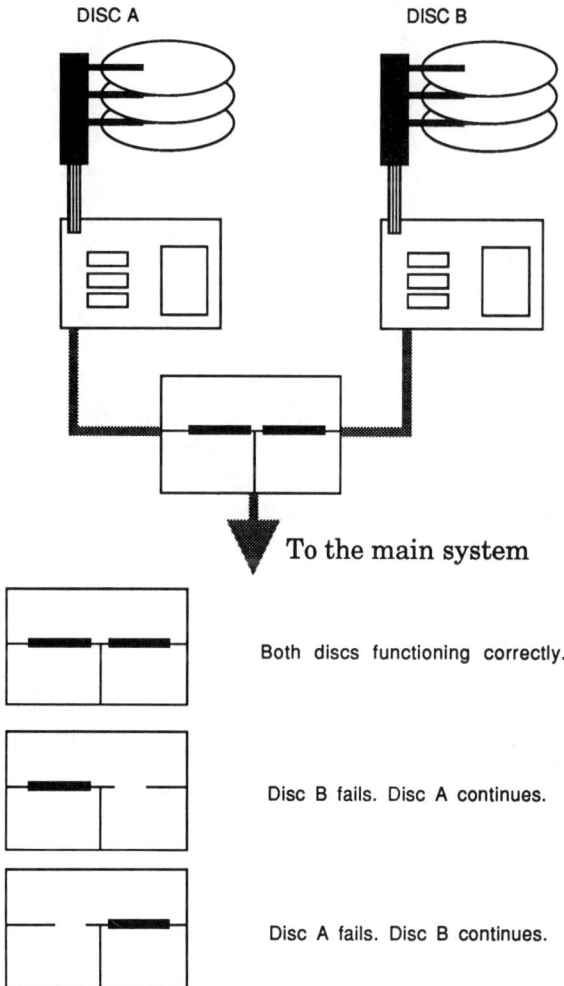

Figure 14.4 *A 'mirror' disc system*

Power supplies

The VMEbus provides a standby 5 V rail and a power fail signal ACFAIL★ to allow power supply failures to be easily handled. A more recent trend in critical systems is the use of uninterruptable power supplies, which use batteries to back up a more standard mains electrical supply. Such power supplies are rated at so many amp-hours, in similar fashion to batteries, which specifies the time a certain current can be supplied. The designer then has to decide how long the batteries have to last before the mains supply can be restored or replaced by an external generator. Small versions are now commonly used in personal computer environments to prevent sudden failures from losing data entered or created over many hours.

Mirror discs

Mass storage is another weak link, due to the mechanical nature of the disc. A common technique is to use a disc controller which drives two winchesters or floppy discs, where exact copies of the data are maintained on both discs. Because the data storage format has extensive error detecting and correcting codes associated with each sector, the controller can detect and correct any errors. If an error occurs which cannot be corrected, data are taken from the good disc to maintain integrity. An error is then flagged so that the faulty disc can be replaced and the 'mirror' status restored. A typical system is depicted in Figure 14.4.

Many systems use a combination of uninterruptable power supplies and mirror discs to provide a pseudo fault tolerant configuration. History or log files record every transaction or command received from each terminal. These files are stored on both mirror discs and updated continually. The operating system reacts to a power failure by first saving the current terminal displays and system status and then shutting down the system, in an orderly manner, before the battery backed up power supply fails. When the power supply is restored, the history files are used to reconstruct the database to its status immediately before the failure. In this way, the system restores itself and can be described as fault tolerant, albeit partially, as it was non-functional during the power failure.

These three techniques provide redundancy for the three main system areas forming the weak links in any VMEbus system reliability chain.

While providing system backup in these areas will improve system reliability, it does not provide full fault tolerance. It is generally accepted that systems described as fault tolerant have a high availability— individual component failures do not disable the system. For such systems, redundancy must be applied to all areas of the design, allowing any system fault to be recognized, the faulty component to be either replaced or disconnected, and the system restored to the same condition prior to the failure without losing or corrupting any system data. In the meantime, the system must still be available to its users, albeit possibly with some performance degradation, although this is dependent on system design.

The use of redundancy throughout the system is essential to ensure that there is no single point of failure. While EDC RAM, uninterruptable supplies and mirror discs are necessary features of a fault tolerant system, redundant processors and processor bus systems have to be designed which can detect a processor failure and prevent a VMEbus failure from locking up a system.

Redundant buses

The VMEbus provides a central communication link between VMEbus processor boards and, if it fails, will cause chaos within the system. Even if the rest of the system is backed up by redundancy, the use of a single VMEbus backplane can prevent its use and, therefore, multiple communication paths must be used as shown in Figure 14.5.

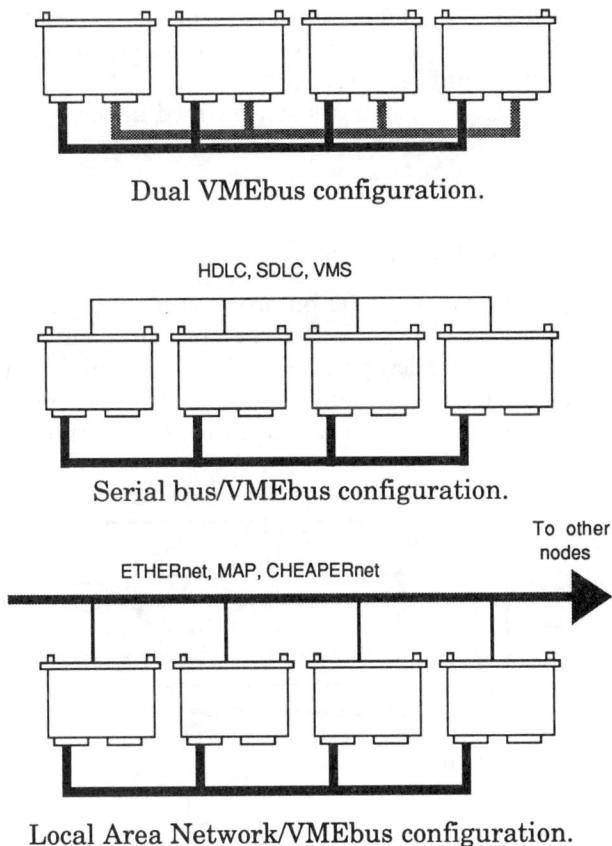

Dual VMEbus configuration.

Serial bus/VMEbus configuration.

Local Area Network/VMEbus configuration.

Figure 14.5 *Examples of redundant bus systems*

The obvious solution is to implement dual VMEbus systems, where processors can communicate over two separate independent buses. For a bus failure to have the minimum possible effect on system throughput, the combined used bus bandwidth must not exceed 100% of a single VMEbus.

An alternative for the redundant bus is VMS, which uses a serial link to pass data and interrupts. Its transfer rate is slower than that of the VMEbus, which would mean a reduced throughput if the VMEbus were to fail. In comparison to using dual VMEbuses, it is simpler to implement, needing only a serial link rather than a full backplane.

Detecting processor failures

There are two methods normally used to detect processor failures: the first is to run two processors in lock step, comparing their output signals to detect errors, and the second is to run the same software task on two independent processor units, comparing the resulting memory structures. Any discrepancy indicates a failure.

Software techniques, similar to those described in the data recorder example, can be used to provide extra confidence with such processor boards.

Lock stepping MC68020 processors

A pair of MC68020 or MC68030 32-bit processors can be configured to run as a redundant pair in lock step because of their interrelated deterministic state machine design. A typical block diagram is shown in Figure 14.6. This means that if inputs to each machine are synchronized to a common clock edge, the internal functions will execute synchron-

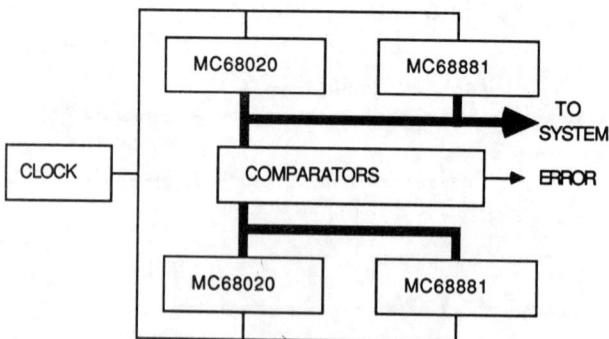

Figure 14.6 *A redundant processing element*

ously and allow the valid comparison of external output signals, such as the address and data buses. A simple flip–flop can be used in most cases.

Figure 14.7 shows a circuit for synchronizing the ADDRESS STROBE signal for a peripheral such as an MC68881 floating point coprocessor. However, this causes a wait state to be inserted in the cycle. This does not greatly affect performance because peripherals, like the MC68881, are calculation bound rather than data bound, and the MC68020 and MC68030 have an on-chip instruction cache to reduce such performance degradation.

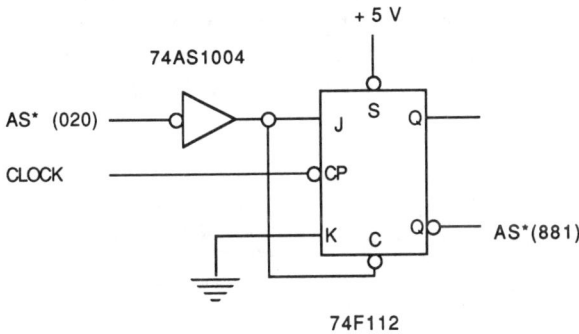

Figure 14.7 *Address strobe synchronizing logic*

The most difficult problem to overcome with lock stepping is the reset initialization sequence, which must set up both the visible and invisible registers.

The programming model can easily be set by a sequence of MOVE instructions. The on-chip cache can be initialized by enabling the cache and generating a code sequence of 128 NOP instructions. To initialize the invisible internal registers, the BFFFO (bit field first find one) instruction with a suitable addressing mode (i.e. address register indirect, with a 32-bit displacement) will initialize all internal registers. The data output buffer can be initialized by executing a MOVE instruction. Alternatively, the Long Bus Cycle Stack Frame, caused by a bus error that is not on an instruction boundary, can be used as an initialization model. The stack frame holds 46 words containing the entire contents of all internal registers. Once generated, all processors can build this frame on their stack and return from the exception. This restarts the cycle, generates the frame again and allows software to remove it from the stack and start code execution proper. However, all processors have now been internally initialized and the comparator logic can be switched on. Similar techniques can be used to initialize peripherals like the MC68881 using the FRESTORE frame restore instruction.

When processors are run in lock step, it is important that each processor node is of the same revision: part of the contents of the stack frame is a mask revision number. Failure to match would be detected as a fault by the comparator logic and therefore it is important that all processors in redundant pairs are of the same mask revision. This can be checked by inspection of the mask set number marked on the top of every device.

Memory structure comparison

An alternative to checking processor boards at the component processor level is to check their integrity by allowing two processor nodes to process data and comparing the results. An extreme example of this is the triplex system, used in the aviation industry, where three system 'vote' to implement a majority decision.

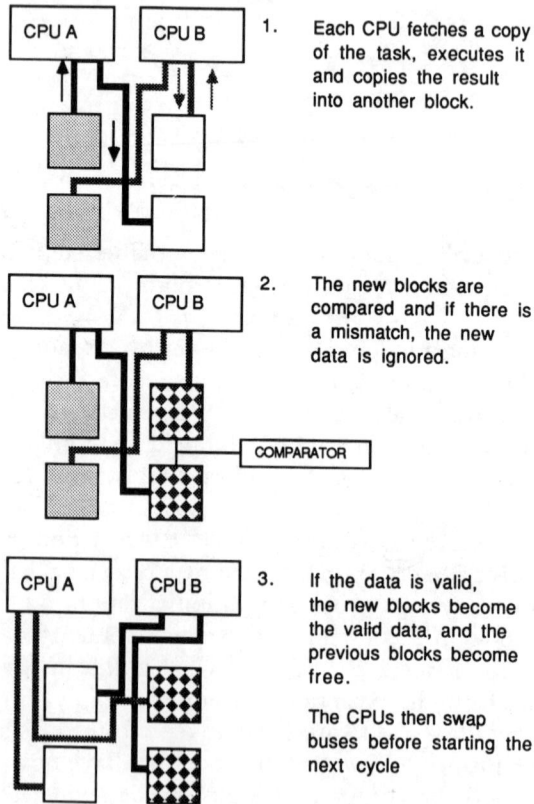

Figure 14.8   *A fault tolerant system using dual processors and memory comparison*

With two processing nodes, four memory areas with battery back up and error detection and correction are used. The mechanism used is shown in Figure 14.8. Two contain valid data from the last successful operation. The other two are then used to hold the results from the next operation. Each processor writes the results into each area and the memory structures are checked. If they are valid, the data from the first two areas are written to main menu and the operation acknowledged as complete; the second two areas are marked as holding the last successful operation. Every time this operation is completed, the processors swap buses so that a bus failure can also be detected. In the event of a failure, there are two copies of known valid data to restart from.

These four memory areas can be implemented within a single global memory area accessed from a single VMEbus by using separate address modifiers to select the appropriate memory block as shown in Figure 14.9. However, if the VMEbus locks up, the entire system crashes and will not recover. To provide an alternative route in case of VMEbus lock up, several VMEbus links or backup are required in the form of alternative buses such as VMS or VSB.

This system does not require the use of lock stepped redundant pairs,

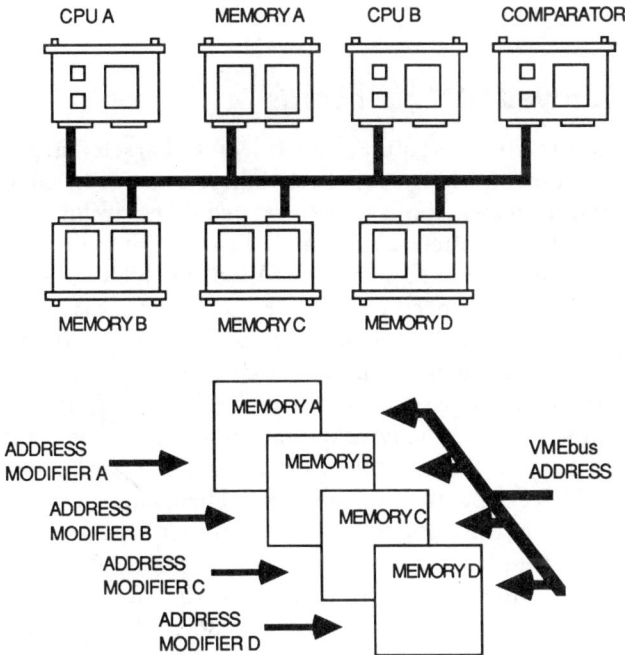

Figure 14.9 *A VMEbus implementation for a fault tolerant system using memory comparison*

but they are often used to provide very early fault warning and protect against both processor boards failing in the same manner.

Multiprocessor systems

The memory structures checking technique is a multiprocessor solution where at least two processors are used. Many fault tolerant systems use multiple processor nodes which perform error checking functions and are on standby to replace faulty units. The processor nodes are designed so that defective units can be electrically isolated from the system and the task running rescheduled to another processor node.

The normal algorithm used is similar to that employed to solve queuing problems in banks and post offices. A single queue, with all the available tasks, is maintained and, as each processor node finishes a task, the task at the head of the queue is dispatched. Removing a faulty node, providing there is at least one node functional, simply reduces the throughput and does not halt the system. Designing the nodes for 'hot' insertion even allows board replacement to be performed without halting the system. Unfortunately, VMEbus does not cater for 'hot' insertion and is generally not used for such applications. Many commercial designs use a proprietary bus with these special features.

Military approved VMEbus boards

Many applications do not require fault tolerant characteristics but do, nevertheless, require a certain level of reliability. This is particularly true for military and high risk applications. In such cases, military specification VMEboards are often used. Such boards are built to certain standards using components approved to MIL SPEC 883C, BS or CECC standards. To meet these specifications, devices and boards are specified to wider temperature limits; they are also specially screened and all the results documented, allowing complete tracing of any component to its manufacturing batch and associated reliability data. Such standards are conservative in nature and many of the techniques used for commercial products, such as double height sockets to allow extra components to be routed under EPROMs, are not allowed. This tends to restrict the functionality of many military versions of commercial boards. It is not uncommon for a single high density VMEbus processor board to be replaced by three military boards to achieve the same functionality. Despite being more expensive, such VMEbus boards are found in many military applications. Radstone Technology of the UK and Dy-4 of Canada both have extensive ranges of state–of–the–art military VMEbus boards, in addition to their commercial product offerings.

Many applications where military boards are used simply require VMEbus boards that can survive more rigorous environmental conditions than are normally specified. Wider operating temperatures and shock specifications are typical. Because of the high costs involved, an alternative solution has arisen, where a commercial product is used in special chambers providing environmentally controlled conditions. Such chambers regulate temperature and humidity and also use suspension systems to reduce shock levels. This technique is often used for VMEbus systems in naval vessels, where systems are protected from the hostile sea water environment by such chambers. The cost of the chamber is recovered from the savings incurred from using commercial boards instead of military approved ones. Roadside installations are another example of this technique.

15
Networking

Networking describes a method of providing communications between various nodes, for example terminals, computers and printers, allowing them to be accessed by the individual members of the network. Such systems are often used within VMEbus designs where there are multiple VMEbus nodes within the system or where the system has to be spread over different physical locations. This chapter describes the basic principles behind networks and gives examples of currently used techniques.

WANs and LANs

There are two basic types of networks used today. Wide Area Networks (WANs) are used to transfer data between nodes that are geographically separated. A great variety of media can be used for such links, such as telephone lines, satellite systems and microwave links. Such facilities are often provided and controlled by the national PTT (public telephone and telegraphic) companies.

Local Area Networks (LANs) are used to join nodes within a single area or building. They are usually controlled by the user and use many different protocols, ranging from international standards to proprietary one-off networks.

Network topologies

Networks can fall into four main organizations:

- point–to–point
- star

- ring
- backbone.

In all of these networks, data are passed around the topology either in asynchronous or in synchronous serial form. The topology refers to the physical arrangement of cabling.

In the point-to-point network, every node has a direct link to every other. A simple intercom, used between a garage and a home, is a good example. However, as the number of nodes increases, so does the number of connections. As the complexity geometrically rises with the number of nodes, such networks can reach the point where they become impractical due to wiring complexities. Figure 15.1 shows how this complexity can increase.

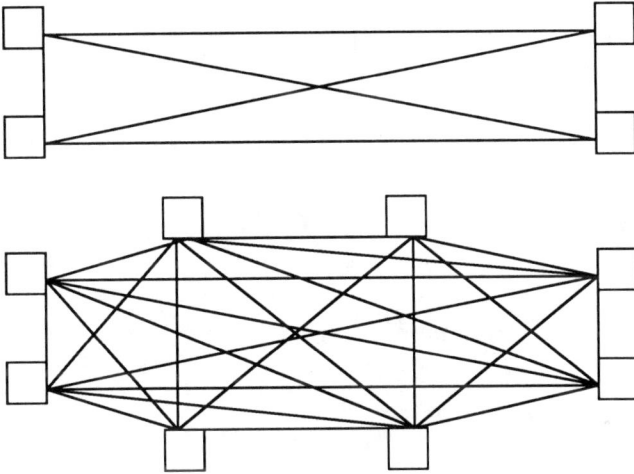

Figure 15.1 *Point-to-point networks*

A method of solving this is to use a star network, Figure 15.2, where the internode communications go through a central point which has a

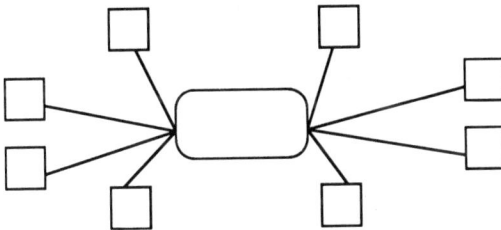

Figure 15.2 *Star network*

single link to all the nodes, which simplifies the wiring. However, this topology limits the communication between the nodes to the number that the central point can handle. An example is a telephone exchange which controls the calls from one telephone to another.

The third topology uses a ring, shown in Figure 15.3, where each node passes the data around the ring until it is received by the recipient node. Such ring systems have extremely simple wiring systems, but as the number of nodes passing data increases, performance decreases. Ring topologies are also susceptible to node failures—if a node fails, or the ring is severed by mechanical means, no data transfer can be achieved until the ring is remade.

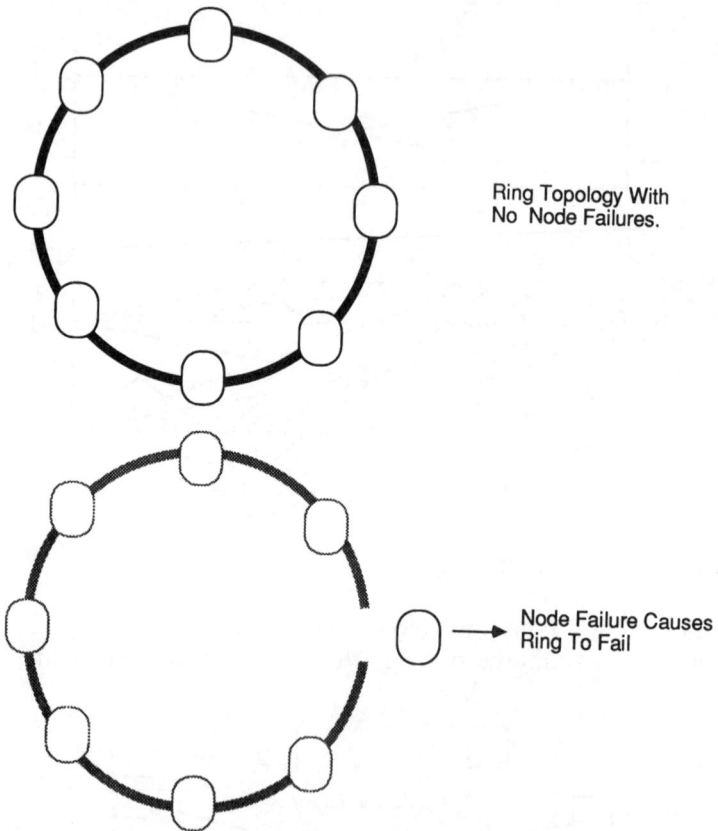

Ring Topology With
No Node Failures.

Node Failure Causes
Ring To Fail

Figure 15.3 *Ring topologies*

The fourth backbone organization, depicted in Figure 15.4, uses a single connection on to which the nodes tap. A good example of this is a

VMEbus system, where the boards are the nodes and the backplane becomes the backbone of the system.

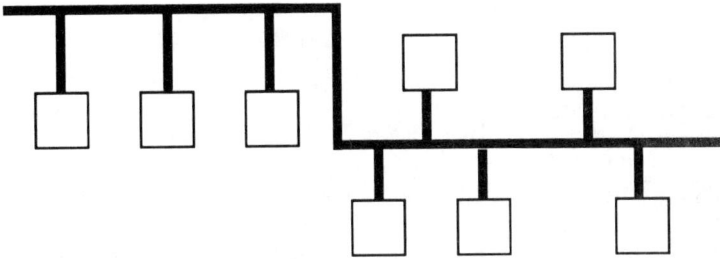

Figure 15.4 *Backbone topology*

Point-to-point and star topologies

For computer system networks, the point-to-point organization is usually only practical for very small networks (less than four nodes) and often uses simple asynchronous or synchronous serial communication to transfer data. Large systems are not really often used due to the complexity of the wiring and the number of communication channels required.

While the star system is less complex to implement, it is not as common because of the wiring costs and the complexity of the central node, when compared with the more common ring and backbone systems. It also has a single point of failure at its central node, which can cause system reliability problems.

The ring topology

The ring topology uses a circular structure, where each node receives the messages from its neighbour and passes them on to the next member of the ring. It potentially has the lowest overhead and the highest throughput of all the topologies—each node has an input and output which can be within the same cable. Such ring structures can greatly reduce the wiring needed to implement networks.

Data are passed circularly round the ring until the sender receives it, together with an acknowledgement that the data have been received. Data can also be broadcast to grouped nodes, at which each recipient reads the passing data. Data transfer rates do not decrease under load due to this circular approach.

The main disadvantage is the dependence of the ring's integrity on each node. If a node fails, the whole network collapses because data sent by a node around the ring would not return and thus complete their transfer. Similar results occur if a node is physically disconnected or the ring is physically broken. To solve this problem requires redundant hardware or additional wiring to remake the connections, should a failure occur.

This ring structure is used by IBM and within the Cambridge and Manchester Ring systems.

The backbone topology

The backbone technology uses a single bus on to which each node connects. This arrangement has the lowest cabling cost and is extremely flexible. Nodes can easily be added or removed and there is no single point of failure. The main disadvantage is the increased overhead required to control access to the bus to therefore prevent message corruption due to simultaneous transmission by more than one node; this overhead may limit throughput. Examples of backbone systems are Ethernet and MAP (Manufacturer's Automation Protocol).

In practice, real life networks are constructed, evolved or developed using combinations of the above topologies. Small networks, using point-to-point communications, often evolve into star networks with the addition of a more powerful processor which starts to function as a file server or central processor. Further communication to a larger network based around Ethernet, for example, further complicates the issue. In such evolutionary developments, much of the data traffic is simply being passed from one network to another to achieve a particular route. Often, if the network had originally been designed with expansion in mind, a more efficient final result could be supported.

SNA, XNS, TCP/IP and ISO OSI

Topologies describe the physical connections between the components of a network. To pass data, each node is required to use standard data formats, commands and responses. This has been performed haphazardly in the past with proprietry systems such as IBM's System Network Architecture (SNA), Xerox's XNS and the US Defense Department's TCP/IP. Unfortunately, their definitions have either not been as comprehensive or as open as the industry has required to provide compatibility, resulting in interest in the International Standards Organisation (ISO) Open System Interconnect (OSI) model.

The OSI model or stack has seven layers, as shown in Figure 15.5, which define the services performed at each layer to allow the transmission of data. Each layer acts on the data to provide data frames in a common format which are then transferred across the physical network.

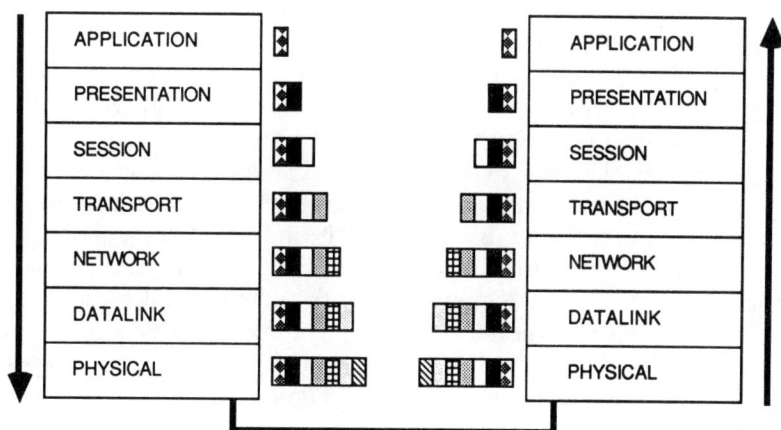

Figure 15.5 *The OSI seven layer stack*

Level 7 is the APPLICATION layer which provides services to process the exchanged information. It is concerned with resource sharing, file transfer and database management.

The PRESENTATION layer formats the data and controls the dialogue between the network nodes.

Layer 5 is the SESSION layer, and is concerned with controlling connection between nodes and access to the lower levels.

The TRANSPORT layer provides functions for error free data delivery such as flow control, error recovery and acknowledgement.

Layer 3, the NETWORK layer, provides the routeing mechanisms between two nodes.

The DATALINK layer controls the rules of transmission on the physical medium such as packet formats, access rights, and error detection and correction.

Layer 1, the PHYSICAL layer, provides the actual mechanical and electrical interconnection between nodes. When data are transferred, they are passed down the seven layers, transmitted and received by the recipient node. They are then processed in the reverse order until they are presented at the second node.

There are currently three protocols defined by the IEEE for LAN OSI model layers 1 and 2:

1   802.3 defines a CSMA/CD or 'Ethernet' scheme
2   802.4 defines a token–passing bus used by MAP
3   802.5 is a token–passing ring.

Each protocol uses a different mechanism for controlling access to the LAN and offers different operational characteristics.

802.3 CSMA/CD

CSMA/CD stands for Carrier Sense Multiple Access with Collision Detect and refers to the mechanism used by IEEE802.3 to control and prevent message corruption. It was derived from the Ethernet specification developed by XEROX and DEC.

The main characteristic of 802.3 is that any station can send a message at any time, irrespective of the line status. If a station wishes to send a message, it listens to see if the line is busy. If it is not, it sends the message and listens to check that no one else is transmitting and therefore corrupting the data. If someone is simultaneously transmitting, the collision is detected and the message jammed to indicate to the recipient that this has occurred. The sender then backs off the line, waits a random time and attempts to retransmit the message. This is shown in Figure 15.6.

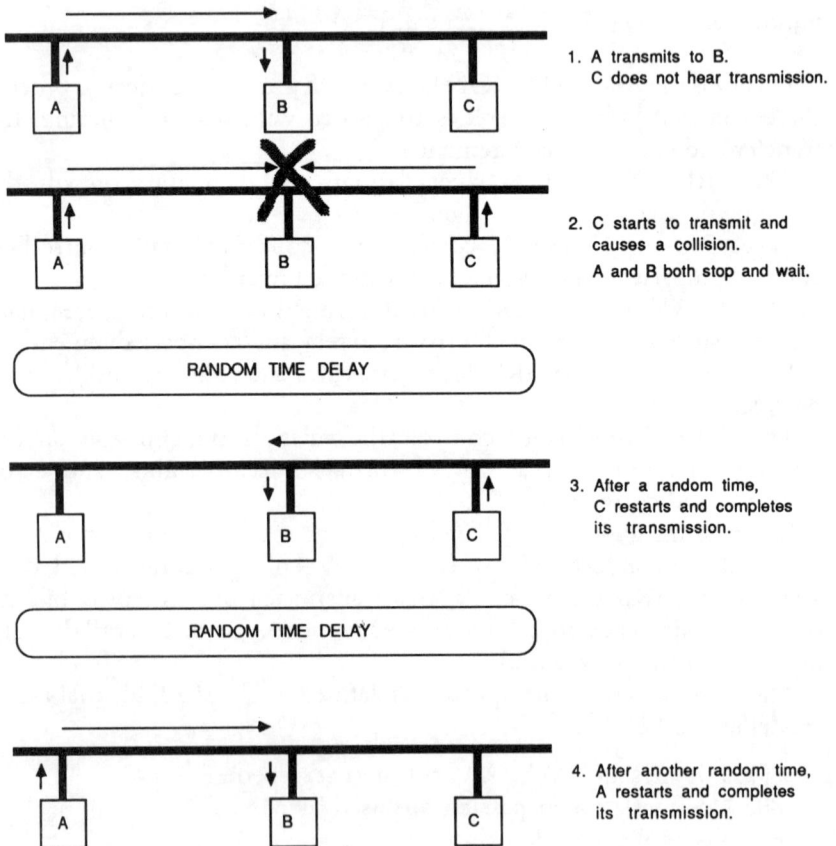

1. A transmits to B.
   C does not hear transmission.

2. C starts to transmit and causes a collision.
   A and B both stop and wait.

RANDOM TIME DELAY

3. After a random time, C restarts and completes its transmission.

RANDOM TIME DELAY

4. After another random time, A restarts and completes its transmission.

Figure 15.6   *CSMA protocol mechanisms*

If no collision is detected, the sender keeps transmitting until the complete message is sent. If the line is busy, the sender waits for a random time and tries again.

CSMA/CD imposes a limitation on the physical length of a network by the propagation delay for collision detection; this limitation depends on the nature of the cabling used for the physical layer, e.g. twisted pair, coaxial cable, etc.

CSMA/CD also has another characteristic in that it is indeterminate. The time taken to send a message can vary and in some cases may not even be received due to the high number of collisions caused when many nodes try to use the network. Every time an attempt is made, the message is aborted through a collision till the node either times out or the message's relevance is lost. The threshold for such performance degradation is dependent on the number of nodes, the message length and the number of attempted accesses per unit time. Once this threshold has been reached, the overall system performance and throughput degrades dramatically. A maximum of about 60 nodes is recommended for many networks, although heavy utilization can start affecting a system with as little as ten nodes. These characteristics effectively rule out 802.3 for real time process control applications—with such a system, it would be impossible to guarantee if a message would actually be received or when. For data interchange, this can be tolerated.

There are many types of cabling used for 802.3 networks, ranging from telephone twisted pair cabling for Starlan, and thin and high grade coaxial cable for Cheapernet and Ethernet, to cable television cable for full broadband implementations. Although the term Ethernet is frequently used in conjunction with the 802.3 standard, the Ethernet specification differs slightly and this reference is technically invalid.

802.4 Token-passing bus

With the increasing demand for LANs, especially in the area of industrial control, the unsuitability of CSMA/CD as a controlling mechanism prompted General Motors to adopt the token-passing bus for the MAP network.

With 802.4, the backbone structure normally associated with 802.3 is used but it is arranged as a logical ring structure. The various nodes are physically connected on to a bus but are all allocated a priority so that each node knows the previous and next nodes in the chain. This then creates the logical ring.

A token is passed around the logical ring, as shown in Figure 15.7, and its possession is required before a sender node can transmit data. This continues until all the data have been transferred or the allotted token possession time has expired. The token is then passed to the next member and the previous sender must wait until it next receives the token before transmitting again.

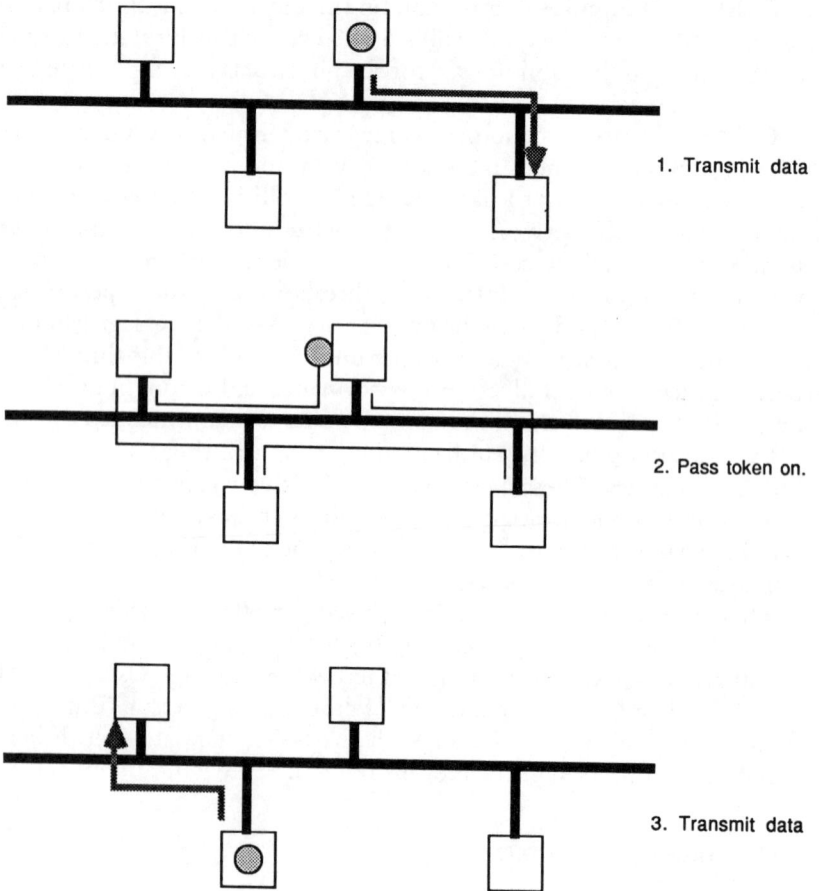

Figure 15.7   *Token-passing bus protocol*

If a node is missing, negotiation takes place within the network to determine which node receives the token next. This means that the logical ring can add or remove nodes dynamically, without having to use bridging hardware.

The system response is deterministic and depends on variables such as the number of nodes, priority and the time slot value. If the backbone is cut, the individual halves remake the logical ring and carry on with the networks, albeit separately.

The MAP standard specifies all the layers from 1 to 7 and allows equipment from many different manufacturers to communicate with each other, enabling large multi-vendor systems to the designed. Many of these component systems are built around VMEbus products; for example, Motorola's MC68824 Token Bus Controller provides hardware support for the lower levels of the OSI MAP model and is used on the MVME372 MAP interface board, which provides the interface for many VMEbus systems.

The TOP (Technical and Office Protocol) comprises the higher layers of MAP, with the 802.3 CSMA/CD protocol replacing the token-passing bus.

802.5 Token-passing ring

The token-passing ring is used by IBM within IBM networks. It is similar to 802.4, in that a token is passed around to control access, but differs in that the ring is physical not logical. Each node receives data and then passes it on. To control access to the ring, a token is passed around the nodes and its possession is a prerequisite for transmitting data. This provides a collision free network allowing high transfer rates. The main problem comes from maintenance of the ring's integrity in the cause of node failure, disconnection or introduction. Relays are often used to

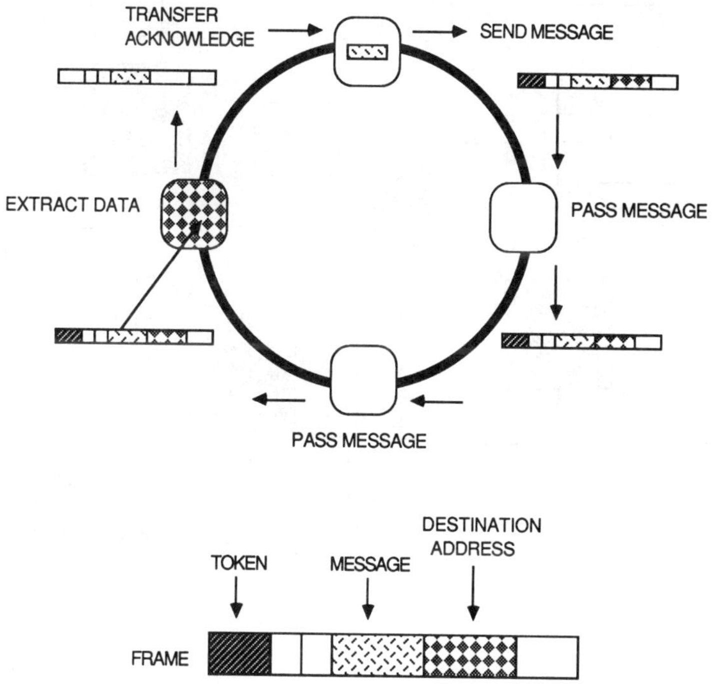

Figure 15.8 *Token ring protocol*

provide ring bypasses to allow the removal of nodes.

The system works by a node deciding that it wishes to transmit data. This is shown in Figure 15.8. It then captures the circulating free token, and then sets the token busy bit and transmits a data frame. This frame circulates around the ring and eventually will return to the originator. The originator strips off the token busy bit, freeing the token for another node to use.

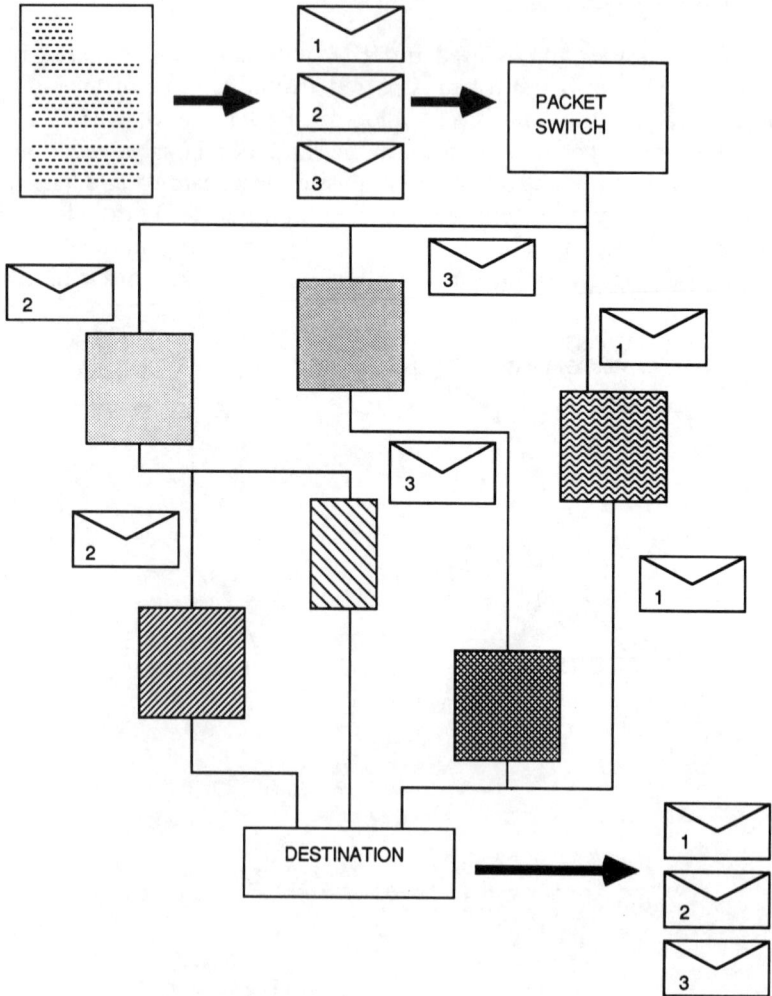

Figure 15.9 *X.25 packet switch*

WANs

Wide area networks provide links between LANs and often cross geographical boundaries. The most commonly used WAN is X.25, which transmits data in packets which may be routed through many different networks before arriving at its destination. As each packet is received, the destination sends an acknowledgement to indicate that all is well. Because of the many possible routes, the packets may arrive non-sequentially or require resending before the complete message is accepted. Figure 15.9 shows how data can travel through such a network. Many PTTs provide X.25 links working up to 64 Kbaud and using standard telephone links. Accunet, Telenet, Transpac and Tymnet are all examples of such services.

A new development in this area is the use of Integrated Services Digital Networking (ISDN) which uses existing twisted pair telephone cabling and digital techniques to carry voice as well as data, network signalling and maintenance information. This allows, for example, two colleagues

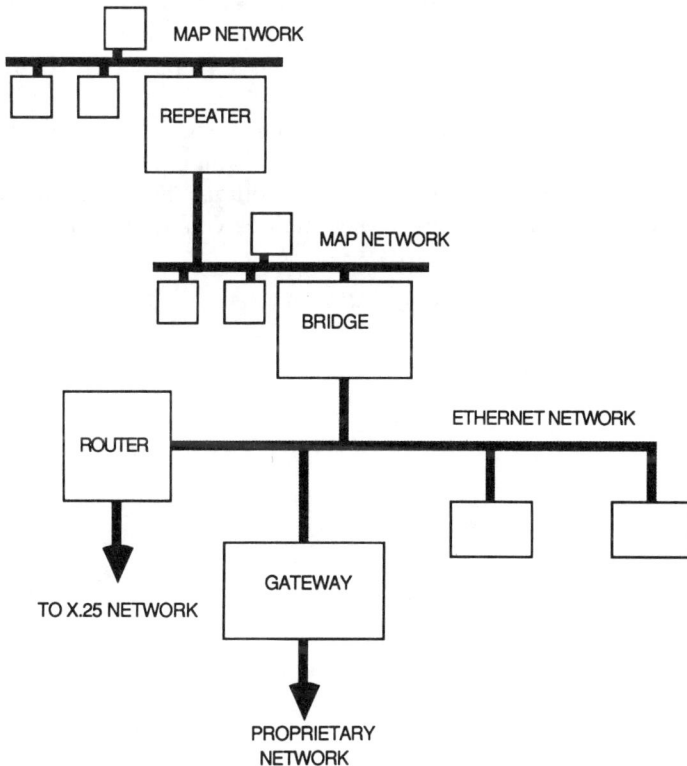

Figure 15.10 *Multi-protocol network using gateways, bridges and routers*

to talk over the telephone while passing information between terminals simultaneously. Another use is a digitizing pad, which allows diagrams to be drawn and transmitted during a telephone conversation.

It is extremely likely that VMEbus systems will start offering ISDN interfaces as well as the more normal terminal connections in the future.

Connecting WANs and LANs

WANs and LANs can be connected by several methods, depending on the similarity between the two networks being connected. Figure 15.10 shows an example configuration involving repeaters, bridges, routers and gateways. A repeater provides an interconnection at the physical level only, and such interconnections are completely transparent to the user. A bridge provides a connection at the next layer where data frames and sizes are consistent between the two networks. A connection between 802.3 and 802.4 networks is a good example. Connection at layer 3 provides a router, which could connect an X.25 packet switch network with a token bus MAP system. The final connection is a gateway where there is little or no similarity and extensive protocol conversion takes place.

The interconnection systems are often designed around VMEbus systems with particular VMEbus boards providing the connections to the networks and a central processor controlling the required protocol conversions. Additional connections/facilities can be provided by adding the appropriate VMEbus boards.

16
Future developments

Processor developments

The VMEbus is now accepted as the most widely used 16/32-bit bus standard and its market and market share continue to grow year by year. With over 300 manufacturers worldwide producing products, it now offers an extremely wide choice to the designer.

More and more integration

The recent exponential growth in the translator density that came from the semiconductor industry has provided the high density integrated circuits that are needed to increase the functionality appearing on VMEbus boards. For example, the members of the MC68000 family have increased in complexity: the MC68000 integrated about 68 000 transistors, the MC68020 and MC68030 increased this to 200 000 and 300 000 respectively, while the forthcoming MC68040 has taken this figure to beyond 1 000 000! The technology appears to be able to go beyond this. Reports of research laboratories producing devices 1.2 inches square containing over 6 million active transistors are now appearing. Memory densities have gone from 1 Kbyte to 4 and 16 Mbytes in a matter of a few years. The development and introduction of such parts has accelerated dramatically resulting in shorter design cycles and product lifetimes. For many applications where it was initially economic to build a system from discrete components, the only cost effective solution now is to use off-the-shelf board level products wherever possible.

These developments have fuelled a similar acceleration within the VMEbus products available since its inception. For instance, the first VMEbus processor boards such as the MVME101 simply had an 8 MHz MC68000 processor, two serial ports, a parallel port, a VMEbus interface and eight 28-pin sockets for ROM and static RAM. In 1982, this was state-of-the-art design. Within three years, boards were appearing which offered a 10 or 12 MHz 68010 with 2/3 serial ports, parallel port, 256K EPROM, 512K or 1 Mbyte of dynamic memory, real-time clock and a winchester disc interface. Such boards effectively replaced three or four of the older generation boards.

This trend has continued unabated: boards are now available which pack a 32-bit MC68030 processor with floating point coprocessor running at 33 MHz clock rates, up to 8 Mbytes of RAM, 512 Kbytes of EPROM, serial ports, VMEbus interface, VSB interface, Ethernet link, winchester interface and real-time clock. Such boards can provide a complete UNIX system without any other additional boards. Such systems easily outperform minicomputers costing more than ten times the price. This trend is not going to stop. The new generations of processor and memory chips will continue to fuel this race towards higher integration.

Faster and faster processors

When the VMEbus first appeared, many sections of the electronics industry were extremely dubious about the need for a high performance 32-bit bus standard. This feeling was based on the gap between the performance offered by the VMEbus and that available from the current technology. An example was the attitude towards processor clock speeds: many of the excuses put forward against the design of microprocessor systems running at 8, 10 or 12 MHz seem to be forgotten when compared with the latest generation designs running at over 33 MHz. Figure 16.1 depicts the performance growth within the MC680x0 processor family. The availability of faster processors coupled with the pioneering spirit of some manufacturers have provided the lower-cost workstations and computer systems to provide the tools necessary to aid and simplify such designs to the point where they now become commonplace. Although concern is expressed that the VMEbus does not provide sufficient bus bandwidth for these new generations, it should be remembered that the original concept for the bus was to provide a global message-passing bus, and not replace the local bus. Message-passing at over 30 Mbytes per second is still extremely good performance.

The advantage that the VMEbus offers to processor users is the ability to take advantage of the new faster processors by simply replacing a processor board, without having to replace other boards in the system. This increases the accessibility to the new technology without having the considerable costs of developing a state-of-the-art board with all the risks associated with it. By using such boards, the risk is taken by the board designers and manufacturers who have the necessary experience to be able to cope with the double edged sword of technology. Design at the

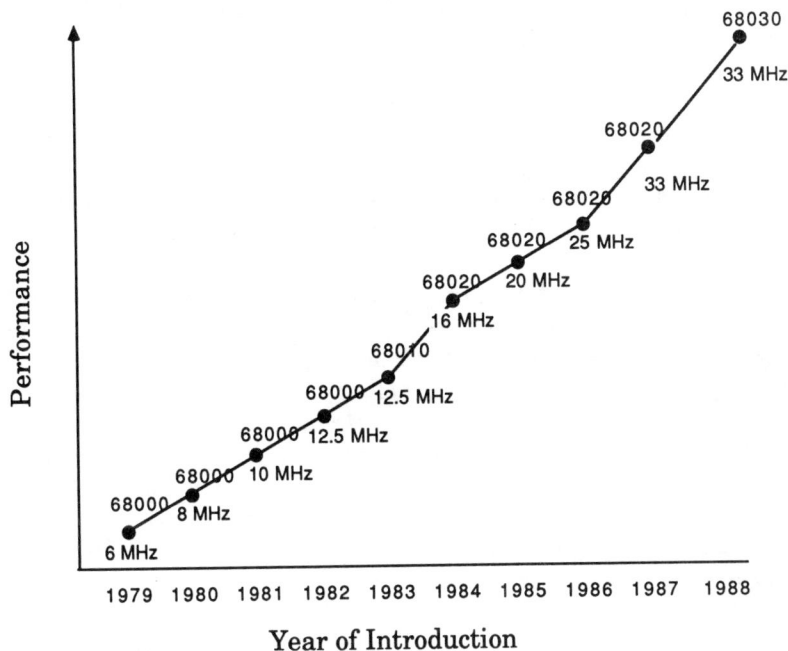

Figure 16.1 *32-bit genealogy*

initial introductory phase of a technology is always more difficult than when it matures. However, the commercial rewards can be extremely large, as shown by the spectacular growth of many start-up VMEbus companies. Although VMEbus is a mature bus standard, the processor families that use it are constantly being further developed.

RISC processors and the VMEbus

Up to about 1987, the majority of microprocessors used within the industry and within the VMEbus community were of a single generic architectural type. These were the CISC (Complex Instruction Set Computers) like the MC68000 family. Since 1987, an alternative processor architecture called RISC (Reduced Instruction Set Computer) has appeared and VMEbus boards with RISC processors from Motorola, AMD and MIPS are now coming on to the market.

CISC: the original architecture

Both architectures have been around a long time: the CISC architectures were the basis of the first 8-bit microprocessors and have since been developed into 32-bit processors such as the MC68020. The RISC was given its Harvard and Berkeley models in the early 1970s but has not really gained prominence within the industry until now. One of the reasons for this was compiler technology, which was not advanced enough to utilize such models efficiently. A second reason was the availability of cheap memory.

In early systems, one of the most expensive components was memory. By using powerful but complex instructions, program storage and memory requirements were reduced. This was beneficial not only in cost savings, but also in keeping program and data needs within a 64 Kbyte memory addressing map. Memory was slow and therefore gave microprocessor designers sufficient time to perform the complex in-struction decoding and execution before the next memory cycle. For some instructions, however, the MPU would need many clock cycles or would wait for memory fetches before it could complete an instruction execution. Both of these cases highlight the major bottlenecks in such a Von Neumann architecture: the serial flow of information from memory to instruction decoder to execution unit results in the overall performance being limited by the slowest member in the chain. As execution unit throughput increased, memory access speed became the limiting factor. It is for this reason that the MC68000 family uses a pipelined architecture which keeps an execution unit filled by pre-fetching instructions and using on-chip caches to provide a fast alternative supply of information. This increases system efficiency when memory fetches are slow or delayed through, for example, bus arbitration.

CISC programming models

In terms of programming models, CISC architectures have a relatively small number of registers which are limited in their functionality by dedicating them to specific roles, such as accumulators, address and data registers. Where there is an extreme case of register dedication, such as with the intel 8086/286/386 architectures, a large proportion of the instructions executed move data from one register to another allowing it to be manipulated by the next instruction. This register swapping is extremely wasteful of system performance and is minimized in the MC68000 family by the provision of eight general data and eight general address registers. There is a condition code register, usually updated after every instruction execution, although its contents may only be interro-gated when a program flow change is executed. It is interesting that the early 8-bit microprocessors did not automatically update this register; this feature only appeared in 16-bit microprocessors, such as the MC68000, where it meant that loops and branches took fewer instructions and therefore less memory storage and time to execute. There are also many addressing modes—the MC68020 has about 54, although the exact number is open to interpretation. All these complexities contributed to the dramatic increase in op code size, and currently instructions can take up to 10 bytes to store all their information.

To implement such architectures, instructions are decoded which then call microcode and nanocode sequences to be preloaded into ALUs etc. and then to be clocked through as shown in Figure 16.2. This results in instruction timings ranging from two to as many as 200 clocks to execute. As the architecture uses more hardware to reduce the Von Neumann bottlenecks, these areas of microcode become dramatically larger until the majority of the microprocessor silicon becomes essentially a ROM area. None of these instructions are hardwired, which makes single clock execution times difficult to achieve.

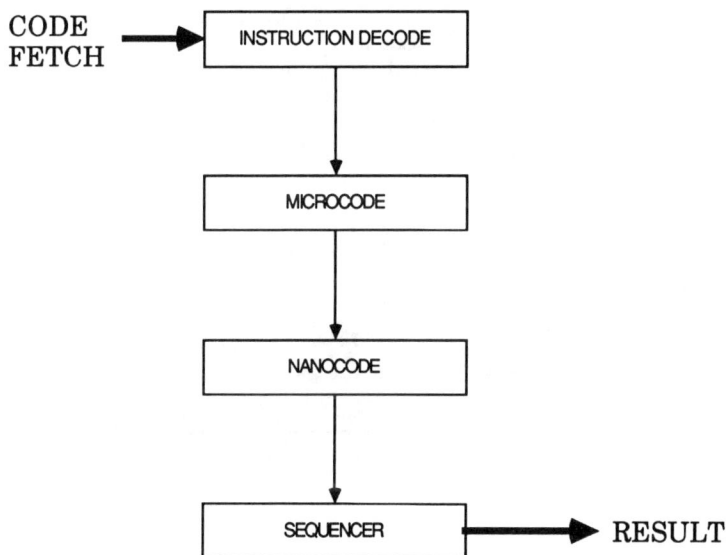

CODE FETCH → INSTRUCTION DECODE → MICROCODE → NANOCODE → SEQUENCER → RESULT

Figure 16.2 *Multi-cycle instruction execution for a CISC processor*

RISC: an alternative approach

The concept behind RISC architecture is to reduce the number of instructions and therefore the complexity of the microprocessor, hence the Reduced Instruction Set acronym. Simple instructions can be implemented in hardwired logic and executed in a single clock cycle. Although more instructions are required to achieve the same function of a more complex CISC op code, the faster total execution time improves performance. Memory is now inexpensive and, coupled with 4 Gbyte linear addressing ranges, additional storage is no longer a problem.

The Von Neumann bottleneck is solved by having separate data and program buses to external memory. This allows the simultaneous access of data and program and increases performance. Typical configurations are shown in Figure 16.3. Hardware design complexity is reduced by passing more responsibility to the software. Most RISC instruction sets and/or architectures are designed around compiler technology: in some current RISC systems, the internal synchronization of the processor is maintained by the compiler when it generates its object codes. This is often achieved by placing NOP op codes in a 'bubble', allowing the processor hardware to synchronize itself; however, this places tremendous responsibility on the compiler supplier who must ensure compatibility, prevents any hardcoding in assembler of time critical paths and poses serious questions for processor architecture development. The

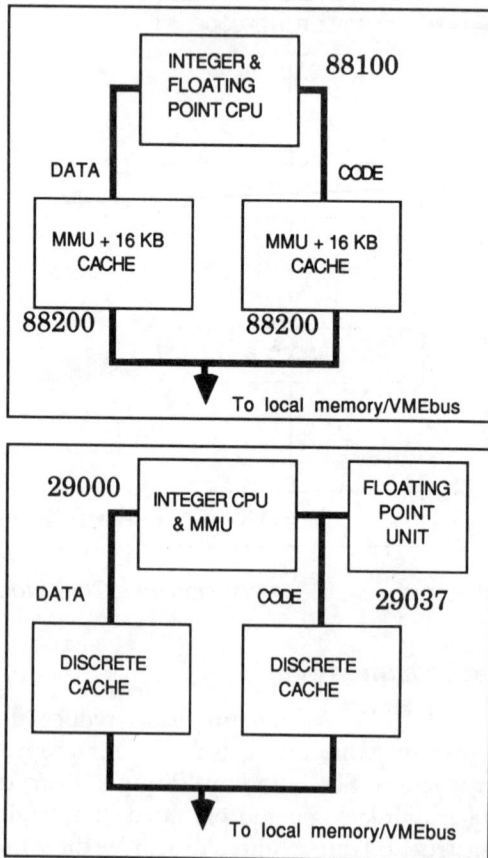

Figure 16.3 *The Motorola M88000 and the AMD29000 RISC processor configurations*

responsibility for interrupt handling is also given to the compiler writer: RISC hardware is designed to have a simple but very fast interrupt response. Interrupt latency is reduced as there are no complex instructions requiring multiple clocks to execute. There are no multiple interrupt levels or vectoring, and the time taken to recognize the exception is therefore reduced. The register set is immediately stored internally and the time consuming stacking operations of CISC architectures are therefore removed. As a result, response times of about 0.5 μs are achievable.

Why the interest in RISC?

The MC68020 and MC68030 state-of-the-art 32-bit CISC microprocessors have proved that the combination of well designed architecture and the right fabrication technology can offer performance rivalling mini- and super-minicomputers at a fraction of the cost. This has provided the catalyst for the market in UNIX systems and graphics workstations to grow rapidly in recent years. This growth, with its penetration into traditional mini- and super-minicomputer markets, has prompted the industry to look at alternative ways of increasing price performance over and above that currently available. Current predictions are that present ECL (emitter coupled logic) and bit-slice computers will be replaced in the 1990s by RISC and CISC microprocessor architectures. In addition, faster ECL and technologies such as gallium arsenide will provide the top of the range in performance. Underlying these predictions is a trend towards more performance. This growth will be exponential, as has already been seen within the MC68000 family, where faster clock speeds and new family members have offered a doubling of performance every 12 to 15 months.

Both CISC and RISC architectures are now limited by external memory performance: execution units can generally process data faster than external memory can supply it. With the RISC tenet of single clock instruction execution, memory fetches must take a single clock cycle to prevent execution times being delayed. The separate data and program buses associated with RISC architectures help solve this problem; consideration must also be given to how the system can supply data and instructions to a processor running at clock frequencies greater than 25 MHz within the single cycle limit. The new VMEbus processor boards that use these fast single clock per instruction CISC or RISC processors will almost certainly feature cache memory systems either integrated into the processor chip itself or as a discrete implementation. Such boards would offer 20–30 MIPS (million instructions per second) performance. A VMEbus rack with twenty processor boards could offer a system throughput of over 400 MIPS! With the MC68000 conservatively rated at

0.75 MIPS, this would be equivalent of 533 MC68000s working in parallel!

The VMEbus provides an ideal vehicle to enable these new generation processors to be used quickly and allow products to be brought to market quickly. The ability to simply change a processor to reconfigure a new hardware platform allows users access to this new technology without the risks and delays associated with designing their own boards.

The future for VMEbus is very bright indeed.

Appendix A: Common system errors

This appendix is devoted to describing and explaining the common system errors that cause most system problems. These errors have been grouped together under main general headings, although there is some overlap. An error may also have more than one symptom—for example, a bus error during the start-up phase of a debugger could cause a double bus fault and halt the processor. Under these conditions, the board would appear to have failed during power-up.

'Board fails on power-up'
1   Incorrect jumper and switch settings.
2   Memory chips inserted incorrectly.
3   Bent leads, wrong orientation, wrong socket, wrong type.
4   Blank EPROMs, odd and even byte EPROMs switched around, wrong access times.

'Bus error or timeout during memory access'
1   Access to non-existent memory
    This is usually caused by a programming error or missing boards. The bus timeout proves that the system watchdogs are correctly functioning and are preventing a 'hang-up'. If the system hangs up with no response, it is likely that there are no watchdogs functioning within the system. Likely causes are incorrect jumpering or control register settings or their corruption by software.
    If memory sockets are left for the user to populate with the various size memory chips required, the wrong size selection can effectively screen the memory: a board may be fitted with a 32K by 8 static RAM but if the size jumpering is for a 16K by 8 chip, this results in a 'missing' 16 Kbytes.
2   Incorrect address modifier
    The address modifier is presented with the address and a slave must match both of them before it will respond. The modifier sent depends on the address width used (16, 24 or 32 bits), the type of access

(USER, SUPERVISOR, PROGRAM or DATA) or be user-defined. These parameters change depending on the environment running at the time. Code which works under a debug monitor may fail under an operating system due to the change from SUPERVISOR to USER mode.

3   Bus arbitration problem: bus not granted or released within a timeout period.

    If the bus is not granted, the transfer cannot be completed and this results in a timeout. Typical bus arbitration problems are described later on.

4   Wrong data bus width used.

    e.g.   a 32-bit long-word access to an 8- or 16-bit slave

          a 16-bit access to an 8-bit slave.

5   Watchdog timeout periods too short for normal system response.

    The speed of a memory access across the VMEbus is dependent on the time taken to obtain the bus and complete a transfer. This time varies with system activity. The maximum time is defined by the watchdog timeout period, which may be set too short. Lengthening the period will therefore solve the problem.

6   Slow VMEbus slave response.

    This is similar to the previous problem. Again, lengthening the timeout period will solve it.

7   Faulty backplane.

    This is extremely rare, providing a good quality backplane is used.

8   Dual ported RAM not enabled.

    Many RAM and ROM banks are accessible from many sources: local RAM from the local processor and VMEbus, VSB memory from the VMEbus, etc. To allow such memory to be declared private to a processor, there are switches or control registers which disable such accesses. If memory can be accessed from one source but not the other, this is most likely to be the problem.

9   Uninitialized memory causing parity errors.

    When a parity protected board is powered up, the parity and data bits will both have random data stored. If the memory is not initialized, by writing data to every location prior to a read, a parity error can occur causing a bus error.

'Memory corruption'

1   Multiple slaves responding to same address information.

    If two or more slaves are responding to the same VMEbus access, the data read or written depend on the individual timings for each board, resulting in data inconsistency. This is usually caused by incorrect jumper settings or multiple mapped boards, which do not fully decode the address data. This forces the memory to be repeated on block boundaries right through the address map.

Another cause is the use of control registers to change the memory mapping of the slave. Again, these can be corrupted through software errors resulting in overlapping memory.

2   Missing or duplicating backplane termination.

These can cause corrupt data on the backplane during VMEbus transfers.

3   Timing problems: insufficient access time for the memory system.

If the DTACK★ signal is returned too early for the memory or peripheral chips being used, corrupt data can be returned or stored. Where empty sockets are available for the user to populate, jumpers are provided to select the DTACK★ for the IC's access time. Usually these are set incorrectly or the wrong chips used.

4   Faulty backplane.

Again this is rare, but does occasionally happen.

'No response to interrupts'

1   Interrupt level masked out.

Interrupts can be masked out by jumper settings, the processor interrupt mask or control register settings. The last two causes can be further complicated due to the dependence on the software environment. These settings change dynamically, depending on what is being executed.

2   Interrupt handled by the wrong handler/processor.

With a distributed interrupt handling scheme, which is often used within a multiprocessor system, the handling of the various levels is determined by jumper settings and/or control registers on each processor board. If these are wrong, the interrupt can either be handled by the wrong processor, which may cause havoc with its software, or may not be handled at all.

3   Wrong level or vector used.

Apart from the obvious wrong settings that can cause this, it is also possible if two interrupters, with interrupts outstanding on the same level, see the IACK★ signal simultaneously.

This is normally prevented by the daisy-chaining hierarchy scheme. An interrupter responding to the IACK★ signal can prevent the signal from going any further down the chain. However, if the signal is jumpered by a backplane signal, it is not stopped and the second interrupter sees it. The two interrupters put out their own vectors and either the wrong vector is generated or the system fails. If the second interrupter does not have an outstanding interrupt, nothing will go wrong. This means that this often appears as a transitory failure, totally dependent on software conditions but caused by hardware.

4   No IACK★ daisy-chain jumpers on backplane or empty VMEbus
slots.

Part of the interrupt acknowledge scheme requires the passing of
the IACK★ signal down the backplane to inform the interrupter
which interrupt is being processed. This requires an unbroken chain
formed by backplane jumpers and boards to be present. Any break in
this link, by an empty slot without a backplane jumper, for example,
prevents the interrupt from being acknowledged and therefore any
further response.

While most VMEbus boards that do not use the IACK★ signal
actually jumper the link internally, there are some that do not. If in
doubt, put a jumper on the backplane.

5   Handler unable to obtain the bus.

Part of the interrupt mechanism requires the handler to request and
obtain the bus so that an acknowledgement cycle can commence. Any
failure in obtaining this prevents the interrupt from being recognized
and handled.

6   Interrupt rate too high.

The time taken for an interrupt to be handled over VMEbus has to
include the software overheads as well as the acknowledgement.
Once the interrupt has been recognized by the handler and has
generated a processor interrupt, the processor automatically masks
out any more interrupts at that level. Therefore, although the
VMEbus is capable of accepting more interrupts, they are masked by
the processor and appear to be missed.

If interrupts are coming at a very high rate, the system software
may spend all its time handling them, with little or no time left for
normal operation. This results in a system that appears to have hung
up with no response at all. Reducing the interrupt rate restores the
system.

A typical response time for an 8 MHz MC68000 based system,
running a real-time operating system like VERSAdos and using the
system calls to handle interrupts, is approximately 125 μs. This is
about 10 to 12 times the processor interrupt latency.

7   Other interrupts taking higher priority.

While the system is servicing an interrupt, any lower level
interrupts are masked out. Therefore, a disc access, which involves
many high level interrupts, may cause lower level interrupts to be
delayed.

8   Multiple handlers for same interrupt level.

In a system that has multiple handlers for a single level, the handler
dealing with the interrupt is chosen almost at random. As a result, the
system is constantly playing 'Russian Roulette' with itself and finally
crashes. As software or other interrupts can dynamically mask the

interrupt recognition, the right handler may actually deal with the interrupt correctly. It is only if a prior activity delays the acknowledgement, and another handler is available, that the wrong one gets involved. The effect of handling an unexpected interrupt is usually fatal to the system.

'Failure to access the bus'

1 Wrong or no arbitration request sent.

   If no arbitration request or a wrong one is sent, the bus cannot be granted. Failures of this type are usually caused by wrong jumper settings or system design. Requesting on bus request level 2 when the arbiter is a single level 3 is a good example.

2 No system controller.

   If there is no system controller, problems are only generally seen if there is a second master in the system. With no arbiter to referee over bus ownership disputes, the master can either be held off the bus or multiple simultaneous access can occur. Both have disasterous results.

3 Single level arbiter used with multilevel requesters.

   Only level 3 requests will be recognized.

4 Bus hogging: masters refusing to relinquish the bus.

   Many bus masters have a 'DMA' mode, where the bus is not relinquished until a certain number of transfers have been completed. This allows the rapid transfer of buffered information, from disc controllers, for instance. With such boards, this bus hogging may prevent other masters, which should have priority from obtaining the bus. In extreme cases, this can cause bus timeouts. The size of the block transfer is usually programmable and may need to be tailored.

   Bus hogging can also occur if a high priority master has an extremely high VMEbus bandwidth requirement. An MC68000 based processor, with little or no local memory, can use in excess of 80% of the available VMEbus bandwidth if global memory is used for code and data. The addition of more masters to such a system is restricted to the remaining bandwidth and subject to the bus hogging. This type of problem is indicative of poor system design.

5 Wrong arbitration scheme.

   For a multiprocessing system requiring an even distribution of bus ownership between the masters, a single level arbitration scheme with priority based on slot position is wrong. Similarly, a multilevel round robin scheme may be inappropriate for a hierarchical priority scheme. Again, these types of problems are indicative of poor design.

6 Multiple system controllers and arbiters.

   With multiple system controllers and arbiters, the result is chaos: masters are granted access simultaneously and the system locks up.

These conditions are again usually caused by incorrect jumper settings. Most processor boards act as system controllers by default and must therefore be set up differently prior to use in multiprocessor systems.

7   Arbiter not in slot 1.

The bus arbiter is part of the system controller functions, and must therefore be in slot 1 so that all boards below it can take part in the bus grant daisy-chaining. If the controller is not in slot 1, boards above it can be locked out from the arbitration scheme.

8   No daisy-chaining connections.

The bus arbitration scheme uses daisy-chaining to provide a hierarchy based on slot position for masters assigned to the same bus request level. If this chain is broken, either by missing backplane jumpers or boards, the bus grant signals may not appear and the master times out while waiting for the bus.

Peripheral problems

'No access to hard or floppy discs'

1   Incorrect cabling.

It is extremely easy to invert the edge connectors used for the majority of disc drive connections. This grounds the active signals.

2   Wrong drive selection.

Unfortunately, there are currently two nomenclatures for disc drive selections: D0 to D3 and D1 to D4. It is extremely easy to mix them up so that a controller and drive are set up for the same 'drive 2' but are incorrect.

3   Either no termination or too much on cabling between discs and controllers.

If multiple drives are daisy-chained together, there must only be one termination pack in the system. Usually, every drive has a pack fitted.

4   Multiple drives with the same drive select number.

This is a simple incorrect jumper setting usually indicated by two drive select lights coming on simultaneously.

5   Wrongly or non-formatted media.

Winchester discs are usually supplied non-formatted and require formatting prior to use. In such errors, it may appear as if the drive is not being accessed. If the drive is being accessed, it should make some noise.

If media are incorrectly formatted, sector starts, for example, are not found and symptoms similar to non-formatted media are observed.

Very high density drives (>1.6 Mbytes) require high density media to function correctly.

6 Power supply insufficient for disc drive.

Specifications for disc drive power supply requirements usually state the typical or quiescent currents and do not take into account the heavy start-up currents when motors start to spin. With winchester discs, these can be up to four times the quiescent.

If a power supply starts to current-limit during this start-up phase, the disc does not reach the desired speed and therefore cannot access any information. If the supply feeds both the VMEbus system and the drives, the current limits may force the voltage rails down and cause the VMEbus boards to crash.

7 Wrong drive configuration.

Accessing non-existent drive heads, cylinders and sectors is easily done. All disc controllers power up with a default configuration which may need changing, prior to any access.

8 Head load and drive motor not activated.

Floppy disc controllers endeavour to reduce motor and media/head wear by only loading heads and spinning the disc when the drive is actually selected. Drive selection may be determined by monitoring special motor on and/or drive select signals supplied to it. Some controllers do not support these signals and therefore the heads and motors are not activated. Visual inspection of the drive during an attempted access can easily confirm this problem.

Most drives can be configured to either permanently spin the motor and load the heads or the controlling signals can be changed by resetting jumpers.

9 No power to drive.

Most drives need a +12 V supply as well as +5 V. This can easily be neglected. Some drives, such as QIC II tape streamers, require two power connections: one for the drive and a second for the controller electronics. It is easy to forget these extra connections.

The +12 V supply is usually for the motor; if the disc either fails to spin up or the floppy disc does not rotate, this could be the problem.

'Terminals'

1 RS232 connections.

The RS232 so-called 'standard' has probably caused more frustration than anything else within the microcomputer world. There is no magic method of connecting up RS232 serial links and there is always a serial port which does not obey the rules waiting for anyone who thinks they have mastered the art. The following method has solved many such problems over the years but is not foolproof.

Pull pins 4, 5, 6, 8 and 20 high, reduce the baud rate to 300 and put an oscilloscope probe on pins 2 and 3 to see which pin transmits data. The transmitting pin should always be connected to the receiving pin. If necessary, trial and error can be used to determine which of pins 2 and 3 are the transmit and receive pins.

One particular problem that has caused much gnashing of teeth is with three-wire RS232 devices, such as the VT100 type terminal. This has no hardware handshaking, which means certain pins on the computer serial port may require configuring. These configuration requirements may also change, depending on the software environment. For example, an RS232 lead may work when the onboard debugger is being used, but fail when the operating system is booted. The debugger does not support hardware handshaking but the operating system configuration does. With no handshake, the terminal just sits there as if the system has crashed. There is no login or failure message and the processor is active apparently in some endless loop. No error has occurred: the system is waiting for the terminal to become ready. Connecting pins 4 and 5 together on the computer board will bring the system to life.

2   Wrong baud rate, number of stop bits, start bits, and data bits, parity settings.

If any of these parameters are incorrect, they usually result in gibberish on the screen. If only some characters are incorrect, it is usually a problem with parity.

Another obscure problem can be associated with stop bits. Stop bits essentially put a small delay between characters as they are sent down the serial line. If the data source is direct from a keyboard, the delay between pressing each key is effectively increasing the number of stop bits between each character. If the number of stop bits is incorrect, e.g. 1.5 instead of 2, no error is seen. If a file transfer is carried out, where there is no delay between characters, then the incorrect stop bit is recognized and the link fails. This results in a system which appears to work correctly from a terminal but fails to allow file transfers or networking.

General
1   A wrong board at a right address.

Most operating systems have a default set of device drivers incorporated and inspect the registers at pre-arranged memory locations to see what hardware is present. If the system responds during such an access, the software assumes that the right type of board is present. Obviously, this may not be the case and by programming the wrong board the system usually crashes.

If other boards are added to a standard working configuration, there must be no conflict with the operating system.

2   A right board with the wrong address.

The factory shipped settings for addresses, interrupt levels, etc. may not be as required by the operating system. At best, the system may not recognize the board; at worse, it may crash.

3   Incompatibility between the board revision and its associated system driver software.

Software drivers require a defined software interface to control many intelligent boards. Some drivers may be totally dependent on a firmware revision to preserve this environment.

Operating system fails to boot

1   Wrong version

It is good practice to change the boot-up message to reflect the changes made to an operating system so that it can be identified, and not confused with any other versions.

2   Operating system not bootable, wrong links etc.

The hardware must reflect the configuration expected by the software.

3   Operating system corrupt.

Check disc media, especially if the disc is a high density version. Always use a copy, never a master disc.

4   Start-up terminal different from boot-up terminal.

UNIX will always start up from the terminal it was shut down from!

Another peculiarity is that sometimes UNIX will default to a 300 baud rate instead of the normal 9600 baud without telling anyone!

5   Operating system terminal configurations different from debuggers.

6   Insufficient memory.

Add more memory after checking that the present memory is accessible and in the right location.

7   Wrong jumper and switch settings.

8   No P2 backplane support.

32-bit data and address accesses will be corrupted.

Appendix B: Installing VERSAdos on an MVME117 system

These notes, when used in conjunction with customer letters, hardware manuals, etc. will help anyone installing VERSAdos 4.4+/4.5 on an MVME117 system. While being specific to this hardware, the principles involved are applicable to any system. They have been included as an example of the information generated during system integration.

Stage 1: Prepare the hardware

The basic system comprises an MVME117–3 with its transition card, an OMTI 5200 SCSI disc controller, a MICROPOLIS 1453 ST506 winchester and a Shugart 96 tpi 5 inch floppy disc. The system cabling is shown in Figure B.1. Note that for this basic system the VMEbus interface is not being used.

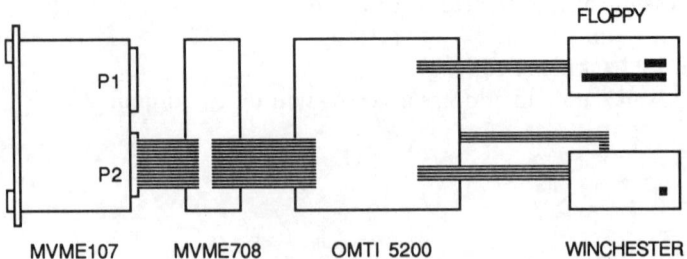

Figure B.1 *Cabling*

VME117bug Rev. 1.0 was used for general testing and to boot VERSAdos up on the system.

The jumper settings are described in Figures B.2, B.3 and Table 1.

Check that these, the cabling and the power rails are correct before powering up. A +12 V line wrongly connected will permanently damage the hardware.

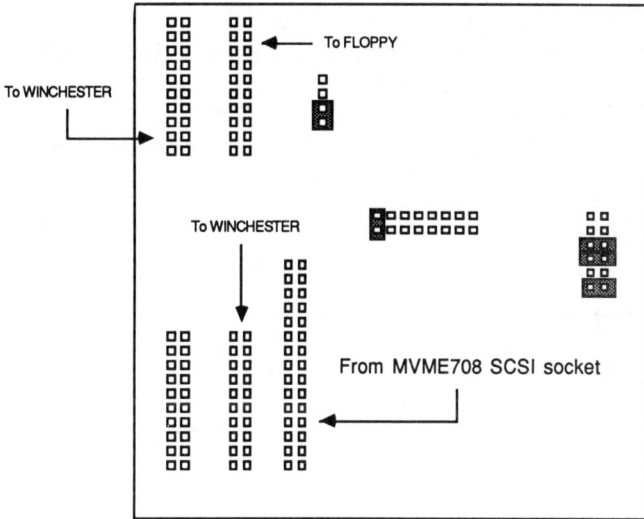

Figure B.2 *Jumper settings for OMTI 5200 SCSI controller*

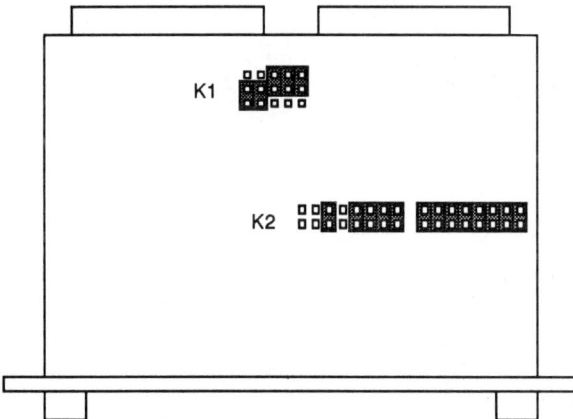

Figure B.3 *Jumper settings for MVME215–1 static RAM board with memory address starting at $80 000*

After powering up, check that the winchester has come up to speed (whirring noises and selected light flashes) and that a floppy disc placed in the drive revolves when used. If nothing happens check the jumpering for motor on selections as described in the relevant manuals. Do not use your boot disc for these tests in case of problems.

The run light on the MVME117 should be on: any red LEDs on indicate a problem. Check the jumpering carefully and that the EPROMs are seated in the sockets correctly if this is the case.

Connect a terminal to the front RS232 port on the MVME117. Check that the RS232 settings on the terminal match those stated in the MVME117bug manual (9600 baud, 8 bit no parity, 1 stop bit). Power up and type Y in answer to the 'size and initialize RAM' question. A message telling you how much RAM and where it is should now appear, followed by a prompt.

Stage 2: Testing the hardware

VME117bug has a nice facility: typing in ST followed by return will start a comprehensive self test. Answer its questions correctly and it will test even the switch settings and panel LEDs. After passing this, reset the SCSI controller using the command RESET. Put a formatted disc into the floppy drive, and rerun the self test with its SCSI test option, i.e. type in ST 2,0 <cr>.

This performs the same self test with an additional SCSI test which fetches sector 0 from the floppy disc (drive 2, controller 0). The error code 20120000 is symptomatic of incorrect cabling and SCSI controller selection. Error codes similar to 20430000 and 20460000 result from not resetting the SCSI controller. This test will fail if the winchester is selected because it has not been formatted. The next step is to boot the operating system.

Stage 3: Booting VERSAdos

This is very simple yet nerve racking for the inexperienced! Power up, size memory, reset the SCSI, place the boot disc into the floppy drive and enter BO 2,0 <cr>. The drive will then start moving, a booting message will appear followed by a boot complete message. Shortly after this, both the winchester and floppy discs will be selected (drive select LEDs will momentarily flash). Then a few seconds later the screen will clear and a logon request will be given. VERSAdos has now been booted. Logon with the volume name of the floppy and proceed to initialize the winchester. The system is now ready to install the 37 or so floppy discs' worth of VERSAdos 4.4. Consult the relevant customer letters for more details.

If nothing happens then check the system for visual indications of problems. If the winchester is not, or incorrectly, connected then the system will hang. VERSAdos appears to check that there is a drive there in its initialization routines, and being a polite operating system waits until it receives an acknowledgement. Another obscure reason for causing the same hang-up is telling the SCSI controller that the winchester is a floppy disc. This can be done by an incorrect jumper setting on the controller.

No messages indicates that booting from an unformatted or different format disc has taken place. No apparent causes are often due to the disc being bootable by default for another system. Consult customer letters if a specific file has to be called:

> e.g. BO 2,0,VME117.VERSADOS.SY
> BO 2,0,9200.VME117.VERSADOS.SY

Red failure LEDs on the CPU usually indicate a hardware problem, a corrupt or incorrectly configured boot disc. A really obscure cause is the boot file IPL.SY's sector locations being incorrect in sector 0 of the disc. This can happen when the original installed boot file is overwritten, usually when files are copied over with the ;Y option (overwrite automatically). It is possible if the new location is known to patch the sector to restore its boot capability. Details are in the VERSAdos System Facilities manual.

Winchester: jumpered for drive select 0 from a choice of 0 to 3.
              jumpered for drive select 1 from a choice of 1 to 4.
Floppy disc: jumpered for drive select 2 from a choice of 0 to 3.
              jumpered for drive select 3 from a choice of 1 to 4.
MVME708:   jumpered for 117 to power SCSI terminators.
              RS232 jumpered to suit application.

Table 1 *Further jumper options*

Expanding the system 1: adding more memory

Adding more memory to the system is very easy providing the additional memory is placed inside VERSAdos's existing memory map. This map is defined by the MEMEND parameters in VME117.SYSTEM.CI. As supplied they assume an upper limit to memory of $200000. To put more memory then simply requires jumpering the addresses and putting the card in the system. VERSAdos will look at what memory is in the system and maintain its system tables accordingly. If there are any problems use VME117bug to check the memory (it does this when sizing memory). The SYSANAL utility with its MEM command will show you what memory VERSAdos thinks it has. Non-existent memory is simply described as 'used'.

To add another partition requires adding additional MEMEND parameters and then additions to the INITDAT.AG file to build the partitions based on these extra parameters. All that is done is to duplicate the entry, modify it and rebuild VERSAdos. More on these topics is given later. The jumper settings for the MVME215–1 are shown in Figure B.3.

Expanding the system 2: altering VERSAdos

This again is a very simple task yet causes the same apprehension as going to the dentist! In essence all that is done is to change some parameters and then issue the SYSGEN command to VERSAdos and it will do the rest.

The most important aspect is to start with a known working set of modules. With the VME117 this requires the loading of about 37 floppy discs in three stages as previously mentioned. The customer letter recommends a manual mounting–copying–dismounting procedure which is tedious. Figure B.5 has a listing of a chain file which will perform this task for you. All that is required is the removal/insertion of discs when prompted. This chain file should only be used for installing VERSAdos 4.4 discs, not the 3rd-quarter update or MVME117 SCSI driver software!! These two last sets of discs must overwrite existing files, but overwriting with the 4.4 discs can destroy the link between sector 0 and IPL.SY and render a bootable disc inoperative. Figure B.6 lists a suitable chain file for these discs. Do not forget to install the new version of INIT.LO. The old version causes a disc format to carry on indefinitely. If this happens the only way to get control is to press reset on the MVME117, and use the RESET command in MVME117bug to reset the controller and stop the disc from formatting.

It cannot be stressed hard enough that the customer letters are essential reading prior to performing these tasks.

```
=/*   This program copies discs to the winchester.
=/*   Existing files will not be overwritten.
=/*
=/*   To exit this chain file, press BREAK and then the
=/*   command END followed by RETURN.
=/*
=/*   It assumes that there is no disc mounted on the system.
=/*
=/*   Insert a disc into drive 2, shut the door
=/&   and press RETURN.
=mt #fd02
=backup #fd02, #hd00;an
a
```

```
=/★  Copy finished.
=/&  Remove disc and press RETURN.
=dmt #fd02
=copyflop.cf
```

Figure B.5   *Listing of chain file COPYFLOP.CF*

```
=/★  This program copies discs to the winchester.
=/★  Existing files will be overwritten.
=/★
=/★  To exit this chain file, press BREAK and then the
=/★  command END followed by RETURN.
=/★
=/★  It assumes that there is no disc mounted on the system.
=/★
=/★  Insert a disc into drive 2, shut the door
=/&  and press RETURN.
=mt #fd02
=backup #fd02,#hd00;an
a
=/★  Copy finished.
=/&  Remove disc and press RETURN.
=dmt #fd02
=overflop.cf
```

Figure B.6   *Listing of chain file OVERFLOP.CF*

Now that the software is installed, the relevant files required for SYSGEN can be copied into a new user number ready for running. This is done by another chain file called 9998.VME117.COPYSGEN.CF. Chain files are very common in this work and a few minutes' reading about them is very worthwhile. Invoke the chain file supplying the necessary arguments, e.g.

9998.VME117.COPYSGEN.CF SYS,SYS,9200

and the files will be copied over from volume SYS to volume SYS user number 9200. If a file is non-existent, usually due to an overlooked floppy, then the chain file will stop. Note the file that is missing and enter PROC followed by RETURN. This instructs the chain file to carry on copying. The missing file(s) can be retrieved later by using the COPYFLOP.CF chain file and starting with the last discs installed, i.e. the MVME117 SCSI driver and 3rd-quarter update. COPYFLOP.CF only copies non-existent files.

Armed with these files, a sysgen can be performed. Logon to the SYSGEN account and start the standard SYSGEN chain file, e.g.:

=USE SYS:9200.VME117
=STD.SYSGEN.CF

The system will then start running and about 45 min later a new version of VERSAdos, 9200.VME117.VERSADOS.SY will be created. For the inexperienced, watching the process run will give insight into the various files and parameters used. Whenever it runs, however, watch for the first few minutes while old file deletions take place. If no file exists, it will carry on but will treat it as an error. At the end, if there are any errors, the SYSGEN will tell you and ask if you wish to proceed. Obviously if the number of errors ties in with that from deleting missing old files you can carry on.

Three additional files, SYSLIST.LS, SYSASML.LS and SYMBOLS.LS, will also be created giving the exact build standard used to create the new VERSADOS.SY. To test the new version, power down the system, reset the SCSI controller and boot, e.g.:

BO 0,0,9200.VME117.VERSADOS.SY

The system should then come up as normal. Should it fail then check using the build listings that PC and STARTUP addresses, and the number of symbols, are reasonable. For a standard SYSGEN they are:

PC	$01B600
STARTUP	$01AA00
NUMBER OF SYMBOLS	258

Should the system come up but disc access is impossible, check that the logon volume was valid. If this is correct then check the value of COMINTZ mentioned in 9200.VME117.SCSIDRV.CI and 9200.VME117.RMS.LL are the same. If there is any difference then re-install the software. This restriction should be removed in VERSAdos 4.5.

The short cut: getting just the relevant files

Once it has been proved that all the relevant files are in the SYSGEN account *and* that they combine to create a valid VERSADOS.SY, then these files can be transferred to a couple of floppy discs for future use. This is easily done by using the COPYSGEN.CF utility mentioned before. The first thing is to format several floppy discs. Mount the first floppy disc and then invoke the COPYSGEN.CF, e.g.:

=9998.VME117.COPYSGEN.CF SYS,BT00,9200
    where BT00 is the floppy disc volume
    and 9200 is the user number for the SYSGEN files.

The chain file will then carry on until the floppy is full. It will print a message stating this and then prompt you. Although still in the chain file, VERSAdos commands can still be executed. Dismount and remove the disc using DMT. Then insert the next disc and mount it using MT. Enter the chain command ARG and a list of the chain file arguments will appear, e.g.:

ARG <cr>

SYS

BT00

9200

N

−PCDRV

ARGS

Then type in the new list, followed by the RETRY command to restart the chain file, e.g.:

ARG SYS,BT01,9200,N,−PCDRV,ARGS <cr>

RETRY <cr>

Once all the files have been copied then they can all be copied on to another system to give the same system build. This technique assumes that no modifications to the RMS68K kernel are required. The RMS68K files are on another user number and a similar technique can be used to copy them.

Appendix C: Common VMEbus specification violations

This list describes the most common specification violations and is based on the specification violations that the **VMETRO VMEbus** conformance tester will identify.

It provides a reasonable check list for any VMEbus design that claims to meet the specification. However it is not definitive and does not cover all the possible violations.

The rules that are referred to can be found in the VMEbus specification revision C1.

- Data lines D31*D00 changing when they should be stable.
  (Rules 2.16, 2.48, 2.54, 2.56, 4.36)
- Address lines A31*A0 changing when they should be stable.
  (Rules 2.30, 2.40, 4.18)
- Multiple bus grants, i.e. more than one at a time.
- Bus request lines aborted prior to BBSY* or bus grant active.
  (Part of rule 3.11, can also be caused by violating rule 3.13)
- Illegal combinations of DS0*, DS1*, A01 and LWORD*.
  (Rule 2.1)
- WRITE* unstable when it should be stable.
  (Rules 2.38, 2.49, 4.23, 4.31)
- Address modifiers AM5*AM0 changing when they should be stable.
  (Rules 2.30 and 2.40)
- DS0* and DS1* asserted before DTACK* released.
  (Rules 2.35 and 4.20)
- IACK* asserted prior to bus granted.
  (Rules 2.28, 4.16)
- WRITE* asserted prior to bus granted.
  (Rule 2.28)
- LWORD* asserted prior to bus granted.
  (Rules 2.28, 4.16)

- DS0★ and DS1★ asserted before bus granted.
  (Rules 2.28, 4.16)
- AS★ asserted before bus granted.
  (Rules 2.20, 4.16)
- New bus grant generated before BBSY★ rescinded.
  (Rule 3.6)
- DS0★ and DS1★ rescinded before DTACK★ asserted.
  (Rules 2.17, 4.30)
- AS★ removed prior to the last falling edge of DTACK★
  (Rules 2.44, 4.27)
- Excessive skewing between DS0★ and DS1★.
  (Rules 2.39 and 4.24)
- BBSY★ removed prior to bus grant going high.
  (Rule 3.10)
- BBSY★ less than 90 ns duration.
  (Rule 3.7)
- AS★ duration insufficient.
  (Rules 2.45 and 4.28)
- IACKOUT★ asserted more than 30 ns after AS★ ends.
  (Rules 4.41, 4.47)
- IACKOUT★ driven low less than 40 ns after DS0★.
  (Rule 4.46)
- +5 V supply rail dips below 4.85 V.
  (Usually during bus accesses involving high order addresses and data)
- SYSRESET★ high before +5 V power rail reaches 4.85 V.
  (Rule 5.1)
- Interrupt request lines aborted prior to acknowledgement cycle.
  (Rules 4.5 and 4.6)
- Insufficient DS0★ and DS1★ de-assertion time.
  (Rules 2.37 and 4.22)
- Insufficient AS★ de-assertion time.
  (Rules 2.31 and 4.17)

Appendix D: VMEbus and VSB connections

VMEbus

PIN	ROW A	ROW B	ROW C
1	D00	BBSY*	D08
2	D01	BCLR*	D09
3	D02	ACFAIL	D10
4	D03	BG0IN*	D11
5	D04	BG0OUT*	D12
6	D05	BG1IN*	D13
7	D06	BG1OUT*	D14
8	D07	BG2IN*	D15
9	GND	BG2OUT*	GND
10	SYSCLK	BG3IN*	SYSFAIL*
11	GND	BG3OUT*	BERR*
12	DS1*	BR0*	SYSRESET*
13	DS0*	BR1*	LWORD*
14	WRITE*	BR2*	AM5
15	GND	BR3*	A23
16	DTACK*	AM0	A22
17	GND	AM1	A21
18	AS*	AM2	A20
19	GND	AM3	A19
20	IACK*	GND	A18
21	IACKIN*	SERCLK	A17
22	IACKOUT*	SERDAT*	A16
23	AM4	GND	A15
24	A07	IRQ7*	A14
25	A06	IRQ6*	A13
26	A05	IRQ5*	A12
27	A04	IRQ4*	A11
28	A03	IRQ3*	A10
29	A02	IRQ2*	A09
30	A01	IRQ1*	A08
31	-12V	+5VSTDBY	+12V
32	+5V	+5V	+5V

PIN	ROW A	ROW B	ROW C
1		+5V	
2		GND	
3		RESERVED	
4		A24	
5		A25	
6		A26	
7		A27	
8		A28	
9	USER	A29	USER
10		A30	
11	DEFINED	A31	DEFINED
12		GND	
13		+5V	
14		D16	
15		D17	
16		D18	
17		D19	
18		D20	
19		D21	
20		D22	
21		D23	
22		GND	
23		D24	
24		D25	
25		D26	
26		D27	
27		D28	
28		D29	
29		D30	
30		D31	
31		GND	
32		+5V	

J1/P1 Pin assignments   J2/P2 Pin assignments

VSB

PIN	ROW A	ROW B	ROW C
1	AD00	+5V	AD01
2	AD02	GND	AD03
3	AD04		AD05
4	AD06		AD07
5	AD08		AD09
6	AD10		AD11
7	AD12		AD13
8	AD14		AD15
9	AD16		AD17
10	AD18		AD19
11	AD20		AD21
12	AD22	GND	AD23
13	AD24	+5V	AD25
14	AD26		AD27
15	AD28		AD29
16	AD30		AD31
17	GND		GND
18	IRQ*		GND
19	DS*		GND
20	WR*		GND
21	SPACE0		SIZE0
22	SPACE1	GND	PAS*
23	LOCK*		SIZE1
24	ERR*		GND
25	GND		ACK*
26	GND		AC
27	GND		ASACK1*
28	GA0		ASACK0*
29	GA1		CACHE*
30	GA2		WAIT*
31	BGIN*	GND	BUSY*
32	BREQ*	+5V	BGOUT*

All unspecified pins are user defined.
In practice, they are usually the
VMEbus extension signals.

J2/P2 Pin assignments

Appendix E: VMEbus suppliers and manufacturers

This is a list of VMEbus suppliers and distributors for the United Kingdom. For a complete world wide list, please consult the VMEbus Product Directory which not only details names and addresses but gives brief product descriptions. It is available from VITA, and is usually updated twice a year.

Aditi Electronics (Distributor), 46B High Street, Hurstpierpoint, West Sussex, BN6 9IT, Tel: 0273 833124.

Amplicon Electronics Ltd (Distributor), Richmond Road, Brighton, East Sussex, BN2 3RL, Tel: 0273 608331.

Anglia Technology Ltd (Distributor), 4 Hellesden Hall, Industrial Park, Norwich, Norfolk, NR6 5DR, Tel: 0603 789432.

Arcon Ltd (Manufacturer), Unit 8, Clifton Road, Cambridge, CB1 4BW, Tel: 0223 411200.

BICC Vero Electronics (Manufacturer), Flanders Road, Hedge End, Hants, S03 3LG, Tel: 04215 66300.

Burr Brown Ltd (Distributor), 1 Millfield House, Woodshots Meadow, Watford, Herts, WD1 8YX, Tel: 0923 33837.

Bus Solutions (Distributor), 85 Weir Road, Milnrow, Rochdale, OL1 3UX, Tel: 0706 354088.

Cambridge RISC Machines (Manufacturer), 26 Mill Road, Cambridge, CB1 2AD, Tel: 0223 350405.

C-Matic Systems Ltd (Manufacturer/Distributor), Fifth Quarter, Lenham Road, Headcorn, Kent, TN27 9LE, Tel: 0622 890737.

Convergent Technologies (Manufacturer), Network Systems Division, 2700 N First Street, San Jose, California, CA95150–6685,

USA. Tel: 0101 408 435 3125.

Comendec (Manufacturer), 6A School Lane, Hopwas, Tamworth, Staffs, B78 3AD, Tel: 0827 286180.

CompControl (Manufacturer), Sratumsedijk 31, PO Box 31, 5600 AD Eindhoven, Holland, Tel: 00 31 40 124955.

Creative Electronics Systems SA (Manufacturer), Route Du Pont Butin 70, Case Postale 107, CH–1213 Petit-Lancy, Geneva, Switzerland, Tel: 01041 22 925748.

Crellon Microsystems (Distributor), 3 The Business Centre, Molly Millar's Lane, Wokingham, Berks, Tel: 0734 776161.

Dage GB Ltd (Distributor), Rabans Lane, Aylesbury, Bucks, HP16 3RG, Tel: 0296 393200.

Data Sud Systemes SA (Manufacturer), Rue de la Croix Verte Prolongee, Bat. 8, Zolad, Miniparc, BP1097, 34007 Montpellier Cedex, France, Tel: 01033 67 525904.

Data Translation Ltd (Manufacturer), Mulberry Business Park, Wokingham, Berks, RG11 2QT, Tel: 0734 793838.

Dean Microsystems Ltd (Distributor), 7 Horseshoe Park, Pangbourne, Berks, RG8 7JW, Tel: 07357 5155.

Diamond Point International (Distributor), Unit 9, North Point Bus Estate, Medway City Estate, Rochester, ME2 4LY, Tel: 0634 722390.

Diode Belgium (Distributor), Keiberg Brussels Airport, Excelsiorlaan, 53–1930 Zaventem, Tel: 02 721 29 92.

Diode Holland (Distributor), Meidoornkade, 22–3992 AE HOUTEN, Tel: 03403 91234.

Dy–4 Systems (Manufacturer), 21 Credit Union Way, Nepan, Ontario, Canada, K2H 9G1, Tel: 0101 613 569 9911.

Electronic Modular Systems (Manufacturer), Unit 5, Ladywood Works, Lutterworth, Leics, LE17 4HD, Tel: 0455 54731.

Europel Systems (Manufacturer), 5 Vo-Tec Centre, Hambridge Lane, Newbury, Berks, RG14 5TN, Tel: 0635 31074.

Ferranti Computer Systems (Manufacturer), Simonsway, Wythenshawe, Manchester, M22 5LA, Tel: 061 499 3355.

Force Computers (Manufacturer), 1 Holly Court, 3 Tring Road, Wendover, Bucks, HP22 6NR, Tel: 0296 625456.

GMT Electronic Systems (Manufacturer), Mole Business Park, Leatherhead, Surrey, KT22 7BA, Tel: 0372 373603.

Hawke Systems (Distributor), Amotex House, 45 Hanworth Road, Sunbury on Thames, Middlesex, Tel: 01 979 7799.

High Technology Electronics (Manufacturer), 303–305 Portswood Road, Southampton, Hants, Tel: 0703 581555.

Hi-Tek Electronics Ltd (Distributor), Ditton Walk, Cambridge, CB5 8QD, Tel: 0223 213333.

Imhof-Bedco (BICC) (Manufacturer), Ashley Works, Ashley Road, Uxbridge, UB8 2SQ, Tel: 0895 37123.

Integrated Micro Products (Manufacturer), Number One Industrial Estate, Medomsley Road, Consett, County Durham, DH8 6TJ, Tel: 0207 503481.

Interphase International Inc (Manufacturer), 93a New Street, Aylesbury, Bucks, HP20 2NY, Tel: 0296 435661.

Kentec (Distributor), 50 London Road, Sevenoaks, Kent, TN13 1AS, Tel: 0732 456188.

Koral Microsystems Ltd (Distributor), Brookfield Business Park, Twentypence Road, Cottenham, Cambridge, CB4 4PS, Tel: 0954 50526.

Logic Replacement Technology (Manufacturer), Arkwright Road, Reading, Berks, RG2 0LU, Tel: 0734 751054.

Lynx Computer International (Manufacturer), 12 Deer Park Road, London, SW19 3RJ, Tel: 01 534 5635.

MCP Electronics Ltd (Distributor), 26–32 Rosemount Road, Alperton, Middlesex, HA0 4QY, Tel: 01 902 6146.

Micro Marketing Electronics (Distributor), Unit 4, Soho Mills Industrial Estate, Wooburn Green, High Wycombe, Bucks, HP10 0PF, Tel: 06285 29222.

Microsystem Services (Distributor), Merlin House, Lancaster Road, High Wycombe, Bucks, HP12 3XY, Tel: 0494 41661.

Motorola (Manufacturer), Fairfax House, 27 Market Street, Maidenhead, Berks, SL6 8AE, Tel: 0628 39121.

Mizar Inc (Manufacturer), 1419 Dunn Drive, Carrollton, TX 75006, USA, Tel: 0101 214 446 2664.

Ovation Systems (Manufacturer), Lower End, Great Milton, Oxon, OX9 7NJ, Tel: 0844 46638.

Pronto Electronic Systems Ltd (Distributor), City Gate House, 399–425 Eastern Avenue, Gants Hill, Ilford, Essex, IG2 6LR, Tel: 01 554 6222.

Quarndon Electronics Ltd (Distributor), Slack Lane, Derby, DE2 3ED, Tel: 0332 32651.

Quin Systems Ltd (Distributor), 35 Broad Street, Wokingham, Berks, RG11 1AU, Tel: 0734 771077.

Radstone Technology Ltd (Manufacturer), Water Lane, Towcester, Northants, NN12 7JN, Tel: 0327 50312.

SBE Europe (Manufacturer), 6 The Old Mill, Reading Road, Pangbourne, Reading, RG8 7HY, Tel: 0735 75577.

Schroff UK Ltd (Manufacturer), Maylands Avenue, Hemel Hempstead, Herts, HP2 4SG, Tel: 0442 40471.

Syntel Microsystems (Manufacturer), Queensmill Road, Huddersfield, HD1 3PG, Tel: 0484 535101.

Tadpole Technology (Manufacturer), Cambridge Science Park, Milton Road, Cambridge, CB4 4BH, Tel: 0223 861112.

Tekelec Communications (Manufacturer), Charles House, Toutley Road, Wokingham, Berks, RG11 5QN, Tel: 0734 771020.

Thame Microsystems Ltd (Distributor), Thame Park Road, Thame, Oxon, OX9 3XD, Tel: 084 421 7272.

Universal Engineering and Computer Systems (UECS) (Distributor), 5–11 Tower Street, New Town, Birmingham, B19 3UY, Tel: 021 359 1749.

Wordsworth Technology Ltd (Distributor), Wordsworth House, Westerham, Kent, Tel: 0959 63208.

XIXIN Ltd (Distributor), Cosgrove Way, Luton, Beds, LU1 1XL, Tel: 0582 20121.

Xycom (Manufacturer), Nendex House, Ross Road, Northampton, NN5 5AX, Tel: 0604 587401.

Appendix F: Useful contacts and publications

VITA User Groups

The VITA groups can supply copies of all the VMEbus specifications and the VMEbus product directory. Membership is either individual or corporate. Typical fees at the time of writing were US$20 and US$200 respectively.

1   Belgium, Netherlands, Luxembourg

Prof. dr. ir. Timmerman, L. van Beethovenstraat 2, 1070 Brussel.

2   Finland

Mr. M. Nordberg, Tekniikantie 17b, SF–02 150, Espoo.

3   Germany

Mr. M. Adams, FZI, Haid and Neu Str. 10–14, D–7500, Kahlsruhe.

4   United Kingdom

Mr. B. Squirrell, Bob Squirrell Marketing, Unit 6, The Old Mill, Reading Road, Pangbourne, RG8 7HY.

There is a VMEbus magazine published on a quarterly basis by the VITA USERGROUPS EUROPE organization. It is free to VMEbus users. Please contact the local user group or Prof. Timmerman in Brussels to join the circulation list.

The following journals/magazines often feature VMEbus topics:

Microsystem Design   – English monthly
Electronics and Wireless World   – English monthly

Microsystems and Microprocessors	– English monthly
New Electronics	– English monthly
Elektronik	– German monthly
VMEbus	– German monthly

Appendix G: Silicon support for the VMEbus

This is a list of interface chips suitable for use with VMEbus designs. For further information contact either the manufacturer or your local distributor.

Part Number	Manufacturer	Function	Pins
MC68153	Motorola	BIM—Bus Interrupter Module	40
MC68452	Motorola	BAM—Bus Arbitration Module	
MVME6000	Motorola Computer Systems	Complete VMEbus interface	134
MVSB2400	Motorola Computer Systems	Complete VSB interface	120
PT–VSI	Performance Technologies	VMEbus SLAVE interface	84
SCC68154	Signetics	Interrupt Generator	40
SCC68155	Signetics	Interrupt Handler	40
SCC68171	Signetics	VMS interface	16
SCC68172	Signetics	VMEbus controller	28,44
SCC68173	Signetics	VMS controller	28
SCC68175	Signetics	VMEbus MASTER controller	24

Appendix H: Operating systems

This appendix lists the most commonly used operating systems within the VMEbus community for the MC680x0 family of processors, and all have been ported to VMEbus hardware. Most VMEbus users choose a suitable operating system from those that are available off the shelf for various hardware configurations and direct from the supplier. This removes or reduces any porting work, and provides a single source for support which is always beneficial.

UNIX is best purchased already ported to hardware unless access to source can be easily achieved. The current source costs usually prohibit most users from porting a form of UNIX to their hardware themselves, and this is usually performed by a specialized porting house. For this reason, UNIX has been omitted from this list.

Operating System	Supplier	Notes
Concurrent DOS	Digital Research 160 Central Avenue Pacific Grove CA 93950 408 649 3896	Single and multi-user multitasking operating system with graphics, LAN and window support.
PDOS	Eyring Research 1455 West 820 Nth Provo, UT. 84601 801 375 2434	ROMable multitasking kernel with file support. Real-time.
VRTX	Ready Systems 445 Sherman Ave Palo Alto CA. 94036 800 228 1249	ROMable kernel, uses IOX and FMX extensions. Real-time.

MTOS	Industrial Programming 100 Jericho Quad. Jericho, NY 516 938 6600	ROMable kernel with multiprocessor support. Real-time.
PSOS	Software Components 4655 Old Ironsides Dr. Suite 370 Santa Clara CA 95054	Plug-in ROMable kernel. Real-time.
VERSAdos	Motorola Computer Systems 2900 Sth Diablo Way Tempe AZ 85282 602 438 3500	Based around RMS68K kernel. Real-time.
OS–9/68K	Microware 1866 N.W. 114th St. Des Moines, IA 515 224 1929	Real-time, ROMable, UNIX like interface and file structure.

Index